PREVENTING WAR

PREVENTING WAR

The United Nations and Macedonia

ABIODUN WILLIAMS

ROWMAN & LITTLEFIELD PUBLISHERS, INC.
Lanham • Boulder • New York • Oxford

ROWMAN & LITTLEFIELD PUBLISHERS, INC.

Published in the United States of America
by Rowman & Littlefield Publishers, Inc.
4720 Boston Way, Lanham, Maryland 20706
http://www.rowmanlittlefield.com

12 Hid's Copse Road
Cumnor Hill, Oxford OX2 9JJ, England

British Library Cataloguing in Publication Information Available

Library of Congress Cataloging-in-Publication Data

Williams, Abiodun, 1961–
    Preventing war : the United Nations and Macedonia / Abiodun Williams.
      p.   cm.
    Includes bibliographical references (p. 185) and index.
    ISBN 0-7425-0907-9 (cloth : alk. paper) — ISBN 0-7425-0908-7 (pbk. : alk. paper)
    1. United Nations—Macedonia.   2. Peacekeeping forces—Macedonia.   I. Title.

JZ4997.5.M27 W55   2000
  341.5'84—dc21   00-036857

Printed in the United States of America

♾™ The paper used in this publication meets the minimum requirements of American
National Standard for Information Sciences—Permanence of Paper for Printed Library
Materials, ANSI/NISO Z39.48-1992.

AHF-1645

CONTENTS

Preface   *vii*

List of Acronyms and Abbreviations   *xi*

1   Preventive Diplomacy and the Evolution of UN
    Peacekeeping   *1*

2   The Burden of History   *17*

3   Making a New Beginning   *41*

4   Composition, Organization, and Structure
    of UNPREDEP   *67*

5   Keeping Watch   *87*

6   The Good Offices Function   *109*

7   Withdrawing a Winning Team   *151*

Epilogue   *179*

Selected Bibliography   *185*

Index   *193*

About the Author   *203*

PREFACE

In the last decade of the twentieth century, the bloodiest century in recorded history, the United Nations devised a new instrument, preventive deployment, to deal with the age-old problem of war. During the last few years, several friends and colleagues within the United Nations and academia have urged me to write about the United Nations Preventive Deployment Force (UNPREDEP), the first and so far only United Nations peacekeeping operation with a preventive mandate. This book is the result.

While teaching at the Edmund A. Walsh School of Foreign Service at Georgetown University, I became particularly interested in the crucial nexus between the theory and practice of international peacekeeping. My experience in peacekeeping operations has provided me with new perspectives on the United Nations' efforts to prevent, manage, and resolve international conflicts. As if in Parliament, I must declare an interest. From 1994 to 1998, I served as political and humanitarian affairs officer with UNPREDEP, in the former Yugoslav Republic of Macedonia.[1] Despite my professional ties with UNPREDEP, I have tried to present a balanced picture of the operation.

It is a cliché among advocates of preventive action that conflict, like disease, is easier and less costly to prevent than to cure. To accept that preventive action is worthwhile is one thing; knowing how to implement it is quite another. Advocating preventive measures does not entail an obvious course of action. Although there is a substantial theoretical literature on conflict prevention, there is a dearth of empirical studies on the subject. This volume is a case study of UNPREDEP, a story that has not been told before. It attempts to illuminate the limits and possibilities of preventive deployment in general and UNPREDEP in particular. To know how to prevent war and other forms of deadly conflict, we must study specific cases of preventive action.

Macedonia was an ideal "test case" for preventive deployment. Situated on the strategic crossroads of the southern Balkans, Macedonia has been the cockpit of conflict throughout the centuries. According to Otto von Bismarck, the nineteenth-century German chancellor, "Those who control the valley of the River Vardar in Macedonia are the masters of the Balkans." The contemporary state of Macedonia is beset with formidable external and internal threats to its stability: neighbors with competing historical claims on its territory, old animosities between ethnic groups, and economic stagnation. It is remarkable that the country has survived in very trying conditions.

The fear of a spillover of conflict from other parts of the former Yugoslavia into Macedonia—the vital link in the stability of the southern Balkans and the traditional crucible of trouble—led to the UN's first preventive military deployment in December 1992. The mandate of the Force was to monitor and report any developments that could threaten Macedonia, to deter such threats by its presence, and to use good offices to contribute to the maintenance of peace and stability in the country. During the six years it was deployed in Macedonia, the operation assumed greater duties and responsibilities that were not foreseen by the Security Council.

The mandate of UNPREDEP raises a broader question of the role of the UN in the post–Cold War world: whether the organization's fundamental purpose is to deter aggression and interstate conflict or whether it should also include dealing with the underlying causes of conflict within society.

The story of UNPREDEP is that of continuity and change. It was an unprecedented mission that combined the elements of first and second-generation peacekeeping operations. It blended the old with the new, tradition with innovation. While UNPREDEP was the first case of preventive deployment of peacekeeping troops, it was consistent with the essential principles of traditional peacekeeping.[2] Though the preventive nature of the mandate made it unique, the way it was implemented was not. At the same time, during the six years it was deployed in Macedonia, UNPREDEP evolved into a multidimensional mission which monitored and reported developments on borders, monitored sanctions, observed national elections, provided humanitarian assistance, engaged in peace-building activities, and used its good offices to promote peace and stability.

UNPREDEP is generally regarded as one of the more successful UN operations, which raises important questions to which there are no quick answers: What is success? Can it be defined? What in the end did UNPREDEP achieve? Causation is a controversial and problematic issue in the social sciences. And it is not easy to evaluate cause and effect in a preventive deployment operation. It is impossible *to prove* the deterrent effect of UNPREDEP in preventing threats to Macedonia's security, an external attack, or the spillover of conflict. We do not know what would have happened within and around Macedonia without UNPREDEP, any more than we know what would have happened in the Cold War without nuclear deterrence.

Another difficulty is comparing the deterrent value of UNPREDEP with other factors that have contributed to the security and stability of Macedonia. Other international actors such as the Organization for Security and Cooperation in Europe (OSCE), the International Conference on Former Yugoslavia (ICFY), and nongovernmental organizations (NGOs) have worked closely with the Macedonian government and the various ethnic groups in the country to prevent a spillover of war and to maintain domestic stability. Although I have given some attention to the role of the OSCE and the ICFY, this book is by no means a comprehensive account. The roles of these organizations merit greater study, but such a discussion would go beyond the scope of this volume.

To write about UNPREDEP, which ended active service in February 1999, is to plow new ground. It offers the opportunity for fresh reflections and observations. I have tried in this book to say why the operation was established, how it implemented its mandate, and what it accomplished. In addition, I have attempted to draw lessons from the experience of UNPREDEP. The lessons learned in Macedonia are important to understand the requirements of preventive operations. While every peacekeeping operation is *sui generis*, it may be that some of these lessons could be applied to future peacekeeping operations.

A word about terminology is in order. Although the acronym UNPREDEP only appeared in 1995, and the mission became an independent one only in 1996, I will refer throughout to it as UNPREDEP unless otherwise specified.

It would have been impossible to write this book without the help of many people. I am grateful to the many colleagues at the United Nations who willingly discussed various aspects of the UN mission with me and made every effort to respond to my requests for documentation. They are too numerous to name individually, and any attempt to do so would be invidious. I wish to pay special thanks to Nidija Cilimanova, Susana Fidanova, Naser Maksut, Burim Sadiku, Daniela Stefanovska, Sonja Stefanovska, Ilja Todorovski, and Arsim Zekolli, who helped me to understand something of their country. This book has benefited from the constructive criticisms and invaluable suggestions of Alan James, John McNeill, Michael Pugh, and James Sutterlin. I thank Tom Weiss for his assistance in finding a publisher. I am indebted to my friends, Isabel and David Taylor, without whose support I would never have gone to Macedonia. My gratitude to my sister, Valerie, is profound; she kindly read drafts of the man-

uscript and made helpful comments on the text. I remain solely responsible for
the opinions expressed and for any errors. The views expressed herein are those
of the author and do not necessarily reflect those of the United Nations.

Abiodun Williams

NOTES

1. In 1993, the newly independent state was admitted to the United Nations under
the provisional name of the former Yugoslav Republic of Macedonia as a result of a dispute with Greece over its constitutional name, the Republic of Macedonia. For the sake
of brevity, I refer to the country as Macedonia, but this should be interpreted neither as
an endorsement nor as a rejection of the term. For a discussion of the Greek-Macedon-
ian dispute, see chapter 2.

2. Sir Brian Urquhart has summarized these principles as: the consent of the parties
involved in the conflict to the establishment of the operation, to its mandate, to its composition, and to its appointed commanding officer; the continuing and strong support of
the operation by the mandating authority, the Security Council; a clear and practicable
mandate; the nonuse of force except in self-defense, including resistance to attempts by
forceful means to prevent the peacekeepers from discharging their duties; the willingness
of troop-contributing countries to provide adequate numbers of capable military personnel and to accept the degree of risk that the mandate and the situation demand; and,
less often noted, the willingness of member states, and especially the permanent members of the Security Council, to make available the necessary financial and logistical support. See Brian Urquhart, "Beyond the 'Sheriff's Posse,'" *Survival* 32, no. 3 (May–June
1990): 198.

ACRONYMS AND ABBREVIATIONS

ARM	Macedonian Army
ASNOM	Anti-Fascist Assembly of National Liberation of Macedonia
AVNOJ	Anti-Fascist Council for the National Liberation of Yugoslavia
CAC	Civil affairs coordinator
CRS	Catholic Relief Services
CSCE	Conference on Security and Cooperation in Europe
DPA	Democratic Party of Albanians
DS	Democratic Party (Serbia)
EAPC	Euro-Atlantic Partnership Council
EC	European Community
ECMM	European Community Monitoring Mission
EU	European Union
FINCOY	Finnish Company
FYROM	Former Yugoslav Republic of Macedonia
GOC	General officer commanding
GSS	Serbian Civic Alliance
ICFY	International Conference on Former Yugoslavia
ICRC	International Committee of the Red Cross
IDF	Israel Defense Forces
IFOR	Implementation Force
IFRC	International Federation of Red Cross and Red Crescent Societies
JNA	Yugoslav National Army
JTF-PP	Joint Task Force–Provide Promise
KLA	Kosovo Liberation Army
MACSAM	Macedonia Sanctions Assistance Mission

MINUSAL	UN Mission in El Salvador
MOU	Memorandum of Understanding
NATO	North Atlantic Treaty Organization
NDP	National Democratic Party
NGO	Nongovernmental organization
NLAOO	Northern Limit of the Area of Operations
NORDBAT	Nordic battalion
NordSamFN	Nordic Committee for Military UN Matters
ONUC	United Nations Operation in the Congo
ONUSAL	UN Observer Mission in El Salvador
OSCE	Organization for Security and Cooperation in Europe
PDD	Presidential Decision Directive
PDP	Party for Democratic Prosperity
PDPA	Party for Democratic Prosperity of Albanians in Macedonia
QRF	Quick reaction force
SAM	Sanctions Assistance Mission
SAMCOMM	SAM Communications Center
SCANDCOY	Scandinavian Company
SDSM	Social Democratic Union of Macedonia
SOFA	Status of Forces Agreement
SPO	Serb Renewal Movement
SRSG	Special representative of the secretary-general
UN	United Nations
UNCIVPOL	UN Civilian Police
UNCRO	UN Confidence Restoration Operation
UNDP	UN Development Program
UNEF	UN Emergency Force
UNFICYP	UN Peacekeeping Force in Cyprus
UNHCR	UN High Commissioner for Refugees
UNIFIL	UN Interim Force in Lebanon
UNIIMOG	UN Iran–Iraq Military Observer Group
UNITAF	Unified Task Force
UNMOGIP	UN Military Observer Group in India and Pakistan
UNOSOM	UN Operation in Somalia
UNPA	UN Protected Area
UNPF	UN Peace Forces
UNPREDEP	UN Preventive Deployment Force
UNPROFOR	UN Protection Force
UNTAG	UN Transition Assistance Group
UNTOFY	UN Transition Office in the Former Yugoslavia

UNTSO	UN Truce Supervision Organization
UNTV	UN Television
USAREUR	United States Army Europe
USBAT	U.S. battalion
VMRO	Internal Macedonian Revolutionary Organization
VMRO-DPME	VMRO-Democratic Party of Macedonian National Unity

1

PREVENTIVE DIPLOMACY AND THE EVOLUTION OF UN PEACEKEEPING

> Preventive deployment, in one particular example, has already had a remarkable effect in the explosive region of the Balkans. Such a force is only a "thin blue line." But the United Nations Preventive Deployment Force's role so far in the former Yugoslav Republic of Macedonia suggests that preventive deployment, adequately mandated and supported, can make the difference between war and peace.[1]
>
> Kofi Annan

Of the UN's peacekeeping operations, UNPREDEP is one of the few that has got less attention than it deserves. This is surprising, not least because there seems to be no shortage of supporters of preventive action who extol its virtues with missionary zeal. Michael Lund notes that this new enthusiasm for preventive action is the result of a convergence of four trends: "the emergence of a new, more cooperative international milieu; the sobering experience of international intervention in already advanced conflicts; the prospect of more threats to international stability; and the growing economic and political constraints on governments' exercise of foreign policy."[2]

Two main reasons account for this apparent lack of interest in UNPREDEP. The first is the international preoccupation with the wars in Bosnia and Croatia and their consequences. Between 1991 and 1995, nearly three hundred thousand people were killed in the former Yugoslavia, the bloodiest conflict in Europe since World War II. Macedonia, however, was the only republic that seceded peacefully from the Yugoslav Federation, an event that is widely, but incorrectly, viewed as incidental in the disintegration of Yugoslavia. The second reason is that UNPREDEP is the victim of its own success, for failure by international institutions seems to command greater attention than success. As Yasushi Akashi, the secretary-general's special representative for the former Yu-

1

goslavia, put it on his departure from Zagreb in October 1995, "[T]he preventive deployment of peacekeeping troops in the former Yugoslav Republic of Macedonia is a shining example of what can be accomplished given implementable mandates and adequate resources in the emerging field of conflict prevention. Since the United Nations was successful in that regard, hardly anyone spoke of it."³

The present chapter will put the concept of preventive diplomacy and UN peacekeeping in historical perspective. It discusses the role of the UN's second secretary-general, Dag Hammarskjöld, in the development of preventive diplomacy. It examines in some detail the ideas on preventive diplomacy of former Secretary-General Boutros-Ghali, summarized in his seminal report *An Agenda for Peace*. The final section will deal with the evolution of UN peacekeeping; peacekeeping was a phenomenon, which was not envisaged by the framers of the Charter. It is convenient to distinguish between two periods: peacekeeping during the Cold War and peacekeeping during the post–Cold War era. The Cold War, now a rapidly fading memory, defined the parameters of peacekeeping. The end of the Cold War opened new possibilities for peacekeeping while at the same time unleashing new threats to world peace and stability.

HISTORICAL ORIGINS

The UN's second secretary-general, Dag Hammarskjöld, coined the term *preventive diplomacy,* and the idea it captured was a cornerstone of his tenure as secretary-general.⁴ For Hammarskjöld, preventive diplomacy referred to efforts by the UN to prevent local disputes and conflicts in the third world from sparking a confrontation between the two superpowers.⁵ This conception of preventive diplomacy was understandable in an era in which the East–West conflict was the matrix of international politics. The secretary-general or his representatives and the Security Council could undertake preventive diplomacy. The mechanisms used included good offices, mediation, fact finding, economic measures, and peacekeeping operations.

However, the term *preventive diplomacy* failed to gain currency. Alan James has suggested that "this was due to Hammarskjöld's reluctance to elaborate and publicize the concept, to the superfluity (in a UN context) of describing its diplomacy as preventive, and the inappropriateness of the word diplomacy in relation to the UN's activity in the field."⁶

In January 1992, the Security Council, meeting at the summit level, requested Secretary-General Boutros Boutros-Ghali to submit an "analysis and recommendations on ways of strengthening and making more efficient within the framework and provisions of the Charter the capacity of the United Nations for preventive diplomacy, for peacemaking and for peacekeeping."[7] The secretary-general's report *An Agenda for Peace* gave a new boost to the concept of preventive diplomacy.[8] He defined preventive diplomacy as "action to prevent disputes from arising between parties, to prevent existing disputes from escalating into conflicts and to limit the spread of the latter when they occur."[9] Boutros-Ghali identified five instruments and mechanisms for implementing preventive diplomacy: measures to build confidence, fact finding, early warning, preventive deployment, and the establishment of demilitarized zones.

With regard to preventive deployment, he noted that this approach could occur in various circumstances:

> For example, in conditions of national crisis there could be preventive deployment at the request of the Government or all parties concerned, or with their consent; in inter-State disputes such deployment could take place when two countries feel that a United Nations presence on both sides of their border can discourage hostilities; furthermore, preventive deployment could take place when a country feels threatened and requests the deployment of an appropriate United Nations presence along its side of the border alone. In each situation, the mandate and composition of the United Nations presence would need to be carefully devised and be clear to all.[10]

The secretary-general suggested that if the government or all parties within a country in crisis consented, preventive deployment

> could help in a number of ways to alleviate suffering and to limit or control violence. Humanitarian assistance, impartially provided, could be of critical importance; assistance in maintaining security, whether through military, police or civilian personnel, could save lives and develop conditions of safety in which negotiations can be held; the United Nations could also help in conciliation efforts if this should be the wish of the parties.[11]

Nevertheless, he underlined the need for the United Nations to respect the sovereignty of the state: "to do otherwise would not be in accordance with the understanding of Member States in accepting the principles of the Charter."[12]

As to the role of preventive deployment in interstate disputes, the secretary-general wrote that "when both parties agree, I recommend that if the Security Council concludes that the likelihood of hostilities between neighboring countries could be removed by the preventive deployment of a United Nations presence on the territory of each State, such action should be taken. The nature of the tasks to be performed would determine the composition of the United

Nations presence."[13] When both states do not agree, preventive deployment was still possible:

> In cases where one nation fears a cross-border attack, if the Security Council concludes that a United Nations presence on one side of the border, with the consent only of the requesting country, would serve to deter conflict, I recommend that preventive deployment take place. Here again, the specific nature of the situation would determine the mandate and the personnel required to fulfill it.[14]

Four years after *The Agenda for Peace* was issued, in the fiftieth anniversary annual report on the UN, Secretary-General Boutros-Ghali noted that "preventive diplomacy is particularly favored by Member States as a means of preventing human suffering and as an alternative to costly politico-military operations to resolve conflicts after they have broken out." He declared, however, that he had reached the conclusion that "the activity we call 'preventive diplomacy' should be renamed 'preventive action.'" The secretary-general jettisoned the term *preventive diplomacy*, which he had done much to publicize, because, as he put it:

> Diplomacy is certainly a well-timed means of preventing conflict. The United Nations experience in recent years has shown, however, that there are several other forms of action that can have a useful preventive effect: preventive deployment; preventive disarmament; preventive humanitarian action; and preventive peace-building, which can involve, with the consent of the Government or Governments concerned, a wide range of actions in the fields of good governance, human rights and economic and social development.[15]

These remarks were striking for two reasons. First, they recognized that preventive action involves a broader range of activities beyond traditional diplomacy. Second, they acknowledged that multiple preventive measures can be taken depending on the nature of the problem being addressed.

THE BIRTH OF UN PEACEKEEPING

The framers of the United Nations Charter were determined that the UN would not suffer the fate of its predecessor, the League of Nations, in setting up the new organization's mechanisms for the pacific settlement of disputes and a collective security system. The preamble of the Charter states that "armed force shall not be used, save in the common interest." Article 1 (1) makes clear that one of the purposes of the organization is "to maintain international peace and security, and to that end: to take effective collective measures for the prevention and removal of threats to the peace." Under Chapter VI, member states are required to settle their disputes by peaceful means using methods such as negotiation, mediation, and arbitration, and Chapter VII empowered the Security Council, which has primary responsibility for maintaining international peace and security, to take action with respect to threats to peace, breaches of the peace, and acts of aggression. Such action could take the form of diplomatic, economic, or military sanctions or coercion by military enforcement.

As the United Nations would not have its own army, member states undertook "to make available to the Security Council, on its call and in accordance with a special agreement or agreements, armed forces, assistance, and facilities, including rights of passage, necessary for the purpose of maintaining international peace and security" (Article 43). The Charter provided for a Military Staff Committee, composed of the Chiefs of Staff of the five Permanent Members of the Security Council, that was "responsible under the Security Council for the strategic direction of any armed forces placed at the disposal of the Security Council" (Article 47).

The collective security system soon became hostage to the Cold War, as the United States and the Soviet Union used their vetoes to block forceful measures permitted by the Charter. With the paralysis of the collective security system, the UN in a remarkable example of functional adaptation developed peacekeeping as a tool to maintain international peace and security. Dag Hammarskjöld referred to peacekeeping operations as coming under "Chapter Six and a Half" for they fall in the gray zone between Chapters VI and VII. Hammarskjöld, Canadian Foreign Minister Lester B. Pearson, and UN Undersecretary-General Ralph Bunche made signal contributions to the adaptation and refinement of peacekeeping. All UN peacekeeping operations have contributed or tried to contribute to the prevention of conflict in three ways: by defusing a continuing and serious crisis, by maintaining calm in an area of armed confrontation, and by strengthening mechanisms for the settlement of disputes.[16] Therefore, to refer to UNPREDEP as the first preventive operation means that it was the first, which aimed at preventing a *first* round of fighting.

PEACEKEEPING DURING THE COLD WAR

Peacekeeping developed slowly.[17] Between 1945 and 1988, the UN approved only thirteen operations. These traditional or first-generation peacekeeping operations were frequently composed of troops from small or neutral states; they were deployed with the consent of the host government; they had to be impartial; and they could use force, but only in self-defense. The usual tasks of the "blue helmets" or "blue berets" were to monitor cease-fires and armistice agreements, serve as buffers, separate hostile forces, and enable political and diplomatic negotiations to be conducted.

The UN's first experience with peace observation was in the context of the Greek civil war following World War II. In 1946, a UN Investigative Commission was established to look into claims that Albania, Bulgaria, and Yugoslavia were supporting guerrillas in northern Greece. The Commission visited Greece and the neighboring states on a fact-finding mission. However, in light of the Cold War dimension to the civil war, the General Assembly and not the Security Council established an observation force in Greece that monitored its northern border.

During its first decade, the UN established three observer missions for truce supervision, two of which are still operational after half a century. The first mission was the UN observation team in Indonesia deployed from 1947 to 1950, to assist its independence from the Netherlands. The United Nations Truce Supervision Organization (UNTSO) was set up in 1948 in Palestine, under the UN mediator, Swedish Count Folke Bernadotte, to supervise the truce between Israeli and Arab armies. Count Bernadotte's assassination by the Stern Gang in Jerusalem was an early indication that peacekeeping would be a hazardous enterprise. Following Bernadotte's death, his adviser Ralph Bunche stepped into the breach and brokered an armistice between Israel and its Arab neighbors, for which he was awarded the Nobel Peace Prize in 1950.[18] UNTSO, whose headquarters are still at Government House in Jerusalem, has supervised a succession of armistices in the Middle East and reported regularly on the situation in the region to the United Nations. In addition to its observing and reporting functions, UNTSO provides experienced military officers to help in establishing new operations.

Conflict between the newly independent states of India and Pakistan over Jammu and Kashmir led to the establishment of the UN Military Observer Group in India and Pakistan (UNMOGIP) in 1949, which is also still in place. It was deployed in Kashmir to supervise a cease-fire between India and Pakistan after conflict erupted over the disputed territory. The observer force has investigated complaints, reported on troop movements, and helped to maintain order.

In 1956, the UN deployed its first peacekeeping force, the United Nations Emergency Force (UNEF I), to bring about a peaceful end to the Suez Crisis. In a move aimed at reversing Egypt's nationalization of the Suez Canal, British, French, and Israeli forces had invaded Egypt. Because two permanent members of the Security Council with veto power, Britain and France, were involved, the Council was deadlocked. At the initiative of Lester B. Pearson, on 4 November 1956, the General Assembly adopted Resolution 998 creating UNEF I. It monitored the cease-fire between the forces, oversaw the withdrawal of the invading armies from the area, and served as a buffer between the Israeli and Egyptian forces. UNEF I established key principles that guided subsequent operations: the consent of the parties to the dispute for the establishment of the mission; nonuse of force except in self-defense; voluntary participation of contingents from small, neutral countries in the force; strict impartiality; and day-to-day control of peacekeeping operations by the secretary-general.[19] UNEF I remained in the Middle East until 1967, when it was withdrawn at the request of President Gamel Nasser of Egypt. In the aftermath of the Yom Kippur War of October 1973, UNEF II was authorized by the Security Council to act as a buffer between Egyptian and Israeli forces. Following the historic Camp David accords between Egypt and Israel in 1979, UNEF II ended and was replaced by a non-UN, U.S.-sponsored multinational force.

The problems of decolonization led to the UN's second peacekeeping mission, which was deployed in the Congo from 1960 to 1964. The mission foreshadowed the multidimensional peace operations launched by the UN in the 1990s. The Congo gained its independence from Belgium on 30 June 1960, but law and order soon collapsed. Belgium deployed troops to protect its nationals. Civil war erupted when the province of Katanga seceded and declared its independence. Congolese Prime Minister Patrice Lumumba appealed to the United Nations for assistance, following which the UN established a peacekeeping force, Opération des Nations Unies au Congo (ONUC). Its initial mandate was to ensure the withdrawal of Belgian forces, to assist the government in maintaining law and order, and to provide technical assistance. ONUC's tasks were later expanded to include maintaining Congo's territorial integrity and political independence and securing the withdrawal of all foreign military, paramilitary, and advisory personnel not under UN command, as well as all mercenaries. In 1961, in an attempt to reconcile rival factions and establish a cease-fire in the Congo, UN Secretary-General Dag Hammarskjöld, seven UN staff, and the Swedish crew died when their plane crashed. ONUC was the UN's largest and most controversial operation undertaken during the Cold War era. At its height, it had more than twenty thousand personnel, and the financial controversy over ONUC provoked a crisis that threatened the future of the UN. The operation claimed the lives of 250 peacekeepers, the greatest number of fatalities prior to 1991.[20]

The Mediterranean island of Cyprus was the location of the UN's third peacekeeping operation. There is a history of animosity between the Greek and Turkish communities on the island. Cyprus became independent in 1960, and its Constitution included power-sharing provisions to balance the interests of the two communities. The constitutional arrangements had been worked out with Britain, Greece, and Turkey. However, disputes between Greek and Turkish Cypriots over the governing of the island led to a number of constitutional crises. In December 1963, violence erupted. Diplomatic efforts to resolve the conflict were unsuccessful, and on 4 March 1964, the Security Council unanimously adopted Resolution 186 (1964) authorizing the establishment of the United Nations Peacekeeping Force in Cyprus (UNFICYP). The mandate of the Force was to prevent a recurrence of fighting, restore law and order, and contribute to a return to normal conditions.[21]

In July 1974, Turkish troops invaded Cyprus and occupied the northern half of the island. UNFICYP has supervised the cease-fire, which came into effect on 16 August 1974 and maintained a buffer zone between the lines of the Cyprus National Guard and the Turkish Forces. A Greek Cypriot administration, internationally recognized as the government of Cyprus, controls the south, while Turkish Cypriots, recognized only by Ankara, control the north. Various attempts to reach a political settlement have failed, and UNFICYP remains deployed on the partitioned island.

The United Nations Interim Force in Lebanon (UNIFIL) was the last major peacekeeping operation established during the Cold War. In the early 1970s, a pattern of Palestinian terrorist attacks began against Israel, followed by Israeli reprisals against Palestinian targets in Lebanon. On 11 March 1978, Palestinian guerrillas at a base in southern Lebanon attacked a tourist bus in Israel, killing thirty-seven people and wounding many more. In response, the Israeli army invaded Lebanon and in a few days had occupied the south of the country.

The Lebanese government protested to the United Nations, and on 19 March the Security Council adopted Resolution 425 (1978) and 426 (1978) authorizing the creation of UNIFIL. The peacekeeping force was to supervise the withdrawal of Israeli forces, restore international peace and security, and assist the government of Lebanon to reestablish its effective authority in the area. UNIFIL's capacity to implement the mandate was impeded by lack of cooperation from the Palestine Liberation Organization (PLO) and Israel.[22]

In June 1982, Israel invaded Lebanon again and reached the outskirts of Beirut. UNIFIL's role became limited to providing humanitarian assistance to the local population. Israel carried out a partial withdrawal in 1985 but retained control of its "security zone" in southern Lebanon through the Israel Defense Forces (IDF) and its Lebanese auxiliary de facto forces (DFF). The IDF and DFF have been targets for attacks by groups opposed to Israel's occupation of South Lebanon. In 1993 and 1996, Israel launched massive strikes against Palestinian targets in Lebanon, in which many civilians were killed. Although UNIFIL has not succeeded in preventing armed conflict, many observers believe its presence has been a restraining influence, and the Security Council has regularly extended its mandate.[23]

The contribution of United Nations peacekeepers to maintaining international peace and security was recognized with the award of the Nobel Peace Prize in 1988. This was the high-water mark of peacekeeping. But it would be wrong to regard the first forty years as the "golden age" of UN peacekeeping. As the Charter did not deal with peacekeeping, the early operations were marked by a great deal of ad hocery and improvisation. At the establishment of UNEF I in 1956, there was widespread skepticism about its utility and value. Peacekeeping also sparked serious controversy among UN member states during the Cold War. The UN was polarized along East–West lines over ONUC, and some permanent members of the Security Council questioned the independence and integrity of the secretary-general and the Secretariat. UN peacekeeping would face even sterner tests in the aftermath of the Cold War.

PEACEKEEPING IN THE POST–COLD WAR WORLD

The end of the Cold War in 1989–90 ended the Security Council's institutional paralysis. There was a new spirit of cooperation among the permanent members and much less use of the veto. The UN seemed to begin to function as its founders had intended. Many commentators talked of a renaissance of the organization, saying that like the phoenix it had been reborn. The improved international climate led to three new UN peacekeeping operations in 1989: Angola, to verify the staged withdrawal of Cuban troops from the country; Namibia, to supervise its transition to independence; and Central America, to monitor a cease-fire and the demobilization of guerrilla forces.

Although the shadow of possible nuclear confrontation had lifted, a resurgence of ethnic conflicts and civil wars occurred after the Cold War, followed by a dramatic increase in the number and scope of peacekeeping operations. Peacekeeping was seen as a panacea for international disorder. These second-generation or multidimensional operations were quantitatively and qualitatively different from those undertaken during the Cold War. In the space of only six years, 1988 through 1994, the UN established twenty-two new peacekeeping operations. The total number of UN peacekeepers serving in the field grew from ten thousand military personnel in 1987 to nearly eighty thousand in 1994. The UN also expanded the level of involvement by civilian police and international civilian personnel. In contrast to the Cold War era, most of the new missions were deployed to deal with conflicts within states, and some were established without the consent of a host government. The mandates were more complex and included observing elections, demobilizing and rehabilitating armed factions, delivering humanitarian aid, removing antipersonnel mines, protecting safe areas, training civilian police, investigating human rights violations, ensuring the return and resettlement of refugees, and monitoring no-fly zones.

The UN mounted relatively successful operations in Namibia, El Salvador, and elsewhere. The United Nations Transition Assistance Group (UNTAG) in Namibia was the first multidimensional operation and combined peacekeeping and peacemaking. It was deployed in April 1989, over ten years after it had initially been authorized by Security Council Resolution 435 (1978) of 29 September 1978. It was charged with ensuring the independence of Namibia through free and fair elections under the supervision of the UN. UNTAG was also to help ensure that South African forces withdrew from the country, political prisoners were released, all discriminatory laws were repealed, Namibian refugees were allowed to return, and law and order impartially administered and maintained. To accomplish its mandate, the mission had political, military, civilian police, legal, quasi-judicial, public information, and administrative components. UNTAG successfully supervised Namibia's first democratic elections, which led to its independence in 1990. Supervising the elections was not easy, the main problems being the lack of a forum to mediate electoral disputes, the inadequate size of the Force, and the enormous size of the mission area.[24]

The United Nations Observer Mission in El Salvador (ONUSAL) was established in July 1991 to verify the agreements between the government of El Salvador and the guerrilla resistance movement, Frente Farabundo Marti para la Liberacion Nacional (FMLN), ending a long and bitter civil war. ONUSAL was responsible for monitoring the cease-fire and separation of forces, as well as maintaining public order while a new police force was being created. It was also the first operation with a specific mandate to verify compliance with human rights. After the end of armed conflict and demobilization, ONUSAL observed presidential, legislative, and municipal elections in March and April 1994. After the withdrawal of the military and civilian police personnel in April 1995, a small group of UN civilian personnel known as the United Nations Mission in El Salvador (MINUSAL) remained in the country to provide good offices to the parties, to monitor implementation of outstanding points of the peace agreements, and to report regularly to the United Nations.[25]

Perhaps because of the UN's more successful operations, little consideration was given to whether the organization had the capacity to respond effectively to all the new demands that were being placed on it. Establishing a peacekeeping operation was sometimes the easy option chosen by the major powers between doing nothing and taking decisive military action. Peacekeeping troops were deployed where there was no peace to keep. Some of the mandates were either too vague or too ambitious. Sometimes the necessary resources were not provided to implement the mandates, as Secretary-General Boutros-Ghali noted pointedly in *An Agenda for Peace*: "A chasm has developed between the tasks entrusted to this Organization and the financial means provided to it."[26]

Setbacks followed the successes in Somalia, Rwanda, and Bosnia. It is instructive to reflect on the UN's experience in Somalia; it exemplifies a number of the problems that the UN would face in its less than successful operations. President Mohammed Siad Barre, a general who came to power by a military coup, had ruled Somalia since 1969. As a client of the Soviet Union and later the United States, Somalia received a substantial amount of weapons. In January 1991, Siad Barre's government collapsed and Somalia was plunged into anarchy. There was no central government, no common power. Fighting among rival factions and clans was the order of the day. The political problems were compounded by widespread famine, especially in the provinces.

A year after Barre's government was toppled, in January 1992, UN Undersecretary-General for Political Affairs James Jonah went to Somalia to mediate between the two major warlords, Mohammed Farah Aideed and Mohammed Ali Mahdi. His efforts eventually resulted in a cease-fire agreement in April. The Security Council authorized the deployment of some fifty military observers as part of the United Nations Operation in Somalia (UNOSOM I). They were required to monitor the cease-fire in the capital Mogadishu; provide protection for UN personnel, equipment, and supplies; and escort humanitarian relief supplies in the city and immediate area.[27] In August, a battalion of five hundred troops to enable it to protect humanitarian convoys in the more remote parts of the country enlarged the strength of the mission.

However, the UN Force could not operate in the rural areas of the country where the cease-fire was not observed. Feuding militias regularly attacked the peacekeepers, humanitarian convoys were looted, and emergency relief workers were prevented from reaching those who needed help the most. Images of emaciated Somalis appeared in the Western media, prompting calls for more effective international intervention.

Faced with the deterioration in the situation in Somalia, President George Bush, in the twilight of his presidency, decided to send U.S. troops to Somalia. On 3 December 1992, the Security Council, acting under Chapter VII of the Charter, unanimously adopted Resolution 794 authorizing UN member states to "use all necessary means" to establish a secure environment for humanitarian relief operations in Somalia. The Unified Task Force (UNITAF), including twenty-eight thousand U.S. troops, entered Somalia on 9 December 1992. Secretary-General Boutros-Ghali was, however, concerned about UNITAF's limited mandate. He wanted UNITAF to disarm the Somali militias because, as he wrote in a letter to President Bush:

> without this action I do not believe that it will be possible to establish the secure environment called for by the Security Council resolution or to create conditions in which the United Nations' existing efforts to promote national reconciliation can be carried forward and the task of protecting humanitarian activities can safely be transferred to a conventional United Nations peacekeeping operation.[28]

But this was not to be, for the Pentagon was opposed to the idea. The failure to disarm the various factions would pose difficulties for the UN successor mission and impede the search for a negotiated political settlement.

Nonetheless, UNITAF had significant accomplishments. It halted the fighting and ensured that humanitarian assistance reached the more inaccessible areas of the country. The number of deaths from hunger and starvation dropped significantly.

UNOSOM II was established on 26 March 1993 by Security Council Resolution 814 and took over from UNITAF on 4 May 1993. The new Force was authorized to take enforcement measures to establish a secure environment throughout Somalia. UNOSOM II was given a broad mandate that included disarming rival factions, assisting Somalis in rebuilding their economy and social and political life, reestablishing the country's institutional structure, achieving national political reconciliation, recreating a Somali state based on democracy, and rehabilitating the country's economy and infrastructure.[29] It was a tall order.

The UN peacekeepers' efforts to disarm the Somali militias were met with strong opposition. On 5 June 1993, twenty-six Pakistani peacekeepers carrying out weapons inspections were killed in an ambush, and fifty-six were wounded. The Security Council's response was swift. The following day, 6 June, the Council adopted Resolution 837 authorizing the secretary-general "to take all necessary measures against those responsible for the armed attacks . . . including their arrest and detention for prosecution, trial, and punishment." In the words of William J. Durch, "This paragraph—made in the USA—set UNOSOM II on the path that led to the firefight of 3 October 1993, the U.S. pullout from UNOSOM II, and an uproar in the United States over the role of American forces in UN peace operations."[30] A UN investigation confirmed that General Aideed and his supporters were responsible for the attacks. A manhunt for Aideed began.

UN troops and the U.S. Quick Reaction Force (QRF) launched a number of attacks against Aideed's strongholds in south Mogadishu. They destroyed much of Aideed's heavy weaponry but failed to capture the wanted man. Some UN and U.S. troops were killed in the raids, as were some of Aideed's followers. On 26 August, a U.S. Delta Force of commandos and Rangers arrived in Mogadishu and conducted six raids against Aideed's followers over the next month. However, a raid by the Rangers on 3 October went terribly wrong and resulted in the deaths of eighteen U.S. soldiers. Supporters of Aideed dragged the body of one U.S. soldier through the streets of Mogadishu. On 6 October, President Bill Clinton announced that U.S. troops would withdraw from Somalia at the end of March 1994. Efforts to capture Aideed were abandoned, and the UN continued its elusive search for a political solution. The security situation deteriorated following the departure of U.S. troops, and political reconciliation made little headway. In March 1995, UNOSOM II was withdrawn from Somalia.

The UN missions in Somalia dramatized the perils of conducting operations in a state lacking central authority. UNOSOM II had an ambitious mandate of nation building but lacked the requisite resources and the sustained support of the major powers. Traditional peacekeeping principles were inappropriate in the conditions that existed in Somalia. And the efforts to arrest Mohammed Aideed were a departure from two cardinal principles of peacekeeping: neutrality and impartiality.

CONCLUSION

In the Cold War era, traditional UN peacekeeping was the norm for field operations. With the end of the Cold War, the UN embarked on more ambitious ventures with varying degrees of success. The limits of the UN's capacity became clear with its reversals. Peacekeeping was discredited and seemed to be the god that failed. Governments were reluctant to authorize new operations, and as a result, UN peacekeeping was dramatically reduced in the late 1990s. In 1998, only thirteen thousand personnel were serving in fifteen operations. Nonetheless, UN peacekeeping is still good value. The cost of U.S., British, French, and German defense in 1994 was more than $400 billion. That of UN peacekeeping in the nineteen major trouble spots around the world during that peak year was some $3.6 billion, less than 1 percent of the former figure.

History demonstrates that it is unwise to exaggerate or underestimate the potential of peacekeeping. The sobering experiences of the 1990s have helped to create a more realistic view of peacekeeping. It is unlikely that UN peacekeeping, which has consistently defied predictions of demise, will soon cease to be a tool for the prevention and management of international conflict.

NOTES

1. Kofi Annan, "The Challenge of Conflict Prevention," address to the James A. Baker III Institute for Public Policy at Rice University, Houston, Texas, SG/SM/6535, 23 April 1998.

2. Michael S. Lund, *Preventing Violent Conflicts: A Strategy for Preventive Diplomacy* (Washington, D.C.: U.S. Institute of Peace, October 1996), chap. 1. For a skeptical view of the merits of preventive diplomacy, see Stephen John Stedman, "Alchemy for a New World Order: Overselling 'Preventive Diplomacy,'" *Foreign Affairs* 74, no. 3 (May/June 1995): 14-20. See also the response by Michael S. Lund, "Underrating Preventive Diplomacy," *Foreign Affairs* 74, no. 4 (July/August 1995): 160-63.

3. Press briefing by Yasushi Akashi, United Nations Peace Forces Headquarters, Division of Public Information, *Daily Public Information Summary,* Zagreb, 31 October 1995. In Yasushi Akashi, "The Dilemmas of Peacekeeping," *Brown Journal of World Affairs* 3, no. 1 (Winter/Spring 1996): 79, he again pointed to the success of the UN's mission in Macedonia:

> There is no question in my mind that preventive diplomacy is the most effective and most cost-effective way of dealing with conflicts. Take the former Yugoslavia. There are people who say that the UN experience there was a failure. I do not subscribe to that at all and if you turn your attention to the former Yugoslav Republic of Macedonia where the UN has a preventive deployment, it is a resounding success. Through its preventive deployment the UN has been able to make sure that the interethnic conflict which prevailed elsewhere in the former Yugoslavia did not permeate into Macedonia, and although it is suffering from serious economic dislocation and unemployment, Macedonia has been able to maintain its political independence and ethnic stability, thanks partly to the wise leadership of President Gligorov. But I think—and I had many occasions to speak to President Gligorov—I think the primary factor for stability in Macedonia is the UN preventive deployment where Nordic and U.S. troops are there in the framework of the UN. This is one example in which preventive diplomacy and preventive deployment have been successful.

4. For an excellent discussion of the contributions of the second secretary-general, see the magisterial biography by Brian Urquhart, *Hammarskjöld* (New York: Knopf, 1972).

5. Dag Hammarskjöld, *Introduction to the Annual Report of the Secretary-General on the Work of the Organization, 16 June 1959–15 June 1960,* UN General Assembly, Official Records, Fifteenth Session, Supplement No.1A.

6. Alan James, "UN Preventive Diplomacy in Historical Perspective," paper presented at the international workshop on "An Agenda for Preventive Diplomacy: Theory and Practice," Skopje, 16-19 October 1996.

7. Quoted in Boutros Boutros-Ghali, *An Agenda for Peace* (New York: United Nations, 1992), para.1.

8. For a useful discussion of the drafting of *An Agenda for Peace,* see Jean Krasno, *The Quiet Revolutionary: A Biographical Sketch of James S. Sutterlin* (New Haven, Conn.: Academic Council on the United Nations System, 1998), 32-34.

9. Boutros-Ghali, *An Agenda for Peace,* para. 20. For a critical view of Boutros-Ghali's definition of preventive diplomacy, see Lund, *Preventing Violent Conflicts*, chap. 2.

10. Boutros-Ghali, *An Agenda for Peace*, para.28.

11. Boutros-Ghali, *An Agenda for Peace*, para.29.

12. Boutros-Ghali, *An Agenda for Peace*, para.30.

13. Boutros-Ghali, *An Agenda for Peace,* para.31.

14. Boutros-Ghali, *An Agenda for Peace,* para.32.

15. Boutros Boutros-Ghali, *The 50th Anniversary Annual Report on the Work of the Organization* (New York: United Nations, 1996), para. 652.

16. See Alan James, "UN Preventive Diplomacy in Historical Perspective," paper presented at the international workshop on "An Agenda for Preventive Diplomacy: Theory and Practice," Skopje, 16-19 October 1996.

17. The historical review of peacekeeping in this section draws on Alan James, *Peacekeeping in International Politics* (London: Macmillan, 1990); Paul F. Diehl, *International Peacekeeping* (Baltimore: Johns Hopkins University Press, 1994); William J. Durch, ed., *The Evolution of UN Peacekeeping* (New York: St. Martin's, 1993); William J. Durch, ed., *UN Peacekeeping, American Policy, and the Uncivil Wars of the 1990s* (New York: St. Martin's, 1996); and Thomas G. Weiss and Jarat Chopra, *United Nations Peacekeeping: An ACUNS Teaching Text* (Providence, R.I.: Academic Council on the United Nations System, 1992).

18. For a splendid biography of Ralph Bunche, see Brian Urquhart, *Ralph Bunche: An American Life* (New York: Norton, 1993). Sir Brian was a close associate of Bunche in the United Nations Secretariat.

19. A. B. Fetherston, *Toward a Theory of United Nations Peacekeeping* (New York: St. Martin's, 1994), 13.

20. *United Nations Peacekeeping: 50 Years 1948–1998* (New York: United Nations Department of Public Information, October 1998), 18.

21. On the origins of UNFICYP, see Alan James, "Reluctant Heroes: Assembling the United Nations Cyprus Force, 1964," *International Journal* (Autumn 1998): 734-52.

22. Diehl, *International Peacekeeping*, 57.

23. *United Nations Peacekeeping: 50 Years 1948–1998*, 80-81.

24. Diehl, *International Peacekeeping,* 159-62.

25. For a detailed discussion of the ONUSAL operation, see Fen Osler Hampson, "The Pursuit of Human Rights: The United Nations in El Salvador," in Durch, ed., *UN Peacekeeping,* 69-102.

26. Boutros-Ghali, *An Agenda for Peace*, para.69.

27. *United Nations Peacekeeping: 50 Years 1948–1998*, 28.

28. Boutros Boutros-Ghali, *Unvanquished: A U.S.–UN Saga* (New York: Random House, 1999), 59-60.

29. *United Nations Peacekeeping: 50 Years 1948–1998*, 29.

30. William J. Durch, "Introduction to Anarchy: Humanitarian Intervention and 'State-Building' in Somalia," in Durch, ed., *UN Peacekeeping,* 332.

2

THE BURDEN OF HISTORY

The challenges facing the new former Yugoslav Republic of Macedonia must be understood in history's light but can be resolved only by moving out from under history's shadow.[1]

David Fromkin

To understand contemporary Macedonia requires an understanding of its past, especially as the apple of discord in the Balkans. In the turbulent Balkan region, history is a vital dimension of the present. Macedonia, a small landlocked country, about the same size as Vermont, and with a population of some two million, is of strategic importance to the security of the southern Balkans and the eastern Mediterranean. In the words of Misha Glenny, "The Balkan mountains can only be traversed through Macedonia—either north to south, from Orthodox Belgrade to Orthodox Thessaloniki, or from west to east, from Muslim Durrës in Albania to Muslim Istanbul; all main trading routes in the southern Balkans pass through Macedonia."[2] During the last two hundred years, major powers have fought one another for control of this strategic territory. For centuries, Macedonia has been the home of various ethnic groups with different cultures and languages, which prevented the development of a national identity. At the end of World War II, Josip Broz Tito, the new head of state of Yugoslavia, recognized Macedonia as one of the Yugoslav republics and encouraged a separate national consciousness among Macedonians. The regional rivalries for control of Macedonia through the ages, and the relations among the ethnic communities, which inhabit the territory, have profound effects on the modern Macedonian state.

At independence, the new state faced a number of external and internal threats to its stability and survival. It had troubled relations with its neighbors, which challenged its right to exist as an independent country. The main goal of its foreign policy was to gain recognition and membership of international organizations, but Macedonia's dispute with Greece was a major obstacle to achieving this objective. The political conflict between the two neighbors resulted in Macedonia becoming the first state to be admitted to the United Nations under a temporary name.

Internally, ethnic tension was growing, especially between ethnic Macedonians and Albanians. The two communities have existed separately for generations, largely in mutual incomprehension and suspicion. For contemporary Macedonia, as for most countries in the twentieth century, the state preceded the nation at independence. Creating a sense of nationhood—across ethnic lines—is a major challenge confronting the Macedonian government and its peoples. This is not an easy task, for the ethnic cleavages are deep. The poorest of the former Yugoslav republics, Macedonia's weak economy compounded ethnic and social problems.

In September 1991, the United Nations took the first steps that would lead to the most complex and expensive peacekeeping operation in its history. This chapter includes an examination of the original mandate of the United Nations Protection Force (UNPROFOR) and its initial implementation in Croatia and Bosnia.

WHAT'S IN A NAME?

The term *Macedonia* refers to a new independent and sovereign state, and it is also a geographic and historical concept. The former Yugoslav Republic of Macedonia is landlocked and bordered by four countries: Albania, Bulgaria, the Federal Republic of Yugoslavia (Serbia and Montenegro), and Greece. Today, geographically, the historical region of Macedonia overlaps four countries: Albania, Bulgaria, Greece, and the former Yugoslav Republic of Macedonia. During the nineteenth and twentieth centuries, Albania, Bulgaria, Greece, and Serbia coveted all or parts of the geographic territory.

Macedonia has ancient roots that can be traced to the reign of King Karan, 808–778 B.C. Under Philip II, who reigned from 359 to 336 B.C., Macedonia became a formidable military power, and his kingdom included present-day Kosovo, Albania, Thrace, and the former Yugoslav Republic of Macedonia.[3] His son Alexander the Great, in a relatively short reign of thirteen years, extended the Macedonian Empire from the Adriatic Sea to the Indus River. Following his death in 323 B.C., the empire disintegrated, and Macedonia eventually came under Roman and later Byzantine rule.

In the sixth century, the Slavs settled in Macedonia. During the medieval period, Macedonia became part of short-lived Bulgarian and Serbian empires. In the fourteenth century, it became part of the Ottoman Empire, under whose control it remained for more than five hundred years. With the weakening of the central authority of the Ottoman Empire by the eighteenth century, lawlessness and banditry became the norm in Macedonia, which by then had a mixed population of Albanians, Bulgarians, Greeks, Jews, Roma (Gypsies), Turks, and Vlachs.

THE "MACEDONIAN QUESTION"

In the late nineteenth and early twentieth century, the "Macedonian question" was a major preoccupation of the European powers and a cause of much bloodshed. Its origins go back to the Treaty of San Stefano of 3 March 1878, which ended the war between Russia and the Ottoman Empire. Russia led the move for the creation of a new Bulgarian state, much larger than Greece and Serbia, and which included the geographic region of Macedonia. The presence of a large Bulgarian state in the Balkans, allied with Russia, was unacceptable to other European powers. Three months later at the Congress of Berlin, Macedonia was returned to a weak Ottoman Empire. Commenting on this reversal, Duncan Perry writes, "this great power action inflicted a deep gash in the psyche of the Bulgarian nation, depriving it of its perceived Macedonian birthright, [an] objective that Bulgarians pursued with vigor throughout [the] remainder of that century and into the present one."[4]

The first signs of a Macedonian national identity were evident in the late nineteenth century, mostly among intellectuals called "The Macedonianists." The Ilinden ("St. Elijah's day") Uprising of 2–3 August 1903 has an important place in Macedonian mythology and historiography. The Internal Macedonian Revolutionary Organization (VMRO) organized a revolt against Ottoman rule. It established the Krushevo Republic for a week, before Ottoman forces crushed it. Meanwhile, Bulgaria, Greece, and Serbia, which did not recognize the existence of a separate Macedonian nation, continued to support guerrilla movements in an effort to gain control of Macedonia.

Macedonia was the focus of bitter struggle in the two Balkan Wars of 1912 and 1913. In the First Balkan War, Bulgaria, Greece, and Serbia formed an alliance and defeated Turkey, liberating most of the Balkan Peninsula from Ottoman control. Following their victory, the three countries fought among themselves in the Second Balkan War, this time with Greece and Serbia allied against

Bulgaria. The Balkan Wars were marked by much brutality, which presaged the ethnic violence of the wars of Yugoslav secession eight decades later. On 10 August 1913, the Treaty of Bucharest carved up Macedonia among the victors. Aegean Macedonia, 34,356 square kilometers (representing about 51 percent of the total original area), was incorporated into Greece; Vardar Macedonia, 25,713 square kilometers (39 percent), became part of Serbia; Pirin Macedonia, 6,798 square kilometers (9 percent), was given to Bulgaria; and Albania got a sliver of 1 per cent. At the start of the Balkan Wars, a variety of different ethnic groups lived within geographic Macedonia: Albanians, Slavs, Vlachs, Jews, Roma (Gypsies), and Greeks. There was also a religious split between Orthodox Christians and Muslims. For example, there were both Christian and Muslim Slavs, Albanians, and Roma. The partitioning of Macedonia resulted in a patchwork of different peoples in the four states.

During World War I, Greece and Serbia supported the Western Allies, while Bulgaria supported the Central powers. In 1915, Bulgaria occupied most of Vardar Macedonia and eastern Aegean Macedonia. Following the war, Vardar Macedonia became part of the newly established Kingdom of Serbs, Croats, and Slovenes and was referred to by the Serbs as "South Serbia." Ethnic Albanians and Slav Macedonians alike faced official repressive policies of Serbianisation and assimilation. The Vardar Macedonian Orthodox Church came under the jurisdiction of the Serbian Orthodox Church, and Albanian schools in western Vardar Macedonia were closed. Slav Macedonians, led by VMRO, and ethnic Albanians took up armed resistance and attacked Serb officials and other civilians, government offices, and trains.[5]

After King Boris of Bulgaria was pressured to join the Axis powers in 1940, the Bulgarians took over most of Vardar Macedonia, as well as eastern Aegean Macedonia and Thrace. The Germans occupied Thessaloniki because of its strategic location, and Italy controlled part of western Aegean Macedonia. The vast majority of the Slavs in Vardar Macedonia initially welcomed the Bulgarians as liberators after the oppressive years of Serbian rule. However, when the Bulgarians imposed an insensitive and corrupt centralized bureaucracy, resentment quickly grew which resulted in several uprisings.[6]

The Communist partisan leader Josip Broz Tito advocated that Macedonia should be an integral part of a new federal Yugoslavia. The second congress of the Anti-Fascist Council for the National Liberation of Yugoslavia (AVNOJ) held at Jajce on 29 November 1943 granted Macedonia equal status to that of the other five federal entities: Serbia, Croatia, Slovenia, Montenegro, and Bosnia-Herzegovina. Tito's ultimate goal was to incorporate most Macedonian territories—not only Vardar Macedonia—within the Yugoslav Federation. On 2 August 1944, the anniversary of the Ilinden Uprising, Tito organized the first

Anti-Fascist Assembly of National Liberation of Macedonia (ASNOM) at the St. Prohor Pchinski monastery. ASNOM affirmed that Macedonia was a federal state within the Yugoslav Federation and decided that Macedonian would be the official language of Macedonia.[7]

At the end of World War II, Macedonia became one of the six republics of the Yugoslav federation. It was also the poorest. Tito encouraged Macedonia to develop a separate national identity, as part of his strategy to establish a new Yugoslavia. As Duncan Perry points out:

> Tito's recognition of the Macedonian nationality and creation of a separate Macedonian republic within the Yugoslav federation, served to set apart the Slavs living there from Bulgarians and Serbs, a fundamental [tenet] of his Yugoslav nation building program. Tito thus undermined Bulgarian territorial claims by reinforcing that Macedonians were a separate nationality and blocked Serbia from claiming that Macedonians were part of the "Greater Serbian" nation that had dominated interwar Yugoslavia politically and demographically and that had sought to Serbianize Macedonia in the interwar period.[8]

The authorities in the new Socialist Republic of Macedonia made concerted efforts at nation building. They developed a new Macedonian language, alphabet, and orthography; commissioned new history textbooks for use in schools; and established the autocephalous Macedonian Church. The extent to which Tito succeeded in developing a separate Macedonian national identity would be tested during the dissolution of Yugoslavia.

THE OUTBREAK OF WAR IN YUGOSLAVIA

The disintegration of the former Yugoslavia is well documented and has produced a steady stream of books advancing contending explanations of the wars of secession that followed in its wake.[9] Undoubtedly, the debate on the causes of Yugoslavia's dissolution will continue for many years to come. To some observers, Serb aggression and President Slobodan Milosevic's unrelenting determination to create a "Greater Serbia" caused the war. A second interpretation focuses on "ancient hatreds," frozen by communism for fifty years, which made the war historically inevitable. Other commentators argue that Yugoslavia's disintegration was due to the rise of ethnic nationalism, primarily in Serbia but also in Bosnia, Croatia, and Slovenia. The fourth thesis emphasizes the destabilizing role of the Great Powers in seeking to reestablish their influence in the Balkans after the end of the Cold War. To other observers, the war was attributable to a "clash of civilizations," a conflict among Latin Christianity, Ortho-

dox Christianity, and Islam. A final view sees the origins of the war in competing claims for self-determination within an artificially constructed federation.

In March and April 1990, Slovenia and Croatia held their first multiparty
elections in nearly fifty years. Parties advocating national sovereignty within a
new Yugoslav federation defeated the Communist reformers. In November and
December 1990, multiparty elections were also held in Macedonia and Bosnia-
Herzegovina. In Macedonia, over 80 percent of eligible voters participated in
the two rounds of elections for 120 representatives to the National Assembly.
The largest number of seats, thirty-eight, was won by the nationalist Internal
Macedonian Revolutionary Organization–Democratic Party of Macedonian
National Unity (VMRO-DPMNE), followed by the Party for Democratic
Transformation (the former Communists), later known as the Social Democra-
tic Union of Macedonia, with thirty-one seats, the moderate ethnic Albanian
Party for Democratic Prosperity with seventeen seats, and the Reform Forces
of Macedonia-Liberal Party with sixteen seats. The remaining eighteen seats
were won by five political parties and three independent candidates.

In January 1991, Parliament elected Kiro Gligorov of the Social Democratic Alliance as the first president of Macedonia. Gligorov had been a Partisan
fighter in the struggle against the Nazis in World War II. A prominent member
of the old Communist elite, he had been a member of the Presidency of Yugoslavia. Of the leaders of the former Yugoslav republics, Gligorov had a reputation for wisdom and level-headedness. A non-partisan government of experts
was formed, but it collapsed in July 1992 after losing a vote of no confidence.
VMRO-DPMNE was unable to form a government due to its unwillingness to
govern with former Communist and ethnic Albanian parties. In September
1992, a coalition government was formed of the Social Democratic Union of
Macedonia, the Reform Forces of Macedonia–Liberal Party, and the Party for
Democratic Prosperity. Thirty-year-old Prime Minister Branko Crvenkovski
led it. Following his graduation from the Faculty of Engineering at Sts. Cyril
and Methodius University in Skopje in 1986, he worked for a computer firm
before being elected to Parliament in 1990.

During early 1991, Macedonia's President Kiro Gligorov and the president
of Bosnia, Alija Izetbegovic, made concerted efforts to find a solution to the crisis within a decentralized and reorganized Yugoslav federation. However, Gligorov and Izetbegovic made it clear that should Slovenia and Croatia decide to
leave the federation, Macedonia and Bosnia would do the same. In the view of
Macedonia's leaders, independence was preferable to remaining in a rump Yugoslavia dominated by Serbia.

Western governments initially insisted that Yugoslavia should remain
united but this was not to be. On 25 June 1991, Slovenia and Croatia simulta-

neously declared their independence from Yugoslavia. A short war broke out between Slovene forces and the Yugoslav National Army (JNA), but less than a fortnight later the JNA withdrew on orders from Milosevic. On 7 July 1991, European diplomacy resulted in the Brioni Accords, which stipulated that the Serb, Croat, and federal leaders respect an immediate cease-fire and accept a three-month moratorium on the declarations of independence of Slovenia and Croatia. However, Milosevic and Slovenian President Milan Kucan had agreed on Slovenia's departure from the federation. In the words of Richard Holbrooke, "Slovenia's departure from Yugoslavia made it easier for Milosevic to create a Yugoslavia dominated by the Serbs, since it removed from the country a republic with almost no Serbs."[10]

The independence of Croatia, which had a larger Serb population, was quite another matter. The JNA, Serb paramilitary units, and Serbs in the Krajina region mounted stiff resistance. Throughout the second half of 1991, the JNA fought an "undeclared and dirty war" in Croatia.[11] The war of Croatian independence lasted six months until UN negotiators brokered a cease-fire.

On September 8, 1991, a referendum for independence was held in Macedonia; 72 percent of eligible voters went to the polls, and 99 percent of those voted supported Macedonian independence. However, ethnic Albanians and Serbs boycotted the referendum. According to the 1991 census, the last conducted by the Socialist Federal Republic of Yugoslavia, 65.3 percent of Macedonia's two million inhabitants were ethnic (Slav) Macedonians. Ethnic Albanians boycotted the census because of concern that they would not be counted accurately, and thus their size was estimated at 21.7 percent by the Macedonian authorities. Ethnic Albanian parties, however, refused to accept this number. The ethnic composition of the rest of the population was as follows: Turks, 3.8 percent; Roma, 2.6 percent; Serbs, 2.1 percent; and Vlachs, 0.4 percent. The vote for independence was the fulfillment of the national aspirations of ethnic Macedonians. The National Assembly adopted a declaration of independence on 17 September, which stated that in the referendum "the citizens of the Republic of Macedonia democratically wrote a new page in the Macedonian centuries-long history for completing the independence and sovereignty of the Republic of Macedonia as a state."[12]

A constitution, as its Latin roots suggest, is something that enables a state to stand together, but in Macedonia it is a source of friction and contention. On 17 November, Parliament adopted a new constitution, which guarantees the rule of law, a democratic political system, and individual rights. However, ethnic Albanian members of Parliament abstained from the vote. They were particularly concerned about the preamble to the constitution, which declares that Macedonia is a "national state of the Macedonian people." Ethnic Albanians, and other minorities, maintain that this implies a second-class status for non-Slavic citizens. For many ethnic Macedonians, the abstention on the vote was evidence of disloyalty by ethnic Albanians to the Macedonian state. A major complaint of ethnic Serbs is that they are not recognized in the Macedonian constitution, unlike Albanians, Turks, Vlachs, and Roma who are mentioned as nationalities. In 1993, the ICFY Working Group on Ethnic and National Communities and Minorities negotiated an "Agreed Minutes" between the government and ethnic Serb political leaders, under which the government pledged that Serbs would be included in the constitution. Similarly, the Council on Interethnic Relations established by the constitution suggested to Parliament that Serbs should be listed, but to date the constitution has not been amended.

The declaration of independence was the prelude to a difficult struggle for international recognition under the constitutional name of the country, "The Republic of Macedonia." On 19 December, the National Assembly adopted a declaration calling for recognition of Macedonia.[13] President Gligorov later wrote to other heads of state requesting that Macedonia be recognized as an independent state. He stated that Macedonia met all the international legal requirements for recognition. Gligorov also appealed for recognition on the basis of justice and in the interest of Macedonia's national security:

> Our claim to recognition as an independent state, thus, rests on the foundation of simple justice, to hold our destiny in our hands, and on a desire of our people to join the family of nations in a constructive effort toward peace and prosperity. A failure to recognize the existence of the state of Macedonia as an independent state can be seen by some as an invitation to interfere in affairs which are properly Macedonia's, and to create tensions and frictions, from which Macedonia has for some time now been free, but have often been experienced in our history.[14]

However, despite the recommendation of the European Community's (EC) Banditer Commission in January 1992 that Macedonia be recognized by EC member states, they initially rejected that view due to Greek opposition.[15]

Greece opposed recognition of Macedonia because of a dispute over the country's name, flag, and constitution. Greece claimed that "Macedonia" is a Greek name and that articles of the Constitution implied territorial claims to its northern province of Macedonia. Greece also objected to the use of the sixteen-pointed star of Vergina found on the tomb of Philip of Macedon on the new republic's national flag. To alleviate Greek concerns about possible irredentist intentions, Macedonia had amended its Constitution on 6 January 1992 to state that the republic had no territorial claims against any neighboring state; its borders can only be changed in accordance with the principle of voluntariness and generally accepted international norms; and it would not interfere in the sovereign rights of other states and in their internal affairs.[16] The position of Greece stemmed from an underlying fear about closer links between Macedonia and Turkey, and that recognition would focus international attention on minority issues within Greece. Nonrecognition of Macedonia was also popular domestically.[17]

Macedonia's independence only became a reality five months after it was proclaimed. In February 1992, following negotiations between President Gligorov and President Milosevic, the JNA withdrew from Macedonia without a shot being fired. The JNA took all its weaponry, including border-monitoring equipment, leaving Macedonia with a small, lightly armed and poorly equipped army. The peaceful withdrawal of the JNA was a tribute to Gligorov's political and diplomatic skills.

There were, however, other reasons for this notable and uncharacteristic decision by Milosevic. First, Serbia was involved in the wars in Bosnia and Croatia, and opening a third front would have put severe strains on the army. Second, Macedonia historically had close links with Serbia, which was its largest trading partner. The use of force to halt Macedonia's secession would have jeopardized bilateral economic ties in the future. Third, Serbs constituted only 2 percent of the ethnic composition of Macedonia, in contrast to much higher percentages in Bosnia and Croatia at the time.[18] Milosevic evidently felt less compelled to use force to protect the ethnic Serbs living in Macedonia. Finally, Macedonia made it clear that it wanted to secede peacefully and there would be no impediments to a withdrawal of the JNA. As President Gligorov recalled:

> We had no wish to take part in war, and we did not repeat the mistakes made in Croatia and Bosnia. We did not surround the soldiers' barracks. We did not try to confiscate their arms. We did not harass their families. The greatest interest of the former Yugoslav army was in their arms. We said they could leave Macedonia peacefully, and take their arms with them.[19]

SURVIVING IN A DANGEROUS NEIGHBORHOOD

Through a combination of history and geography, neighbors surround the independent state of Macedonia with historical claims to its territory and who deny the existence of a Macedonian nation. For reasons already discussed, Macedonia's most difficult relations were with Greece, its southern neighbor. Greece did not recognize Macedonia and blocked its membership of international organizations. On 8 April 1993, Macedonia was admitted to the United Nations as its 181st member, under the provisional name of the "former Yugoslav Republic of Macedonia," as a compromise, in light of the objections of

Greece to the name *Macedonia*.[20] Macedonians were dismayed that their country had not been admitted under its constitutional name, "The Republic of Macedonia." Demonstrations were held in Skopje, Kochani, and Resen. Six hundred Macedonian intellectuals protested in front of Parliament and signed a manifesto promising to take to court President Gligorov and the government on the grounds that they exceeded their authority in agreeing to join the UN as the former Yugoslav Republic of Macedonia. The Macedonian Orthodox Church released a statement saying it did not approve of changing the name of the country. It suggested that it might be asked to change its name to the "FYR Macedonian Orthodox Church," which it would not do. The National Assembly narrowly approved the temporary name by a vote of thirty in favor, twenty-eight against and thirteen abstentions. On 13 April the government survived a vote of no confidence called by the nationalist opposition party VMRO-DPMNE, over the name issue and the economy.

After April 1993, the UN mediator, Cyrus Vance, played an active role in efforts to reach a settlement of the differences between the two countries. The Greek prime minister, Constantine Mitsotakis, was receptive to most of Vance's proposals but would not accept "New Macedonia," which was reportedly the proposed name for the new state. Mitsotakis indicated that Greece would agree to hold face-to-face negotiations with Macedonia, but after his defeat in the October 1993 parliamentary elections, this did not materialize. The new Greek prime minister, Andreas Papandreou, set three preconditions for resuming UN-sponsored talks with Macedonia: it had to change its flag and constitution and cease its anti-Greek propaganda.[21]

However, the hard-line approach of the Papandreou government was counterproductive for Greece. It prompted Western states to reassess their policy of nonrecognition of Macedonia. The European states saw recognition as a means to prevent the spread of the conflict in Bosnia-Herzegovina, to uphold Macedonia's territorial integrity and security, and to contribute to the country's internal stability. Belgium recognized Macedonia in October 1993, followed by Denmark, France, Germany, Italy, the Netherlands, and the United Kingdom in December. Russia, however, angered Greece by its recognition of the state as "The Republic of Macedonia." The United States recognized Macedonia in February 1994, although it did not accredit an ambassador to Skopje.

Incensed by the U.S. recognition of Macedonia, Papandreou imposed a trade embargo against Macedonia on 16 February 1994, effectively preventing imports to Macedonia through Greek territory and denying the landlocked country access to the port of Thessaloniki. The Macedonian government estimated that the blockade resulted in losses of U.S.$40 to 50 million every month and possibly more. Greece rejected appeals by the EU presidency that it reconsider its decision, and efforts by Hans van den Broeck, the EU's Foreign Affairs Commissioner, to resume talks between the two countries were unsuccessful. The combined diplomatic efforts of Cyrus Vance and the Clinton administration eventually bore fruit. As a result of a compromise worked out by U.S. Assistant Secretary of State Richard Holbrooke, Greece and Macedonia signed an Interim Accord on 13 September 1995.[22] Macedonia agreed to change its flag and pledged that it had no irredentist claims and would not interfere in the internal affairs of Greece.[23] The Interim Accord drew strong condemnation from the nationalist opposition parties, VMRO-DPMNE, and the Democratic Party, which denounced the changing of the national flag. But the agreement was of considerable importance for Macedonia. It reestablished diplomatic and economic ties with Greece and provided access to the Aegean. It signified normalization at the country's common border with the European Union. Following the agreement, the United States established full diplomatic relations with Macedonia, and Macedonia was admitted to the OSCE, the Council of Europe, and NATO's Partnership for Peace. At the time of writing, the name issue remains unresolved, but despite this bilateral problem, economic relations between the two countries have continued to grow.

Although the JNA withdrew peacefully from Macedonia in early 1992, Serbia did not recognize Macedonia's independence. Some radical Serbian nationalists rejected the idea of a Macedonian nation and considered Macedonia as "South Serbia." Bilateral relations were also strained because there was no agreement on the demarcation of the border between the two countries.

Recognition by Serbia was slow to materialize, but the recognition of Macedonia by Greece, Serbia's close ally, in September 1995, had a positive effect on President Milosevic. On 2 October 1995, the day before an assassination attempt on his life, President Gligorov met President Milosevic in Belgrade. Milosevic welcomed the Interim Accord between Greece and Macedonia, and both leaders decided to work toward mutual recognition and the establishment of full diplomatic relations between Skopje and Belgrade. On 8 April 1996, Macedonia and Serbia signed an Agreement on the Regulation of Relations and the Promotion of Cooperation, pledging to respect each other's sovereignty, territorial integrity, and political independence.[24] The agreement irritated the Greek government as Serbia recognized Macedonia by its constitutional name.

Following the normalization of relations, a Joint Border Commission was established, but despite protracted negotiations, to date no significant progress has been achieved on the demarcation of the border. In June 1998, Secretary-General Annan reported to the Security Council that the lack of agreement had led to "intensified patrolling by both parties in some of the disputed areas of the border" placing "an additional burden upon United Nations peacekeepers, who have established a presence in those areas to prevent incidents."[25] Nevertheless, relations have been improving in other areas. In July 1997, Serbia and Macedonia signed agreements on education, sports, scientific, and technological cooperation and on the suspension of the visa regime between the two countries.

Albania was one of the first countries to recognize Macedonia. Following the imposition of the Greek embargo in 1994, Albania opened its port of Dürres for use by Macedonia. It initially opposed Macedonia's admission to the OSCE but later supported the country's membership. The main issue of contention between Skopje and Tirana is the status and treatment of the large ethnic Albanian minority in Macedonia. Former Albanian President Sali Berisha frequently and publicly raised the question of the rights of ethnic Albanians, which prompted protests from the Macedonian government that Albania was interfering in Macedonia's internal affairs. Albanian-Macedonian relations were strained in early 1994 when Berisha took sides during the split in the Party for Democratic Prosperity. He supported the radical faction led by Arben Xhaferi and criticized the moderate wing for remaining part of the coalition government. A further complication in bilateral relations was the open support of the Berisha government for the legalization of the Albanian-language University of Tetovo.

The crisis in Albania in early 1997, sparked by the collapse of pyramid investment schemes, led to an increase in illegal border crossers and cross-border shootings along the Macedonian-Albanian frontier. The deterioration in the security situation in the border areas put further stress on relations between the two countries. With the election of President Rexhep Meidani in the summer of 1997, relations improved, with a number of agreements on bilateral cooperation having been signed and several official visits having taken place. The assurances of the Socialist Party government that Albania will not support radicalism by ethnic Albanian parties in Macedonia have contributed to warmer relations.

Bulgaria was the first country to recognize the Macedonian state, a remarkable fact in light of Bulgaria's nationalist aspirations to Macedonia for a century. But Bulgaria qualified its recognition of Macedonia with a policy of nonrecognition of a Macedonian nation and language. Bulgaria maintained that the Macedonian national identity was an artificial creation of Tito's, and Macedonians were really Bulgarians who were unable or unwilling to recognize this fact. It also claimed that the Macedonian language was a dialect of Bulgarian. This language dispute prevented the two countries from signing a number of bilateral agreements, as they could not agree on a formula to describe the two languages. Skopje wanted the languages to be referred to as "Bulgarian and Macedonian," while Sofia preferred "the official languages of both countries" without naming them.

Despite the dispute, the Greek embargo and international sanctions against Serbia helped to foster Macedonian-Bulgarian cooperation. Bulgaria gave Macedonia access to the port of Burgas, and agreement was reached on the construction of the Kumanovo-Gjueshevo railway linking the two countries. In April 1994, President Gligorov visited Bulgaria and addressed the National Assembly for the first time.

In February 1999, Macedonian Prime Minister Ljubco Georgievski and his Bulgarian counterpart, Ivan Kostov, signed a declaration resolving their bilateral dispute. The declaration was made possible by a compromise formula: two copies were signed in the official languages of both countries described as "Bulgarian, according to the constitution of the Republic of Bulgaria, and Macedonian, according to the constitution of the Republic of Macedonia." It was agreeable to both sides because for Macedonia the Macedonian language was specifically named, and Bulgaria could continue to regard Macedonian as merely a constitutional description. Macedonia also declared that it would not interfere in the internal affairs of Bulgaria, which, like Greece, had been concerned about Article 49 of the Macedonian constitution obliging Macedonia "to care for the status and rights of persons belonging to the Macedonian people in neighboring states." Macedonia has considered ethnic Macedonians in Bulgaria as a minority, while Bulgaria regards them as one of a number of regional groups among Bulgarians.

Macedonia pursues a policy of "equal distance" toward its neighbors—that is, having good relations with all four, but not having a special relationship with any of them. This requires a delicate balancing act given Macedonia's strategic position in the southern Balkans and the shifting tides of loyalties in the region. For pragmatic reasons, a priority of Macedonia's foreign policy is regional cooperation. Since its independence, Macedonia's ties with its neighbors have grown slowly but steadily. A small and weak state, the military, economic, demographic, and power relationships will remain major determinants in Macedonia's relations with Albania, Bulgaria, Greece, and Serbia.

Turkey, while not contiguous with Macedonia, has important interests in the country. Having recognized the new state as the Republic of Macedonia, its constitutional name, Turkey developed close ties with Macedonia with a view to increasing its influence in the southern Balkans. It was also interested in the fate of ethnic Turks and Albanians in Macedonia, who are overwhelmingly Muslim. Greece's hostility toward the new Macedonian state provided a unique opportunity for Ankara to cement its links with Skopje. And for Macedonia, Turkey was a strategic counterweight to Greece and Serbia. In May 1993, Turkish Ambassador Süha Noyan became the first foreign ambassador to take up residence in Skopje. Ten months later, in March 1994, the two countries signed a

Trade and Economic Cooperation Agreement, and Turkey granted Macedonia Most Favored Nation status.

The number of visits by high-ranking Turkish government officials to Skopje reflected the importance that Turkey attached to its relations with Macedonia. President Ozal's visit in 1993 served to strengthen bilateral relations. In August 1994, the president of the Turkish Parliament, Husametin Djindoruk, visited Macedonia and met his Macedonian counterpart, Stojan Andov, Prime Minister Branko Crvenkovski, and Foreign Minister Stevo Crvenkovski. During these meetings, both sides underlined the necessity of strengthening economic and cultural cooperation between the two countries. When President Suleyman Demirel paid a state visit to the country in July 1995, it was the second visit of a Turkish head of state in two years. His delegation included businessmen who established a bilateral working group to explore investment opportunities. The Turkish Red Crescent presented forty tons of humanitarian aid for the victims of a flood that had devastated several towns and villages in southern Macedonia earlier that month. Following Demirel's visit, the Turkish and Macedonian armed forces signed agreements on cooperation in the field of defense.

SETTING THE NATIONAL HOUSE IN ORDER

Having gained its independence, Macedonia faced many internal challenges. It had to construct democratic institutions, reform its legal system, and enact new legislation on various matters. A multiethnic and multicultural society, it experienced tensions among its ethnic groups, in particular between ethnic Macedonians and Albanians. There is a long history of animosity and distrust between both communities. Like many former communist countries in a state of transition, it had to create a free market economy, but in particularly difficult circumstances.

Presidential and the second parliamentary elections were held in October 1994. International observers from the Council of Europe, the OSCE, and UN-PROFOR's FYROM Command monitored the elections. The general conclusion of the observers was that in spite of outdated election laws, the elections were conducted in an orderly, regular, and peaceful manner. The elections were won by the Alliance for Macedonia, composed of the Social Democratic Union of Macedonia, the Liberal Party, and the Socialist Party, and its presidential candidate, the incumbent Gligorov. The two main opposition parties, VMRO-DPMNE and the Democratic Party, boycotted the second round of the elections, alleging that they had been rigged. They were therefore not represented in Parliament. The opposition parties never accepted the results of the elections and the legitimacy of the government. They launched a national campaign, which raised over 150,000 signatures in support of a referendum on early parliamentary elections. However, neither the National Assembly nor the courts accepted the constitutional basis of this initiative.

The government's majority in the legislature made it possible to enact new legislation on many issues including local government, the courts, criminal law and procedure, the intelligence services, and education. The government sought and obtained advice on legal reform from outside experts and international organizations such as the UN, the Council of Europe, and the OSCE to ensure that new legislation conformed to international standards.

On 3 October 1995, President Gligorov was seriously injured in an assassination attempt not far from his office in the Parliament Building in the center of Skopje. The car bomb killed his driver instantly. The government suggested that an international company operating in Bulgaria, Multigroup, was responsible, but the perpetrators were never apprehended, and the crime has not been solved.

President Gligorov resumed office in January 1996, but the assassination attempt underlined the important issue of succession to the octogenarian president, who in many ways personifies the Macedonian state. Gligorov was a leading Communist official in the former Yugoslavia and a longtime advocate of economic liberalization. He was head of Yugoslavia's first economic reform commission formed in 1965 but dissolved three years later by Tito out of fear that economic reforms would encourage nationalism and erode the political influence of the Communist Party. At the start of the conflicts, which destroyed Yugoslavia, Gligorov returned from Belgrade to lead Macedonia to independence. A shrewd political juggler, he has had a calming influence on the tense relations between ethnic Macedonians and Albanians.

In the third Parliamentary elections held in the autumn of 1998, the "For Change" coalition of the nationalist VMRO-DPMNE and the Democratic Alternative secured an absolute majority of 62 seats in the 120-seat Parliament. A tripartite coalition government of VMRO-DPMNE, the Democratic Alternative, and the Democratic Party of Albanians, led by the new prime minister and VMRO-DPMNE leader, thirty-four-year-old Ljubco Georgievski, was approved by Parliament on 30 November. Despite its majority, the VMRO-DPMNE and the Democratic Alternative included the Democratic Party of Albanians in the coalition government to maintain a multiethnic government and to increase the chances of gaining a two-thirds majority required for constitutional change.

On the interethnic front, tension between ethnic Macedonians and Albanians remains Macedonia's most serious domestic problem. Most ethnic Albanians live in the western part of the country near the border with Albania and Kosovo, but a significant number also reside in the capital Skopje. Since Macedonia's independence, ethnic Albanians have been demanding greater political, educational, and cultural rights. As suggested earlier, the Macedonian constitution incorporates an ethnic rather than a civic definition of the state. Its preamble defines Macedonia as the "national state of the Macedonian people," although it goes on to proclaim that "full equality as citizens and permanent coexistence with the Macedonian people is provided for Albanians, Turks, Vlachs, Romanies and other nationalities." Ethnic Albanians oppose this conception of the state as it relegates them to an inferior status. They demand to be recognized as a "constituent nation," on par with ethnic Macedonians, as they had been in the 1974 Yugoslav constitution. Ethnic Macedonians, who have no "mother country," often see ethnic Albanians as disloyal to the state and their demands as a threat to Macedonia's territorial integrity. However, as the International Commission on the Balkans noted in its 1996 report, "As long as this concept of statehood prevails (even including any rights granted to the minority), the state is unlikely to be accepted as legitimate by the minority (even without explicit encouragement from their 'mother nation')."[26]

More fundamentally, the two communities cannot agree on the number of ethnic Albanians in Macedonia. The size of a minority group in a country's population is an important element in all ethnic disputes. Ethnic Macedonians view the higher birthrate of Albanians as a demographic time bomb threatening a fundamental shift in the interethnic balance. In 1994, a census was conducted in Macedonia, financed, monitored, and partly organized by the European Union and the Council of Europe. It was hoped that the new census would ease interethnic tension and help resolve the disputes between the Macedonian government and the ethnic Albanian community. During the census, UNPROFOR FYROM Command provided logistical help, including transportation and communication, to the international observers. According to the results of the census, 66.5 percent of the country's 1.94 million citizens are ethnic Macedonians, 22.9 percent are ethnic Albanians, 4 percent are ethnic Turks, 2.3 percent are Roma, 2 percent are ethnic Serbs, 0.4 percent are Vlachs, 1.8 percent belong to other ethnic groups, and 0.1 percent did not state their ethnic affiliation. The international observers confirmed that the "overall results were of acceptable reliability" and stressed that from their "examination of the data on ethnic affiliation and on the basis of the earlier observation in the field . . . the figures derived from the responses on the census forms are a true reflection of the ethnic affiliation that respondents gave of their own free will."[27]

All ethnic Albanian leaders, however, dispute this figure, claiming that it was reduced for political reasons. Some insist that ethnic Albanians constitute as much as 40 percent of the population. When the results were announced in November 1994, a spokesperson for the Party for Democratic Prosperity alleged that the census was plagued with technical and legal irregularities and that the results were suspect as no ethnic Albanian was employed in the Government Statistical Office.[28] The Albanian-language media shared these views.[29] The 1994 census neither eased the tension between ethnic Albanians and Macedonians nor lessened the demands of the former.

Ethnic Albanian parties have continued to press the Macedonian government to address other grievances, including recognition of the Albanian-language University of Tetovo, recognition of Albanian as a second official language, proportional representation in all state and public institutions, and greater access to the media. The grievances stem from very real discrimination against ethnic Albanians in Macedonia. One of the main causes of the disintegration of multiethnic states is the failure to give various ethnic communities compelling reasons to see themselves as part of the same country. National institutions are a unifying force in multiethnic societies, as they are in relatively homogenous ones. However, in the former, all ethnic groups must be fairly represented in national institutions if they are to command their loyalty.

Economically, Macedonia was the poorest republic in the former Yugoslavia, and its main industries are light manufacturing, agriculture, and tourism. Following its declaration of independence, Macedonia faced external and internal shocks, which caused considerable damage to its economy. The disintegration of the Yugoslav Federation meant the end of an internal market of twenty-three million. The UN sanctions against Serbia imposed from mid-1992 until the end of 1995 disrupted Macedonia's economic ties with its most important trading partner. In February 1994, Greece imposed an economic embargo that lasted twenty months and blocked access to the port of Thessaloniki, the gateway for the bulk of Macedonia's imports and exports. The twin embargoes led to widespread smuggling and other illegal activities. The shocks cut per capita income from about $2,200 in 1990 to $700 in 1995, and industrial production declined by almost 50 per cent during the same period. Unemployment rose to more than 30 per cent in mid-1995, thousands of employed workers did not receive regular wages, and the purchasing power of pensions declined dramatically.

The coalition government led by the SDSM undertook painful economic restructuring, including privatization and bank reform, in cooperation with the World Bank and the IMF. Inflation was reduced from about 2,000 percent annually in 1992 to about 16 per cent in 1995. The macro-economy and the denar, the national currency, were stabilized. However, the privatization program was plagued by numerous claims of irregularities. Most of the state enterprises were privatized through management buyouts, which gave rise to the perception among Macedonians that the Privatization Agency had instituted a buyout system that was biased in favor of insiders and allowed them to purchase companies at preferential prices.

ENTER THE UNITED NATIONS

The crisis in the former Yugoslavia posed perhaps the greatest challenge dealt with by the United Nations in its fifty-year history. The United Nations began its involvement in Yugoslavia on 25 September 1991, when the Security Council, meeting at the ministerial level, adopted by unanimous vote Resolution 713 (1991) imposing an embargo on all deliveries of weapons and military equipment to Yugoslavia. The Council invited the secretary-general to offer his assistance in ending the crisis and to report on the situation in Yugoslavia. In early October, UN Secretary-General Javier Perez de Cuellar appointed former U.S. Secretary of State Cyrus Vance as his special representative for Yugoslavia. Vance worked closely with the EC mediator, former British Foreign Secretary Lord Carrington to find a peaceful solution to the conflict.

On 23 November, Vance organized a meeting in Geneva attended by the presidents of Serbia and Croatia, the defense secretary of Yugoslavia, and Lord Carrington. An agreement was reached on an immediate cease-fire, and all the parties indicated strong support for the deployment of a United Nations peacekeeping force. In Resolution 721 (1991) of 27 November, the Security Council encouraged the secretary-general's negotiator to continue his efforts but stressed that deploying a peacekeeping force in Yugoslavia could not be envisaged unless all the parties fully observed the Geneva Accord. On 15 December, the Security Council, in Resolution 724 (1991), decided to send a small group of military personnel to Yugoslavia to prepare for the possible deployment of a peacekeeping operation.

The Macedonian government was enthusiastic about the mediation by the UN and the establishment of a peacekeeping operation. On 19 December, the Macedonian Parliament adopted a "Declaration on the international recognition of the Republic of Macedonia" that stated, "The Republic of Macedonia welcomes and fully supports the efforts of the United Nations made through the Secretary-General and the Security Council for a peaceful resolution of the Yugoslav crisis, including the deployment of peacekeeping UN forces."[30]

As the 1992 New Year began, there were signs of real progress toward a solution to the conflict when Vance negotiated an agreement to end the fighting in Croatia. With the approval of the Security Council, the new secretary-general, Boutros Boutros-Ghali, dispatched some fifty military liaison officers to monitor the cease-fire. On 15 February 1992, despite objections to the UN plan from some political leaders in Yugoslavia, notably Milan Babic, the self-proclaimed president of the "Serbian Republic of Krajina," the secretary-general recommended to the Security Council the establishment of the United Nations Protection Force (UNPROFOR). He noted that the danger that a peacekeeping force would fail for lack of cooperation from the parties was less grievous than the danger that delay in its dispatch would lead to a breakdown of the cease-fire and to a new conflagration.[31]

On 21 February, the Security Council in Resolution 743 (1992) established UNPROFOR for an initial period of one year. The Council stressed that the Force should be "a provisional solution aimed at creating the conditions for peace and security necessary to negotiate a comprehensive settlement of the Yugoslav crisis." It requested the secretary-general to deploy immediately those elements of UNPROFOR, which could assist in developing an implementation plan for the earliest possible full deployment of the Force. The secretary-general was also asked to submit a report on the establishment of the Force within two months following the adoption of the Resolution and to report at least semiannually "on progress made toward a peaceful political settlement and a settlement of the situation in the field." Boutros-Ghali's initial report indicated that there was strong support in Yugoslavia for the full deployment of the Force at the earliest possible time. On 7 April, the Security Council authorized the full deployment of UNPROFOR.

UNPROFOR was deployed in three United Nations Protected Areas (UNPAs) in Croatia: Eastern Slavonia, Western Slavonia, and Krajina.[32] The original mandate of the Force was to ensure that the UNPAs were demilitarized and that all residents were protected from fear of armed attack and to monitor the work of the local police to promote nondiscrimination and the protection of human rights. Three successive enlargements of UNPROFOR's mandate in Croatia occurred in 1992. By Resolution 762 (1992) of 30 June, the Security Council authorized UNPROFOR to monitor the so-called "pink zones"—areas controlled by the JNA and in which Serbs were in the majority but that were outside the UNPAs. It also recommended the establishment of a Joint Commission of representatives of the Croatian government and local authorities to monitor the restoration of authority by the Croatian government in the "pink zones." The Joint Commission was chaired by UNPROFOR, with the participation of the European Community Monitoring Mission (ECMM).

On 7 August, the Security Council approved in its Resolution 769 (1992) the enlargement of UNPROFOR's strength and mandate to enable the Force to control the entry of civilians into the UNPAs and to carry out immigration and customs duties at the UNPAs' international borders.

The third extension of the Force's mandate occurred on 6 October 1992, when the Security Council by Resolution 779 (1992) authorized UNPRO-FOR to assume responsibility for monitoring the demilitarization of the Prevlaka Peninsula near Dubrovnik. As the conflict intensified and spread to Bosnia-Herzegovina, UNPROFOR's mandate and strength were enlarged.

Following Bosnia's declaration of independence in March 1992, the Bosnian Serbs, with the support of Serbia, demanded that Bosnia rescind its declaration. President Izetbegovic did not acquiesce and ordered the mobilization of the country's territorial defense forces. The Bosnian Serbs launched a vicious campaign of "ethnic cleansing," and Bosnia was plunged into war. People who had lived together for decades turned on each other with unimaginable brutality. The outbreak of violence prompted the secretary-general to deploy forty military observers to Mostar on 30 April, but security concerns led to their withdrawal a fortnight later. On 30 May, acting under Chapter VII of the United Nations Charter, the Security Council, in Resolution 757 (1992), imposed mandatory economic sanctions against the Federal Republic of Yugoslavia (Serbia and Montenegro). It also demanded that all parties create the conditions necessary for unimpeded delivery of humanitarian supplies to Sarajevo and other areas in Bosnia and the establishment of a security zone around Sarajevo. The Security Council again extended UNPROFOR's mandate and strength on 8 June by its Resolution 758 (1992) and authorized Secretary-General Boutros-Ghali to deploy military observers in Sarajevo to supervise the withdrawal of antiaircraft weapons at specific areas in the city. By early July, United Nations observers and troops were deployed at the airport and around the city, and the airport was reopened for humanitarian flights.

As the war in Bosnia intensified, the delivery of humanitarian assistance to Sarajevo and other parts of the country was impeded. In September, the secretary-general proposed that UNPROFOR's mandate be enlarged to assist the United Nations High Commissioner for Refugees (UNHCR) in delivering humanitarian relief in Bosnia, to provide protection for UNHCR, and to protect convoys of released civilian detainees on the request of the International Committee of the Red Cross (ICRC) with the approval of the Force Commander. UNPROFOR would be deployed in four or five new zones, with an infantry battalion in each zone. In Resolution 776 (1992) of 14 September, the Security Council approved Boutros-Ghali's recommendations, and a separate Bosnia and Herzegovina Command was created within UNPROFOR.

There were two further enlargements of UNPROFOR's mandate in Bosnia in 1992; the first concerned the No-fly Zone and the second, Border Control. On 9 October 1992, the Security Council adopted Resolution 781 (1992) banning all military flights in Bosnian airspace, with the exception of UNPROFOR's and other flights in support of United Nations operations. The Council requested the Force to monitor compliance with the ban and to establish "an appropriate mechanism for approval and inspection" to ensure that other flights to and from Bosnia did not violate its resolutions. On 16 November, the Security Council adopted Resolution 787 (1992) in which it considered that observers should be deployed on Bosnia's borders to facilitate implementation of its resolutions and requested the secretary-general to present his recommendations on this matter. In his report to the Council on 21 December, Boutros-Ghali stated that it would be necessary to give UNPROFOR the authority not only to search but also to turn back or confiscate military personnel, weapons, or contraband goods whose passage into or out of Bosnia would violate the Council's resolutions. He proposed an enlargement of UN-PROFOR with some ten thousand additional troops to provide for a twenty-four-hour observation and search operation at 123 crossing points on Bosnia's border with its neighbors. In recommending this expansion, the secretary-general observed that a symbolic presence at selected crossing points would "not only fail to fulfill the Council's requirements, but would also undermine the already strained credibility of UNPROFOR." The stage was now set for the United Nations to extend its peacekeeping operation to Macedonia.

CONCLUSION

This review of Macedonian history provides the context for analyzing the UN's first preventive operation. The roots of many of Macedonia's problems can be found in history. Its strategic location in the southern Balkans makes it the most potentially explosive country in the region. George Santayana famously observed that "those who cannot remember the past are condemned to repeat it." Yet, in Macedonia, like the rest of the Balkans, history is an obsession. It is a burden handed down to successive generations. In the Balkan region, five hundred years are but yesterday. It is a place where people speak of the Ottoman occupation, the Balkan Wars in the early twentieth century, and UN peacekeeping operations in the same sentence with no sense of strain. The challenge for Macedonia is to remember the past but not to be held captive by historical memory.

NOTES

1. David Fromkin, "Dimitrios Returns: Macedonia and the Balkan Question in the Shadow of History," *World Policy Journal* 10 (1993): 71.
2. Misha Glenny, "The Birth of a Nation," *New York Review of Books*, 16 November 1995, 24.
3. The discussion of Macedonia's history is based on Duncan M. Perry, *The Politics of Terror: The Macedonian Liberation Movements 1893–1903* (Durham, N.C.: Duke University Press, 1988), and Hugh Poulton, *Who Are the Macedonians?* (Bloomington: Indiana University Press, 1995).
4. Duncan M. Perry, "Crisis in the Making? Macedonia and Its Neighbors," *Südosteuropa* 43, no.1–2 (1994): 48–49.
5. Poulton, *Who Are the Macedonians?* 90–94.
6. Poulton, *Who Are the Macedonians?* 100–1.
7. Poulton, *Who Are the Macedonians?* 105.
8. Perry, "Crisis in the Making?" 34–35.
9. The history of the disintegration of Yugoslavia has been discussed in a number of books. See Misha Glenny, *The Fall of Yugoslavia: The Third Balkan War*, revised and updated edition (New York: Penguin, 1993); Roy Gutman, *A Witness to Genocide* (New York: Macmillan, 1993); Robert D. Kaplan, *Balkan Ghosts: A Journey through History* (New York: Vintage, 1993); Laura Silber and Allan Little, *Yugoslavia: Death of a Nation*, revised and updated edition (New York: Penguin, 1997); Susan Woodward, *Balkan Tragedy: Chaos and Dissolution after the Cold War* (Washington, D.C.: Brookings Institution, 1995); Warren Zimmermann, *Origins of a Catastrophe: Yugoslavia and Its Destroyers* (New York: Times Books, 1996).
10. Richard Holbrooke, *To End a War* (New York: Random House, 1998), 29.
11. See Silber and Little, *Yugoslavia,* 169–89.
12. *Republic of Macedonia: Independence through Peaceful Self-Determination* (Skopje: Balkan Forum/Nova Makedonija, 1992), 11.
13. "Declaration on the international recognition of the Republic of Macedonia as a sovereign and independent state," in *Republic of Macedonia,* 26.
14. *Republic of Macedonia,* 22.
15. On 15 January 1992, the EC recognized the independence of Slovenia and Croatia. Bosnia declared its independence on 3 March 1992 and was recognized by the EC and the United States on 6 April 1992.
16. The third amendment was added to Article 49 of the Constitution, stating that the Republic cares "for the status and rights of those persons belonging to the Macedonian people in neighboring countries." See *The Republic of Macedonia* (Skopje: Goce Delcev, 1994), 65–66.
17. Robert W. Mickey and Adam Smith Albion, "Success in the Balkans? A Case Study of Ethnic Relations in the Republic of Macedonia," in *Minorities: The New Europe's Old Issue,* ed. Ian M. Cuthbertson and Jane Leibowitz (Prague: Institute for East-West Studies, 1993), 58.

18. Bosnia-Herzegovina's prewar population was 31 percent Serb and Croatia's 12 percent.

19. John Corry, "Why Are We in Macedonia?" *The American Spectator*, November 1995, 31.

20. Security Council Resolution 817 (1993) of 7 April 1993 stated that Macedonia would be "provisionally referred to for all purposes within the United Nations as 'the former Yugoslav Republic of Macedonia' pending settlement of the difference that has arisen over the name of the State." It is interesting to note that on 9 April 1993, UN-PROFOR's Macedonia Command issued a press release stating, "On the occasion of *Macedonia's* admission into the United Nations as its 181st member state, the peacekeepers of UNPROFOR would like to express their warmest wishes for peace, stability and friendship to all the people of *Macedonia*" (SP0021; emphasis added).

21. Stephane Lefebvre, "The Former Yugoslav Republic of Macedonia (FYROM): Where To?" *European Security* 3, no. 4 (Winter 1994): 713-14.

22. For details of the agreement, see S/1995/794, annex 1. Richard Holbrooke gives a fascinating account of the negotiations that led to the Interim Accord in *To End a War* (New York: Random House, 1998), 121-27.

23. As a result of the dispute with Greece, Macedonia's original flag was never hoisted at the United Nations headquarters in New York. Following the signing of the Interim Accord, the country's new flag was raised on 21 October 1995.

24. On 25 April 1996, the Macedonian National Assembly ratified the Agreement by a vote of seventy-five in favor, eleven against, with one abstention. The negative votes were cast by the ethnic Albanian parties not part of the coalition government.

25. "Report of the Secretary-General on the United Nations Preventive Deployment Force Pursuant to Security Council Resolution 1142 (1997)," S/1998/454, 1 June 1998, para.14.

26. International Commission on the Balkans, *Unfinished Peace: A Report* (Washington, D.C.: Carnegie Endowment for International Peace, 1996), 31-32.

27. Council of Europe-European Union, *First Results of the 1994 Census in the Former Yugoslav Republic of Macedonia,* Statement by the International Group of Experts, Skopje, 14 November 1994. For a critical view of the 1994 census, see Victor A. Friedman, "Observing the Observers: Language, Ethnicity, and Power in the 1994 Macedonian Census and Beyond," in *Toward Comprehensive Peace in Southeast Europe: Conflict Prevention in the South Balkans*, Report of the South Balkans Working Group of the Council on Foreign Relations Center for Preventive Action (New York: Twentieth Century Fund Press, 1996), appendix A, 81-105.

28. *Flaka e Vëllazërimit,* Skopje, 18 November 1994.

29. For example, in a significant article, L. Zelmai and I. Ajdini wrote that the Macedonian government wanted to keep the percentage of ethnic Albanians as low as possible to justify its continued rejection of their demand for constituent nation status. As a result of the census results, "Albanians will again remain in the margins . . . because their position depends on their percentage." See "The 1994 Census: Manipulation or Reality," *Flaka e Vëllazërimit* (Skopje), 19–20 November 1994. The delegate of the SRSG in

Macedonia, Hugo Anson, recognized that the census results were a bitter pill for ethnic Albanians to swallow. He urged the Macedonian government not to use the results in a triumphalist manner or as a justification for refusing to accommodate the demands of ethnic Albanians. In an interview, Anson said:

> Albanians represent a large proportion of the population in Macedonia. It is not too important whether they are 15, 20 or 30 percent. It is most important that they represent a population with a sizeable number and any effort to integrate them, and any other ethnic group, is a good idea. I am convinced that President Gligorov and the Government clearly understand that it is imperative that different ethnic groups should be fairly represented in every area of society and that any other approach would be dangerous.

See *Flaka e Vëllazërimit,* 12 November 1994.

30. Article 4 of the "Declaration on the international recognition of the Republic of Macedonia as a sovereign and independent state," in *Republic of Macedonia,* 26.

31. S/23592 (1992).

32. For administrative reasons, the United Nations divided the UNPAs into four sectors: East, North, South, and West.

3

MAKING A NEW BEGINNING

Come over into Macedonia, and help us.[1]

Acts of the Apostles

President Kiro Gligorov's request for the deployment of United Nations "observers" in Macedonia in 1992 set in motion the events that would lead to
the UN's first preventive deployment operation. For the first time in its history,
the UN's peacekeepers would be deployed before the outbreak of conflict, instead of after hostilities had erupted. The president's main concern was with external threats to the country's stability. In particular, he feared that if conflict
erupted in Yugoslavia's predominantly Albanian province of Kosovo, the fighting would spill over into Macedonia. Another worry was the potential destabilizing effect of an influx of refugees from Kosovo into Macedonia. The Macedonian government did not believe that there were any real internal threats to
Macedonia, and they were united in this belief with the nationalist opposition
parties. However, the United Nations even at the inception of the mission did
not accept this view. This difference in the assessment of the threats to Macedonia by the Macedonian government and the United Nations persisted
throughout the deployment of UNPREDEP.

In late 1992, Macedonia had been independent for barely one year. A
landlocked country, it had troubled relations with all four of its neighbors who
challenged its right to exist as an independent state. It had been recognized by
very few countries and was not yet a member of the United Nations or any of
the key European regional organizations. The presence of UN troops served an
important political purpose—namely, the legitimization of the country's sovereignty and independence.

UNPREDEP was not a leap in the doctrinal dark; it was guided by established principles of traditional peacekeeping. The most notable of these was the

41

request and consent of the Macedonian government to the deployment of UN peacekeepers. The importance of consent is based on legal principles and practical considerations. Sovereignty remains a central pillar of the international system, the ever-growing importance of nonstate actors and transnational forces notwithstanding. As the disintegration of the former Yugoslavia demonstrated the age of nations is not yet over. From an operational perspective, without the consent of the parties in a conflict, it is extremely difficult, if not impossible, for peacekeepers to keep the peace, and they run the risk of becoming targets of disgruntled parties—in other words, becoming soldiers with enemies.[2] While certain segments of Macedonian society—some ethnic Albanians and the nationalist parties—had objections to the deployment of UN troops, these were not strong enough for them to mount serious opposition to the peacekeepers.

The composition of the Force—Nordic and U.S. peacekeepers—was a reflection of traditional and nontraditional peacekeeping. During the Cold War, peacekeepers were frequently provided by neutral states and not by the superpowers. The Permanent Members of the Security Council are now increasingly providing military personnel to serve in UN operations. The operation also provided the opportunity for the Nordic countries to institute an innovation in their peacekeeping role by establishing a composite battalion to serve in Macedonia. The position of force commander rotated among the four Nordic countries on an annual basis.

Macedonia was the first place in the former Yugoslavia where the United States deployed ground troops. The appearance on stage of the United States added a new dimension to the peacekeeping operation and enhanced the deterrence credibility of the Force. It would be illusory, however, to expect that a thousand-strong force, including some five hundred U.S. troops, could have repelled an external attack or stemmed a massive influx of refugees. The value of the peacekeepers lay not in their strength or their arms but in their presence. They symbolized the interest of the United Nations in Macedonia and signaled that it was off-limits to potential aggressors. Equally important, they were a trip wire and could not be attacked with impunity. Their message was simple: "Hands off Macedonia."

The rules of engagement were another link to the past and the product of new realities. The peacekeepers could use force in self-defense or if armed persons tried to prevent them from implementing the mandate. But they were equipped with credible force and weaponry not only to defend themselves but to serve as a deterrent.

Cooperation between the UN and the OSCE was an important factor in the UNPREDEP experience. The OSCE Spillover Mission in Skopje and UNPREDEP established and maintained effective coordinating mechanisms in the mission area. This relationship was symptomatic of a growing trend of greater coordination and consultation between the United Nations and regional organizations. A detailed discussion of these issues will be the concern of this chapter.

PRESIDENT GLIGOROV
REQUESTS A UNITED NATIONS PRESENCE

On 11 November 1992, during a meeting in New York with UN Secretary-General Boutros Boutros-Ghali, President Gligorov requested that the United Nations deploy "observers" in Macedonia "in view of his concern about the possible impact on it of fighting elsewhere in the former Yugoslavia."[3] The following day, Gligorov also discussed the deployment of UN troops with Cyrus Vance and Lord David Owen, cochairmen of the Steering Committee of the International Conference on the Former Yugoslavia (ICFY). A week later, on the urging of the British EC Presidency, the cochairmen wrote to Boutros-Ghali recommending that a small group of UNPROFOR military and police observers, as well as political staff, visit Macedonia and prepare a report on "how a larger deployment of United Nations military and police personnel might help to strengthen security and confidence in Macedonia."[4] Lord Owen has suggested that their letter was an "important factor in persuading the UN secretary-general to write to the Security Council" about a proposal to send an exploratory mission to Macedonia to prepare for the possible deployment of a peacekeeping operation.[5]

The request of President Gligorov for preventive UN intervention was a tribute to his foresight and a reflection of his keen understanding of the volatile Balkan region. The request and consent of the host government are necessary requirements for a preventive deployment operation. Member states are notoriously reluctant to contribute troops to peacekeeping missions without the invitation and cooperation of national authorities. The president's action underlined that other governments must be willing to request UN preventive deployment before hostilities erupt.

With the consent of the Security Council, the secretary-general sent a fourteen-member exploratory mission composed of military, police, and civilian personnel from UNPROFOR headquarters in Zagreb to Macedonia from 28 November to 3 December 1992, to assess the situation and prepare a report on the necessity of deploying UN peacekeeping troops in Macedonia. Boutros-Ghali envisaged that such a deployment would be a practical implementation of the concept of preventive deployment he had elaborated in *An Agenda for Peace*.[6] The mission, led by Brig. Gen. Bo Pellnas, the chief military observer of UN-

PROFOR, met with President Gligorov; Prime Minister Branko Crvenkovski, and other members of the government; representatives of the major parliamentary parties; senior military and police officers; as well as representatives of UNHCR, the Conference on Security and Cooperation in Europe (CSCE) the ICRC, and the International Federation of Red Cross and Red Crescent Societies (IFRC).[7]

The exploratory mission had three important goals in meeting with the president and other government officials: first, to obtain a better understanding of the reasons that lay behind President Gligorov's request for a UN presence in Macedonia; second, to find out the objectives which the Macedonian authorities intended the UN to fulfill; and, finally, to ascertain the government's preferred timing for a UN deployment.[8] In explaining to the exploratory mission why he had requested UN observers, Gligorov painted a nightmarish scenario. He feared that if conflict broke out in Kosovo, it would spill over into Macedonia. Thousands of Kosovo Albanian refugees would flood into Macedonia, Albania would intervene in support of ethnic Albanians in Kosovo, and Serbia would enter northern Macedonia to deal with the Kosovars and their Albanian allies. Turkey and Greece, two NATO allies, could be drawn into a confrontation that would trigger a wider Balkan war. The Macedonian government was also concerned by statements of nationalist elements in Belgrade suggesting that Serbia had territorial designs on Macedonia. In the case of an external attack, Macedonia would be unable to defend itself because the JNA had taken all heavy weaponry, aircraft, and border-monitoring equipment when it withdrew from Macedonia in 1992.[9] In the event of such a conflict, it would take much more than a stone and a sling for the Macedonian David to defeat the Serbian Goliath.

Apart from the stated reasons of the Macedonian leadership for wanting a UN presence in Macedonia, there were probably two important, unstated motives. First, it was hoped that a UN presence would enhance the legitimacy of Macedonia's sovereignty and independence and, second, that it would increase the country's international diplomatic recognition.

The mission gathered that the Macedonian authorities expected a UN presence to have the following objectives: to monitor the country's borders and report any threatening developments, to serve as a deterrent to external aggression, and to assist in keeping "potentially conflicting parties separate" and thereby strengthen regional security.[10] With regard to the timing of a UN deployment, President Gligorov suggested that this should occur "no later than one, or at the most two, months after the 20 December 1992 elections" in Serbia. He feared that if the Serb nationalists did well in those elections, the situation in Kosovo was likely to explode with the terrible consequences he had outlined.[11]

Based on its discussions and findings, the exploratory mission recommended to the secretary-general that an UNPROFOR presence should be established on the Macedonian side of its 240-kilometer border with the Federal Republic of Yugoslavia (Serbia and Montenegro) and its 182-kilometer border with Albania, with the following preventive mandate:

(a) To monitor the border areas and report to the Secretary-General, through the Force Commander, any developments which could pose a threat to Macedonia; (b) By its presence, to deter such threats from any source, as well as help prevent clashes, which could otherwise occur between external elements and Macedonian forces, thus helping to strengthen security and confidence in Macedonia.[12]

UNPROFOR's "Macedonia Command" would have its headquarters in Macedonia's capital, Skopje, and a commander with the rank of a brigadier-general would head it.[13] To implement the mandate, it was recommended that an infantry battalion of up to seven hundred soldiers, composed of three rifle companies, a headquarters, and logistics company, as well as thirty-five UN military observers should be deployed. In addition, twenty-six UN civilian police (CIVPOL) monitors were to be deployed with a mandate "to monitor the work of the local border police." It was thought that on the Macedonia–Albania border, "the UNCIVPOL presence would assist in calming any interethnic tensions arising from perceptions that the Macedonian police had harassed or abused Albanians, mainly in the context of illegal border crossings."[14] The exploratory mission indicated that two civil affairs officers would be required "to perform liaison functions between UNPROFOR and the central and local authorities, as well as to provide political advice to the Commander."[15] In addition, two public information officers would be needed to mount an effective public information program "to ensure that the role of the United Nations presence is fully understood by the population."[16] Macedonia Command would also require forty-five administrative support staff in the areas of communications, transport, maintenance, building management, general services, procurement, finance, and personnel.[17]

In his report to the Security Council of 9 December 1992, Secretary-General Boutros-Ghali endorsed the proposals of the exploratory mission, which had also been supported by the first force commander of UNPROFOR, Indian Lt. Gen. Satish Nambiar.[18] The secretary-general believed that a UN deployment would "help Macedonia and the two neighboring countries concerned to make safe passage through a potentially turbulent and hazardous period."[19] He recommended that the Security Council authorize an "enlargement of UNPROFOR's mandate and strength" in accordance with the recommendations of the exploratory mission. Macedonia, the perennial tinderbox in the Balkans, became the focus of the anxious attention of the United Nations.

On 11 December 1992, the Security Council by resolution 795 (1992) unanimously approved the secretary-general's report; authorized the secretary-general to establish an UNPROFOR presence in Macedonia, and to inform the authorities of Albania and those of the Federal Republic of Yugoslavia (Serbia and Montenegro) of this development; requested the secretary-general to deploy immediately the military, civil affairs, and administrative personnel recommended in his report and to deploy the police monitors immediately after receiving the consent of the Macedonian government; urged UNPROFOR in Macedonia to coordinate closely with the CSCE mission in the country; requested the secretary-general to keep the Council regularly informed of the implementation of this resolution; and decided to remain seized of the matter.

Thus, the Security Council authorized the first preventive deployment in the UN's history, and it would take place in a country that was not yet a UN member state. It was only six months after Boutros-Ghali had enjoined the Security Council: "The time has come to plan for circumstances warranting preventive deployment, which could take place in a variety of instances and ways."[20] Later, Boutros-Ghali wrote in his memoir of his years as UN secretary-general that it gave him "satisfaction to see a concept from *An Agenda for Peace* put into effect on the ground."[21]

This unprecedented decision by the Security Council marked a new beginning for the United Nations. The UN had turned a corner in its history and in the evolution of its peacekeeping operations. For the first time, the UN had been mandated to deploy forces before the outbreak of conflict. For four decades, peacekeeping forces had performed the vital role of separating opposing parties to prevent a resumption of hostilities. But traditional peacekeeping reflected the failure of international efforts to prevent conflict. The organization had now discovered a new formula, preventive deployment, with great potential for strengthening its role in reducing the toll and cost of international crises around the world.

THE NORDICS TO THE RESCUE

As the UN has no army, the secretary-general had to ask member states to contribute troops to its preventive Force. On 15 December 1992, Canadian Lt. Gen. Maurice Baril, the military adviser to the secretary-general, informally requested Sweden to contribute troops for the Macedonian operation. The same day, the Nordic foreign ministers who were meeting in Stockholm decided that their countries would participate in the peacekeeping operation in Macedonia. Finland, Norway, and Sweden indicated that they would provide the necessary troops as a joint Nordic battalion (NORDBAT). Denmark, which already had a significant number of troops serving with UNPROFOR, offered to provide personnel for the headquarters staff. Following the favorable decision by the ministers, the UN Secretariat informally requested Denmark, Finland, and Norway to assist in establishing the mission in Macedonia. On 23 December 1992, the United Nations made a formal request for assistance to the Nordic countries.[22]

Meanwhile, representatives of the Nordic defense and foreign ministries met in Stockholm and began planning for the operation through the Nordic Committee for Military UN Matters (NordSamFN). NordSamFN held three meetings in Sweden in late December 1992 and early January 1993 to discuss NORDBAT's composition, organization, personnel, logistics, equipment, transportation, and training. Following the visit of a reconnaissance team to Macedonia on 6–11 January 1993, NordSamFN held a final preparatory meeting in Denmark on 18–19 January 1993, at which the composition of the advance party, the training program and the transportation principles were decided.[23] The predeployment training of NORDBAT's personnel was conducted in January in their own countries, with the exception of the armored personnel carrier drivers, who were trained together in Sweden and Finland.

The positive response of the Nordic countries to the need for UN troops in Macedonia was not surprising, for they have been staunch supporters of UN peacekeeping operations. Clive Archer argues that the Nordics' involvement was primarily the result of their liberal institutionalist view of European security, with its emphasis on the prevention of conflict.[24] He further explains the role of the Nordic states as a continuation of their active participation in UN peacekeeping operations, a response to their domestic public opinion or to pressure from allies, an opportunity to deploy peacekeeping troops in a "safe" corner of the Balkans, and the result of institutional pressures within their military establishments for continued activism in peacekeeping.[25] Whatever the explanation for the role of the Nordic countries, it is indisputable that it would have been difficult for the United Nations to undertake its experiment in preventive deployment without their active support.

The decision to establish a joint Nordic Battalion was significant as it was the first time all four Nordic countries had agreed that their troops would participate in a UN peacekeeping operation as a unified battalion. In many ways, that decision was a logical progression in the evolution of Nordic military cooperation in UN peacekeeping activities, which began in the 1950s. The early joint efforts of the Nordic countries concentrated on the organization of units, equipment, and transportation of troops to a mission area. In 1964, all four

Nordic governments reached an agreement on the basic composition of their Stand-By Forces that would be placed at the disposal of the United Nations.[26]

During the last three decades, the Nordics have developed an effective structure for their mutual collaboration in UN peacekeeping operations. The Conference of the Ministers of Defense has ultimate responsibility for general policy matters and meets twice a year. NORDSamFN, composed of military representatives of each Nordic country, is the working body for Nordic military UN cooperation and meets several times a year. It arranges peacekeeping training programs for Nordic officers and noncommissioned officers; coordinates plans, transport, and management of Nordic troops taking part in peacekeeping missions; organizes seminars on peacekeeping operations for Nordic commanders and officials of the ministries of foreign affairs and defense; and issues publications on experiences gained in UN missions. The Nordic Economic Working Committee, which holds a few meetings annually, is responsible for the financial aspects of UN peacekeeping activities.[27] The Nordic countries then, had a solid basis of experience in peacekeeping missions and an extensive record of joint military cooperation on which to build in Macedonia.

THE MACEDONIAN REACTION
TO THE SECURITY COUNCIL'S DECISION

There was broad support for a United Nations presence in Macedonia from the Macedonian government, the leaders of the major political parties, and local authorities. The Central Committee of the Social Democratic Union of Macedonia, the senior partner in the ruling coalition, adopted a declaration supporting the Security Council's decision to send peacekeepers to Macedonia and appealing to MPs from other parties to approve their deployment.[28] Nevertheless, the Macedonian authorities hoped that the peacekeeping operation would accomplish its tasks swiftly. As an official in the Ministry of Defense put it in December 1992, "All of us certainly want this mission to last as short as possible."[29]

Ethnic Albanian leaders had some reservation regarding the deployment of UN troops on Macedonia's border with Albania. The leaders of the Party for Democratic Prosperity (PDP), the main ethnic Albanian party, believed that such deployment was not required "because the source of conflict would not come from that direction, but from the north."[30] The mayor and deputy mayor of Debar, a predominantly ethnic Albanian town in western Macedonia, shared this view. On 29 December 1992, the Assembly of the Municipality of Debar adopted a resolution which, while welcoming the Security

Council's decision to dispatch peacekeeping troops to Macedonia, declared that the presence of UN forces on the Macedonian-Albanian border was "unnecessary and tendentious."[31]

The Macedonian government was not enthusiastic about the deployment of CIVPOL monitors whose mandate was "to monitor the work of the local border police" and whose presence, the exploratory mission believed, "would assist in calming any interethnic tensions arising from perceptions that the Macedonian police had harassed or abused Albanians, mainly in the context of illegal border crossings."[32] In the words of President Gligorov, CIVPOL monitors were unnecessary because "the internal situation was stable [and] ethnic concerns were being dealt with through dialogue and negotiation."[33] Following the adoption of Security Council Resolution 795 (1992), UNPROFOR civilian representatives in Macedonia held talks with the Macedonian defense minister, Vlado Popovski, aimed at obtaining the government's approval of the CIVPOL deployment. They stressed that CIVPOL monitors lacked executive powers and would not arrogate the functions of the local police, their mandate was limited to monitoring and observation, and they were highly experienced and would be unarmed. On 19 December 1992, the Macedonian government approved the deployment of monitors.[34]

The UN's insistence on the necessity of CIVPOL's presence, in the face of initial opposition from the Macedonian government, was a signal that there was a link between the country's interethnic relations and its stability and that this matter was of legitimate concern to the world body. The reluctant consent of the Macedonian government to the deployment of CIVPOL monitors was the price it had to pay for UN troops on its borders, who would provide the security and external political legitimization it needed.

In general, the press warmed to the prospect of the arrival of the blue helmets in Macedonia and in one commentary dubbed them the "angels of peace."[35] The media stressed that the presence of UN peacekeepers would have three advantages: first, they would serve as symbolic confirmation of the inviolability of Macedonia's sovereignty and territorial integrity; second, they would provide psychological support for the Macedonian people; and, finally, they would boost the country's economy.[36] Mirka Velinovska, a journalist, expressed a dissenting view in the weekly *Puls*. In an article skeptical about the value of deploying UN peacekeepers in Macedonia, she argued that one thousand peacekeeping troops would not be a deterrent to President Milosevic's "aggressive policy" of creating a Greater Serbia, which included Macedonia. She also suggested that the UN presence would contribute to civil strife by encouraging "reactionary agitators" to dismember the country and predicted that the peacekeeping operation was "doomed to failure."[37]

In contrast to the government, political leaders, and the press, the Macedonian people's attitude toward the deployment of peacekeeping troops was more ambivalent. In a poll taken by the Agency for Public Opinion Survey at the Publishing House of Nova Makedonija in December 1992, less than 50 percent of Macedonians approved of the deployment of UN troops, while 41.8 percent were opposed. A large portion, 43.4 percent, believed that the decision on the deployment should have been made by Macedonians in a referendum, 21.4 percent considered it the president's responsibility, and less than 20 percent believed it was the Parliament's. Roughly half believed that the presence of UN troops would "diminish the danger of war in Macedonia," while some 38 percent agreed with Velinovska and did not think that their presence would be a deterrent.[38]

On 21 December 1992, the Macedonian government formally accepted the Security Council's decision to establish a peacekeeping operation in Macedonia. The government also set up a Coordination Committee to work with UNPROFOR on various matters relating to the deployment, including accommodation and support facilities.[39] The following day, despite some criticism voiced by the nationalist opposition party, VMRO-DPMNE, that President Gligorov had failed to consult the National Assembly prior to requesting the secretary-general for a deployment of UN observers in Macedonia, the Assembly approved the UN deployment.[40]

Most places where peacekeeping operations are deployed share a common feature: a basic contradiction in the attitude of the political class to the presence of the mission. Macedonia was no different. The operation was viewed as tangible evidence of the UN's commitment to and support for the new state. At the same time, there was some resentment at the presence of the UN, especially its possible involvement in political and ethnic problems.

DEPLOYING THE PEACEKEEPERS

Less than a week after the Security Council adopted Resolution 795, a small team of civil affairs officers, a senior military observer, and a senior administrative officer arrived in Skopje to make the necessary arrangements with the Macedonian authorities for the establishment of UNPROFOR Macedonia Command.[41] On 28 December 1992, the sector commander and other officers, as well as a group of military observers, arrived in Skopje.[42] On the same day, a reconnaissance team of twelve members from the Second Canadian Battalion serving in Croatia also arrived to pave the way for the temporary deployment of a Canadian company, pending the arrival of the Nordic battalion. The Canadian company of about 150 soldiers arrived on 7 January 1993, and Colonel Kari Hoglund of Finland, the chief operations officer of UNPROFOR, was appointed acting commanding officer. The Canadian peacekeepers set up their headquarters at Kumanovo, some thirty-five kilometers from the capital Skopje. They established five observation posts at the main crossing points along the Macedonian-Serbian border, which they monitored, on a twenty-four-hour basis.[43] In addition, the Canadians conducted regular patrols along the border between the observation posts.

A reconnaissance mission of senior Nordic officers led by the newly appointed commander of UNPROFOR in Macedonia, Brig. Gen. Finn Saermark-Thomsen, visited the country on 8–11 January 1993, in preparation for the deployment of the Nordic battalion. A Dane, Saermark-Thomsen had more than thirty years of military experience. He had served twice with the UN peacekeeping operation in Cyprus (UNFICYP) and with the UN Iran–Iraq Military Observer Group (UNIIMOG). Brig. Gen. Saermark-Thomsen assumed command of the operation on 25 January.[44] The advance party of NORDBAT, led by the battalion commander, Swedish Col. Jan Isberg, and including some fifty-six military personnel, arrived in Skopje on 4 February.[45] The Nordic soldiers, military equipment, and other materials were transported by air, road, and rail, arriving in Skopje on 11–15 February. The Nordic battalion became operational on 19 February and began keeping watch in Macedonia, and the Canadian troops were redeployed to Sarajevo.[46]

The Nordic battalion of 434 troops from three Finnish, Norwegian, and Swedish rifle companies were deployed on the western border from Debar northward and on the northern border as far as the border with Bulgaria. NORDBAT's headquarters, "Camp Arctic Circle," were established in Cojlija, about eighteen kilometers east of Skopje and included the logistics company. The headquarters of the Finnish company were in Tetovo; those of the Norwegian company were just outside Skopje, in Djorce Petrov; and those of the Swedish company were in Kumanovo.[47] By mid-February, ten observation posts had been established, and the Force periodically manned thirteen temporary observation posts. By May 1993, eighteen observation posts had been established, four along the Macedonian-Albanian border and fourteen along the border with Yugoslavia.

A small team of nineteen military observers was deployed on the northern border and along the western border, south of Debar. The military observers established their headquarters in Skopje and an office in Ohrid.[48]

The twenty-four CIVPOL monitors, like the Nordic battalion, were deployed along the northern and western borders. Those monitoring the western border were based in Ohrid; those monitoring the northern border were based in

Skopje.[49] The headquarters of UNPROFOR Macedonia Command were set up in a former JNA recruitment center, adjacent to the military hospital in Skopje.

The deployment of the peacekeepers in Macedonia took place relatively swiftly for a peacekeeping operation, as it usually takes at least three months for a new mission to become operational. This is particularly notable because in terms of the weather, it was not the best of times to deploy troops, even though the Canadians and the Nordics were not unaccustomed to harsh winter conditions. No doubt, the presence of Canadian troops in Croatia was a major factor contributing to the rapid deployment. Alice Ackermann and Antonio Pala write that the relatively rapid deployment of the force reflected "the critical importance and the necessity the international community was beginning to place on conflict prevention."[50] The Great Powers were also anxious to prevent a particular conflict in the Balkans from spreading and engulfing the entire region, threatening their vital interests.

ESTABLISHING COOPERATION WITH THE CSCE/OSCE

One of the priorities of UNPROFOR Macedonia Command was to establish mechanisms of cooperation with the CSCE Spillover Monitor Mission in Skopje, as mandated by Security Council Resolution 795 (1992).[51] The Mission was opened on 22 September 1992, four days after the Committee of Senior Officials of the CSCE decided to establish it to prevent the spillover of conflict.[52] The mandate of the CSCE Mission was similar to that of the UN operation:

> to monitor developments along the borders of the Host Country with Serbia and in other areas which may suffer from spillover of the conflict in the former Yugoslavia, in order to promote respect for territorial integrity and the maintenance of peace, stability and security; and to help prevent possible conflicts in the region.[53]

To implement its mandate, the Mission was to engage in dialogue with governmental authorities; establish contacts with representatives of political parties and other organizations and with ordinary citizens; conduct trips to assess the level of stability and the possibility of conflict and unrest; in case of incidents, assist in establishing the facts; and engage in other activities compatible with the goals of its mandate.[54]

On 15 April 1993, the UN and the CSCE reached an agreement on Principles of Coordination between their respective missions in Macedonia. The agreement was signed in New York by UN Undersecretary-General for Peacekeeping Operations Kofi Annan and the representative of the CSCE's chairman in office, Peter Osvald, Sweden's ambassador to the United Nations. It was decided that UNPROFOR Macedonia Command and the CSCE Monitor Mission would coordinate their activities and cooperate through weekly consultation meetings at the head-of-mission level, regular exchange of situation reports and other relevant information, and coordination of movements. Both parties also agreed to refrain from commenting on each other's functions or activities, especially in public statements, and to render mutual assistance in cases of emergency, particularly evacuation. Any differences that arose and could not be resolved locally were to be referred to New York for discussion between the UN and a representative of the CSCE chairman in office. Mrs. Margaretha af Ugglas, the Swedish foreign minister and CSCE chairman in office, commented that the agreement confirmed "the willingness of both organizations to coordinate their efforts to contribute to continued peaceful development in the former Yugoslav Republic of Macedonia."[55]

Several international agencies, regional organizations, and nongovernmental organizations were present in Macedonia, as is increasingly the norm in countries facing crisis or going through postwar reconstruction and development. In the early 1990s, hardly any guidelines were available for coordinating the roles of various international players in the field. Furthermore, while coordination is invariably embraced in principle, it is frequently resisted in practice. This is because coordination is viewed as a loss of influence, control, and identity. The early agreement between the UN and the CSCE on principles for coordinating their respective operations in Macedonia laid the foundation for a productive relationship between both organizations in the country. It helped to prevent potential conflicts between the UN, the predominant and most visible international actor in Macedonia, and the CSCE, whose mission was much more modest. An additional advantage of the joint agreement was that it provided a mechanism for resolving disagreements.

THE UNITED STATES JOINS THE OPERATION

In May 1993, the foreign ministers of the United States, Russia, France, the United Kingdom, and Spain met in Washington to consider the crisis in the former Yugoslavia. In a "Joint Program for Action," they indicated that they "will support the increase of an international peacekeeping presence in Macedonia after consulting with the authorities in Skopje . . . [and] the United States is considering contributing forces in this respect."[56] In the view of UNPROFOR Macedonia Command, the Nordic battalion, whose size had reached the mandated number of seven hundred soldiers, was "sufficient" to implement the Security Council's mandate.[57] However, the Macedonian government and the main political parties in the country were strongly in favor of U.S. troops being deployed in Macedonia for military and political reasons. They believed that U.S. troops would increase the military credibility and deterrent effect of UN-PROFOR peacekeeping forces. It was also hoped that American troops would hasten U.S diplomatic recognition of Macedonia, because Washington would realize the essential contradiction in sending its soldiers to aid a country that it had not recognized as a state.

The prospect of an increase in the size of the UNPROFOR contingent in Macedonia was not welcomed by Serbia, which had only grudgingly resigned itself to the presence of UN troops on the territory of its southern neighbor. That the new troops would be from the United States was viewed with particular alarm. Serbian President Slobadan Milosevic hastily arranged a meeting with President Gligorov, which took place on 31 May, at Macedonia's popular resort town of Ohrid. At the presidential villa, which had served as a summer retreat for Tito, Milosevic tried to reassure Gligorov that Serbia had no territorial designs on Macedonia and wished to normalize mutual relations. He argued strenuously that UN peacekeeping troops in Macedonia were unnecessary and urged Gligorov not to accept U.S. troops. Milosevic indicated that he did not believe that Greece would look kindly on the deployment of U.S. forces in Macedonia. The Serbian president also offered to mediate between Greece and Macedonia with a view to creating an Orthodox axis linking Belgrade, Skopje, and Athens, which would serve as a bulwark against putative Muslim expansion in the region. Gligorov politely but firmly rejected the argument and proposal of his Serbian counterpart. Milosevic's fervor produced the opposite effect to that intended: it strengthened Gligorov's conviction that American troops were necessary.

At a meeting of NATO foreign ministers in Athens on 10 June, U.S. Secretary of State Warren Christopher announced that the United States had decided to contribute a reinforced company of three hundred soldiers to augment the UNPROFOR contingent in Macedonia. He stated, "the troops underscore the seriousness of our warning to Belgrade and to the Bosnian Serbs. The offer of United States troops to the United Nations has both symbolic and tangible significance in the region."[58] In explaining the U.S. decision to participate in the Macedonian operation, President Clinton said, "We've said all along that we would support the United Nations in limiting the conflict. It's a very limited thing—no combat—but a chance to limit the conflict."[59] In the same vein, the U.S. Ambassador to the United Nations, Madeleine Albright, declared that this move was "further evidence of [U.S.] commitment to support multilateral efforts to prevent spillover and contribute to stability in the Balkan region."[60] Although Secretary-General Boutros-Ghali had not requested the U.S. troops, he nonetheless expressed the view that "the United States deployment will further strengthen confidence and stability in the former Yugoslav Republic of Macedonia and underscore the message that the international community will not accept any further widening of the tragic conflict in the region."[61]

However, it may be asked, what were the unstated reasons behind the U.S. involvement? During the 1992 U.S. presidential campaign, candidate Bill Clinton had criticized the Bush administration for not intervening in the Bosnian conflict. As president, however, Clinton had to contend with the fact that there was strong congressional opposition to sending U.S. troops to Bosnia. The American public also had a growing hostility to the use of American soldiers overseas. The decision to send U.S. troops to Macedonia gave the administration an opportunity to demonstrate that it was engaging actively in the Balkans. It could also deflect criticism over its refusal to deploy ground troops in Bosnia. Moreover, since Macedonia had not been engaged in war, the deployment came at an acceptable risk and cost. An editorial in the *Washington Post* put it bluntly: "Alone of the former Yugoslav republics, Macedonia has not seen shooting. That made it possible for an otherwise gun-shy American government to order in ground units."[62]

The Macedonian government unanimously accepted the U.S. offer of troops on the same day as Secretary of State Christopher's announcement in Athens. On 18 June, the Security Council adopted Resolution 842 (1993) authorizing the deployment of U.S. troops in Macedonia and expanding the size of UNPROFOR accordingly. The United States agreed that the three hundred U.S. troops would don the blue berets of UN peacekeepers and be under the operational control of the UN commander in Macedonia. It was the first time U.S. troops would serve under a UN commander.

A few hours before the adoption of Resolution 842 (1993), a small party of eight officers from the U.S. Mechanized Infantry Brigade stationed in Berlin, led by the commanding officer, Colonel Jimmy C. Banks, had arrived in Skopje to establish contact with UNPROFOR's Macedonia Command, to receive briefings on the operation, and to visit the Nordic battalion. During their two-day stay, the officers also assessed possible sites for the deployment of the American troops.[63] A preparatory team of about twelve officers arrived in Macedonia on 25 June and carried out the initial logistics work prior to the arrival of the U.S. reinforced company's advance party on 5 July.[64] The main priority of the advance party of some thirty military personnel was to repair the decrepit former JNA quarters at Petrovec, close to Skopje airport. The barracks, which had been vandalized by the JNA troops during their withdrawal from Macedonia in 1992, was to serve as the headquarters of the U.S. company. On 7–12 July, the American troops were deployed in Macedonia, coming from the Sixth Battalion, 502nd Infantry Regiment, of the U.S. Army Berlin Brigade. The operation was called "Able Sentry."

There was much public interest in what the U.S. company was bringing in on the C-141 Starlifter and C-5 Galaxy aircraft. Because of the amount of airport space needed to maneuver the large planes and the number of civil aircraft flying into the small airport in Skopje during the day, many of the transport flights arrived at night, which only fueled public curiosity. Therefore, UN-PROFOR Macedonia Command issued regular press releases giving the number of supply flights arriving from Germany, the times of their arrival, the type of aircraft used, and details of their cargo.[65] This openness in communication generated goodwill in the mission area, while at the same time signaling to potential aggressors that the company was equipped with credible force.

As the American troops were more familiar with training for combat than peacekeeping, they spent their first month in Skopje training with the Nordic battalion on peacekeeping methods, including special patrolling techniques, reinforcement of observation posts by armored personnel carrier and by helicopter, and medical evacuation. The UN commander, Brig. Gen. Saermark-Thomsen, told the new peacekeepers, "Your most important equipment will be binoculars and communications gear, and not your weapons."[66] On 20 August, some of the U.S. troops were deployed on the northeastern section of the Macedonian–Serbian border, assuming responsibility for two observation posts that had been manned previously by soldiers belonging to the Swedish company. The main body of the U.S. contingent was based at "Camp Able Sentry" in Petrovec and was used as a reserve unit, which undertook assignments with the Nordic battalion along the border.[67]

The decision to deploy U.S. troops in Macedonia brought to the fore two persistent issues related to the UN's peacekeeping mission in the country. The first was whether the size of the UN force was sufficient to maintain a credible deterrence. The second was whether the United States would withdraw its troops at the first sign of real trouble or danger. An editorial in the *Washington Post* noted that the soldiers were more equipped for "light seas" instead of the "vicious storm [that] could blow through the southern Balkans."[68] The article continued:

> How much risk and effort is the United States going to extend on behalf of a little country that it does not officially admit exists? If the United States intends to pull out at the first probe, then, although the policy would be shameful, 300 is a good number; 700 Scandinavians are already there. But if the United States is interested in serious deterrence and stabilization and in making good on its repeated warnings to Serbia to back off, then it has to be asked whether 300 is enough.[69]

A British commentator argued that the United States was barking up the wrong tree, for the main threat to Macedonia's stability was internal rather than external:

> In fact, the Americans are in Macedonia for the wrong reasons, and are destined to accomplish nothing whatsoever. The main threat to Macedonia is internal disintegration, not invasion from outside. Despite efforts to integrate its substantial Albanian minority, the Macedonian government is facing a steadily rising Albanian opposition and, when it comes to keeping them down, Macedonia remains Serbia's potential ally. . . . The chances are that once the Albanian question erupts Washington will conclude that it should have stationed its troops in the near-by Greek island of Corfu; at least the weather is more welcoming there.[70]

The debate over the role of U.S. troops was hardly confined to the British and American media. When Brig. Gen. Saermark-Thomsen, the UN commander in Macedonia, indicated in an interview that U.S. troops would be helping to monitor and report any developments that could threaten the country, in conformity with the UN's mandate in Macedonia, his remarks prompted an indignant letter from the Republican Whip, Newt Gingrich, to President Clinton. Mr. Gingrich asserted:

> When American troops and the American Flag arrive in a country, there should be a presumption that we are serious. Potential aggressors should know that violence will be met with overwhelming force. . . . If we are going to be in Macedonia, we must be determined to defend the Macedonians and to use decisive force if necessary.[71]

It was a misinformed assertion, especially as the secretary-general had noted, "The Macedonian authorities did not expect the United Nations to defend its borders. It was the presence of United Nations forces that was most important."[72] In other words, the blue berets were observers; they were not warriors.

In February 1994, there were positive developments in Bosnia and Herzegovina, including a cease-fire in and around Sarajevo. Secretary-General Boutros-Ghali reported to the Security Council that a qualitatively new situation had now developed, which "should provide numerous opportunities for UNPROFOR to make substantial progress" in implementing its mandate. He stressed, however, that UNPROFOR required additional military resources, adding that "it would be a tragedy for the people of Bosnia and Herzegovina if the present opportunity were lost for lack of resources."[73] By resolution 908 (1994) of 31 March 1994, the Council authorized an increase in the Force's strength by an additional 3,500 troops. Consequently, the Swedish Rifle Company of some 140 soldiers serving in Macedonia was redeployed to Tuzla. In

April 1994, two hundred American troops based in Vilseck, Germany, replaced the Swedes. With the additional American troops, there was now a U.S. battalion of over five hundred of all ranks.[74] The United States also sent three UH-60 Black Hawk helicopters and thirty-five personnel to service them, including pilots, crew members, and maintenance technicians. The aviation personnel were from the Fourth Aviation Brigade of the Third Infantry Division based at Katterbach, Germany.[75]

The trip wire function of UNPREDEP gained greater credibility with U.S. troops as part of the operation. Participation in the preventive deployment operation was a cost-effective way for the United States to protect its strategic interests in the southern Balkans. At the same time, it could shoulder its international responsibilities as a vital permanent member of the Security Council.

CONCLUDING THE STATUS OF FORCES AGREEMENT

With the establishment of a peacekeeping operation, the United Nations initiates negotiations with the host country on a Status of Forces Agreement (SOFA) to regulate the relations between the host and the Force and its personnel. The SOFA for UNEF I, which was dispatched to Egypt during the Suez Crisis in 1956, has served as a precedent for subsequent operations. Concluding a SOFA is not assured and often requires protracted negotiations. Secretary-General Kofi Annan has recommended

> that the Security Council, in establishing a peacekeeping operation, prescribe a time-frame for the conclusion of the status-of-forces agreement between the United Nations and the host government for the operation in question and, pending the conclusion of such an agreement, the model status-of-forces agreement would apply provisionally.[76]

It took over two years before the Macedonian government and the UN signed a SOFA. At the start of discussions on the SOFA in early 1993, it emerged that the main problem concerned the designation of the country in the agreement. The Macedonian authorities objected to the use of "the former Yugoslav Republic of Macedonia." In September 1993, Defense Minister Vlado Popovski confirmed to the UN commander, Brig. Gen. Saermark-Thomsen, that Macedonia had no objections to the substantive provisions of the draft agreement, but he reiterated its position on the question of the name. The Macedonian government suggested that a possible modality for signing may be through an annex to the SOFA whereby the designation "the former Yugoslav

Republic of Macedonia" could be transformed into the constitutional name of "the Republic of Macedonia."

However, since the Security Council had decided that the country would be "provisionally referred to for all purposes within the United Nations as 'the former Yugoslav Republic of Macedonia' pending settlement of the difference that has arisen over the name of the State,"[77] and the secretary-general's envoy, Cyrus Vance, was mediating between Greece and Macedonia with a view to resolving the matter, the UN Secretariat did not believe that the SOFA was the appropriate vehicle by which to effect the transformation of Macedonia's temporary name desired by its government. The Secretariat proposed a compromise formula whereby the Macedonian authorities would make a declaration stating their position with regard to the country's designation, which would form an annex to the SOFA. In addition, the Macedonian prime minister, in signing the agreement on behalf of the government, could add in his own handwriting the title "Prime Minister of the Republic of Macedonia."

The UN's formula was unacceptable to the Macedonian government because the draft SOFA still contained references to "the former Yugoslav Republic of Macedonia." During further talks between UNPROFOR officials and the Macedonian authorities in Skopje in mid-October, the Macedonian delegation suggested that the agreement be concluded in the form of an exchange of letters to which a Memorandum of Understanding (MOU) containing the relevant provisions on the status of the Force would be attached. The UN Secretariat accepted the proposal and a draft text in the new format was transmitted to the government. In the MOU, the terms *government* and *territory* were defined to mean "the State as admitted to membership in the United Nations by the General Assembly further to the adoption on 27 April 1993 of resolution 47/225." The MOU referred to both terms without any additional designation. Any reference to the name of the country was thus avoided in the MOU, but this did not preclude Macedonia from using its constitutional name in the exchange of letters.

Although the revised draft was based on the Macedonian government's proposal and took into account its concerns, the government's consent was slow to materialize. On 23 March 1994, the force commander of UNPROFOR, Lt. Gen. Bertrand de la Presle, and the head of civil affairs, Sergio Vieira de Mello, raised the matter with President Gligorov in Skopje. One week later, the Security Council urged "that necessary arrangements be concluded, including, where appropriate, agreements on the status of forces and other personnel with the Republic of Croatia, the former Yugoslav Republic of Macedonia and the Federal Republic of Yugoslavia (Serbia and Montenegro)."[78]

UNPROFOR's direct appeal to President Gligorov and the prodding of the Security Council bore fruit. The Macedonian government indicated that it was ready to give its concurrence to the MOU. The UN and the government agreed that the exchange of letters would be initiated by the SRSG for the former Yugoslavia, Yasushi Akashi. Accordingly, on 1 June 1994, Akashi wrote a letter to the foreign minister, Stevo Crvenkovski, requesting that the status of UNPROFOR and its personnel in Macedonia be regulated by the MOU, which was enclosed with the letter. Akashi proposed that his letter and the minister's written confirmation accepting the MOU would constitute an agreement between the UN and the Macedonian government. In a letter dated 14 June 1994 from Crvenkovski to Akashi, the foreign minister conveyed the Macedonian government's acceptance of the MOU.[79] The original of the foreign minister's letter was in Macedonian, with a courtesy translation into English by the foreign ministry attached.

It is customary that official documents of the UN, especially those concerning relations between the UN and a host country and having legal implications, are written in an official language of the organization. In light of this, and given that the MOU was written in English, the UN requested that the foreign minister's original letter of acceptance be in English. This issue, essentially a technicality, delayed Macedonia's final acceptance of the MOU by a further nine months.

The Macedonian government interpreted the request for an original English reply as, at best, an attempt by the UN to minimize the importance of the country's official language, Macedonian, and, at worst, a deliberate move to deny that it was a separate language. The authorities were particularly sensitive on the matter for two reasons. First, the country was referred to within the UN by its temporary name, the former Yugoslav Republic of Macedonia, and not by its constitutional name, the Republic of Macedonia. This was a cause of continuing resentment. Second, Bulgaria claimed that although Macedonia was an independent "State," it was not a separate "Nation," and Macedonian was not a language but a dialect of Bulgarian. This language-related dispute was unresolved between the two countries. The Macedonian government believed that agreeing to the UN's request would strengthen the hand of two of its neighbors, Greece and Bulgaria, with whom it had differences concerning fundamental issues of name, nationality, and language.

UNPROFOR officials made concerted efforts to explain to the Macedonian authorities that the UN's request for a new letter was routine and should not impede the conclusion of the agreement. They emphasized that it did not imply a lack of respect for Macedonian as the country's official language. In his report on UNPROFOR in September 1994, the secretary-general took the opportunity "to remind the government of the former Yugoslav Republic of Macedonia of the necessity to conclude without further delay a status of forces agreement with UNPROFOR."[80] The delegate of the SRSG in Macedonia, Hugo Anson, reiterated that there were no major differences between the UN and the Macedonian government on this matter:

> The terms of the status of forces agreement, also known as the Memorandum of Understanding (MOU), have already been agreed between UNPROFOR and the Government of FYROM. This is the essential point. The United Nations is now only waiting for a letter of acceptance in the English language from the government of FYROM, because the MOU itself is in English, and it is necessary to provide a measure of uniformity for official documents in a multinational organization such as the United Nations. This is especially true with regard to documents such as the MOU, which sets out the relationship between the host country, in this case FYROM, and UNPROFOR. UN-PROFOR does not, therefore, see this in any way as a major problem. The Secretary-General has simply called for this important matter to be concluded, which it already almost has been.[81]

Despite the secretary-general's reminder and the efforts of UNPROFOR, the Macedonian authorities would not alter their position. To achieve a solution, and taking into account the sensitivities of the government, the UN decided to compromise on the requirement of an original English letter of acceptance. By an exchange of letters dated 13 March 1995 between the SRSG and the Macedonian foreign minister, an agreement was reached on the status of UNPROFOR and its personnel.[82]

The negotiations on the Status of Forces Agreement illustrated that it was not possible to isolate an essentially legal issue from larger political questions. The disputes between Macedonia and its neighbors bedeviled the process of regulating the operation's relations with the host country.

CONCLUSION

UNPREDEP was a major departure in UN peacekeeping. For the first time since the UN was founded in 1945, its peacekeeping forces were deployed before the outbreak of violent conflict, rather than after bloodletting had occurred and a cease-fire had been reached. The major powers on the Security Council demonstrated the requisite political will without which it would have been impossible to mount a preventive deployment operation. The mission was a significant step toward improving the UN's capacity to fulfill its primary purpose—namely, to maintain international peace and security. In financial terms, the operation cost the relatively modest sum of $50 million annually. It is tragic that the UN came to preventive deployment so late, for its use could have averted many seemingly intractable conflicts and saved millions of lives. However, it is hopeful that the UN arrived at it at all.

The slow deployment of UN peacekeepers has long been one of the weaknesses of international peacekeeping. A clear operational lesson from the UNPREDEP experience is the importance of a timely deployment of troops for successful peacekeeping, especially for missions with a preventive mandate. Macedonia represented a critical test of international resolve to prevent the spread of the conflict in the former Yugoslavia. UN peacekeeping troops arrived in Macedonia in time to make a difference to the country's security and stability.

The deployment of the blue helmets was of great benefit to Macedonia. The troops provided a defensive shield to the new state, which lacked an adequate defense system. Their presence was a clear signal of the commitment of the United Nations to Macedonia's security and a legitimization of its sovereignty and independence. They also provided psychological support to Macedonians and boosted their national self-confidence at a vulnerable period in their country's history.

NOTES

1. Acts of the Apostles, chap. 16, verse 9.
2. A generation ago Larry L. Fabian wrote a book on UN peacekeeping entitled *Soldiers without Enemies: Preparing the United Nations for Peacekeeping* (Washington, D.C.: Brookings Institution, 1971).
3. Letter dated 23 November 1992 from the secretary-general addressed to the president of the Security Council, S/24851, 25 November 1992. Following a fact-finding mission to Bosnia and Croatia organized by the International Rescue Committee in August 1992, Richard Holbrooke, then still a private citizen, wrote an article for *Newsweek* proposing that "international (presumably United Nations) observers should be deployed along the borders and in Kosovo and Macedonia immediately, before fighting spreads to these two critical regions." See Richard Holbrooke, *To End a War* (New York: Random House, 1998), 39.
4. Letter, S/24851, 25 November 1992.
5. David Owen, *Balkan Odyssey* (New York: Harcourt Brace, 1995), 68.
6. Letter, S/24851, 25 November 1992.
7. "Report of the Secretary-General on the former Yugoslav Republic of Macedonia," S/24923, 9 December 1992, Annex, para. 3.
8. "Report," S/24923, 9 December 1992, Annex, paras. 6, 11, and 15.

9. "Report of the Secretary-General on the former Yugoslav Republic of Macedonia," S/24923, 9 December 1992, Annex, paras.6–10.

10. "Report," S/24923, 9 December 1992, Annex, para.12.

11. "Report," S/24923, 9 December 1992, Annex, para. 15.

12. "Report," S/24923, 9 December 1992, Annex, para.17.

13. In August 1993, the name "UNPROFOR Macedonia Command" was changed to "UNPROFOR FYROM Command."

14. "Report," S/24923, 9 December 1992, para. 26. It was recommended that thirteen UNCIVPOL monitors would be deployed on the northern border and thirteen on the western border.

15. "Report," S/24923, 9 December 1992, Annex, para.28.

16. "Report," S/24923, 9 December 1992, Annex, para.28.

17. "Report," S/24923, 9 December 1992, Annex, para.30.

18. Lt. Gen. Satish Nambiar served as force commander of UNPROFOR in former Yugoslavia from 1992 to 1993.

19. "Report," S/24923, 9 December 1992, para.5.

20. Boutros Boutros-Ghali, *An Agenda for Peace* (New York: United Nations, 1992), 16.

21. Boutros Boutros-Ghali, *UnVanquished: A U.S.–UN Saga* (New York: Random House, 1999), 50.

22. *Nordic UN Stand-By Forces,* 4th ed. (Helsinki: Nordsam FN, 1993), 180-81.

23. *Nordic UN Stand-By Forces,* 181.

24. Clive Archer, "Conflict Prevention in Europe: The Case of the Nordic States and Macedonia," *Conflict and Cooperation* 29, no. 4, 376.

25. Archer, "Conflict Prevention in Europe," 380.

26. *Nordic UN Stand-By Forces,* 9-10.

27. *Nordic UN Stand-By Forces,* 10-12.

28. *Nova Makedonija,* 19 December 1992.

29. Interview with Todor Malezanski, undersecretary in the Ministry of Defense and coordinator of the Macedonian Government Coordination Committee for UNPROFOR, *Puls,* Skopje, 31 December 1992.

30. "Report," S/24923, 9 December 1992, para.16.

31. Resolution of the Assembly of the Municipality of Debar, Sixteenth Session, 29 December 1992.

32. "Report," S/24923, 9 December 1992, Annex, para. 26.

33. "Report," S/24923, 9 December 1992, Annex, para. 13.

34. "Report," S/26099, 13 July 1993, para.4.

35. Pajo Avirovic, "Vikings Move South," *Puls,* 31 December 1992.

36. See, for example, Avirovic, "Vikings Move South."

37. Mirka Velinovska, "Blue Color, Red Reaction," *Puls,* 3 December 1992.

38. "Survey of 'Nova Makedonija': Peace Forces in Macedonia," *Nova Makedonija,* 29 December 1992. The telephone poll was conducted 21–24 December 1992, with a sample of 605 Macedonian adults.

39. The Coordination Committee was composed of seventeen members from the Ministries of Defense, Foreign Affairs, Internal Affairs, Finance, Justice, Health and Urbanism, as well as from Macedonian Customs, Radio and Television, and Post, Telegraph, and Telephone.

40. This issue, however, remained a sore point with VMRO-DPMNE. In June 1997, during a ministerial meeting of the Euro-Atlantic Partnership Council (EAPC) in Brussels, Defense Minister Lazar Kitanovski offered the use of Krivolak as a military training site for the Council's proposed center for peacekeeping operations. During the same month, President Gligorov also offered to base SFOR troops in Macedonia should they be withdrawn from Bosnia and Herzegovina. These offers evoked strong criticism from the leader of VMRO-DPMNE, Ljubco Georgievski:

> Such ideas are worrying. Let me remind you, Kiro Gligorov personally sent the invitation for the deployment of UN peacekeeping troops in Macedonia, thus violating the Macedonian Constitution, which is clear that it is a task of the Parliament. Macedonia's sovereignty is questioned. I believe it is time to consider for how long Macedonia will need the UN peacekeeping forces. Are we a serious state, that is, a state with its own defense system, capable of keeping peace and stability in the country or are we not interested in our sovereignty at all? The announcement that SFOR may come from Bosnia to Macedonia is nothing but a complete loss of sovereignty.

See Dnevnik, 20 June 1997. The suggestion of the possibility of stationing SFOR troops in Macedonia also prompted a critical article by retired General Mitre Arsovski, who was serving as the chief of staff of the Macedonian Army when UN troops were deployed in 1992. He wrote:

> Our State already has had this experience with the deployment of UN foreign armed forces, namely UNPROFOR, which is better known now as UNPREDEP. Before this Force arrived, the decision to allow it was made rather clumsily with no prior in-depth analysis. Also, no decision was sought before hand from the institutions that are otherwise responsible for such decision-making, such as the Parliament of the Republic of Macedonia, and its citizens, who have the right to express their view on these issues through a referendum.

"Foreign Armed Forces in Macedonia—For or Against," Dnevnik, 5 July 1997, 14.

41. UNPREDEP in the Former Yugoslav Republic of Macedonia, Brief Summary, Skopje, 30 May 1995, 10.

42. UNPREDEP in The Former Yugoslav Republic of Macedonia, 10.

43. An observation post was permanently occupied by peacekeeping troops from where they monitored and reported activities in the border areas. A temporary observation post was occupied on an ad hoc basis for a minimum period of three to four hours. Both were usually painted in the distinctive white and black colors of UN peacekeeping equipment and prominently displayed the UN flag.

44. "Report of the Secretary-General Pursuant to Security Council Resolution 795 (1992)," S/26099, 13 July 1993, para. 6. Brig. Gen. Finn Saermark-Thomsen served as

general officer commanding, UNPROFOR Macedonia Command, from 20 January 1993 to 24 January 1994.

45. UNPROFOR, Press Release 00SP8, Skopje, 4 February 1993.

46. *Nordic UN Stand-by Forces,* 182.

47. "Report," S/26099, 13 July 1993, para.7.

48. "Report," S/26099, 13 July 1993, para.9.

49. "Report," S/26099, 13 July 1993, para.4.

50. Alice Ackermann and Antonio Pala, "From Peacekeeping to Preventive Deployment: A Study of the United Nations in the Former Yugoslav Republic of Macedonia," *European Security* 5, no.1 (Spring 1996): 90.

51. In January 1995, the CSCE was renamed the Organisation for Security and Co-operation in Europe (OSCE).

52. For a brief description of the activities of the OSCE Mission in Macedonia, see Giorgio Blais, "Experiences with CSCE Monitoring in the Former Yugoslav Republic of Macedonia," in *Verification after the Cold War: Broadening the Process,* ed. Jurgen Altmann, Thomas Stock, and Jean-Pierre Stroot (Amsterdam: VU University Press, 1994), 302-7.

53. Organisation for Security and Cooperation in Europe, *Spillover Monitor Mission, Background Summary* (Skopje: n.d.). Given the dispute between Greece and Macedonia, no reference was made to the latter's name in the mandate of the OSCE mission.

54. Organisation for Security and Cooperation in Europe, *Spillover Monitor Mission, Background Summary.*

55. Permanent Mission of Sweden to the United Nations, "UN and CSCE Agree on Cooperation in the former Yugoslav Republic of Macedonia," press release, New York, 14 April 1993.

56. "Joint Program for Action," Washington, D.C., 23 May 1993.

57. Transcript of interview with Alun Roberts, press and information officer of UNPROFOR Macedonia Command, on CNN International, 12 May 1993.

58. Statement of U.S. Secretary of State Warren Christopher, Athens, 10 June 1993.

59. Quoted in Elaine Sciolino, "U.S. Says It Will Send 300 Troops to Balkan Republic to Limit Strife," *New York Times,* 11 June 1994.

60. Letter dated 15 June 1993 from the Secretary-General addressed to the President of the Security Council, S/25954, 15 June 1993, 2.

61. "Report," S/26099, 13 July 1993, para.24.

62. "Serious about Macedonia," *Washington Post,* 13 July 1993.

63. UNPROFOR Macedonia Press and Information, SP0027, 18 June 1993.

64. UNPROFOR Macedonia Press and Information, SP0028, 25 June 1993.

65. See, for example, UNPROFOR Macedonia Press and Information, SP0030, 4 July 1993, and SP 0033, 10 July 1993.

66. Steve Vogel, "GIs Refurbish Macedonian Barracks, Indicating Commitment to a Long Stay," *Washington Post,* 22 July 1993, 25.

67. UNPROFOR Macedonia Press and Information, SP0043, 18 August 1993.

68. "Serious about Macedonia?"

69. "Serious about Macedonia?"

70. Jonathan Eyal, "From Bad to Worse to Bosnia," *The Spectator,* 17 June 1995.

71. Letter from Newt Gingrich to President Bill Clinton, 7 July 1993.

72. "Report," S/24923, 9 December 1992, para. 21.

73. UN Department of Public Information, "The United Nations and the Situation in the Former Yugoslavia," DPI/1312/Rev. 4, July 1995, 24.

74. UNPROFOR FYROM Command Press and Information, Press Release SP0075, 14 April 1994. The two hundred additional American soldiers were from the same unit as those who had replaced the first American reinforced company in January 1994.

75. UNPROFOR FYROM Command Press and Information, Press Release SP 0080, 27 April 1994.

76. "Renewing the United Nations: A Program for Reform," Report of the Secretary-General, A/51/950, 14 July 1997.

77. Resolution 817 (1993), 7 April 1993.

78. Resolution 908 (1994), 31 March 1994, operative paragraph 7.

79. The foreign minister's letter was, however, only hand delivered to UNPROFOR FYROM Command's headquarters on 30 June 1994.

80. "Report of the Secretary-General Pursuant to Resolution 908 (1994)," S/1994/1067, 17 September 1994, para.50.

81. UNPROFOR FYROM Command, Statement to the Press, Skopje, 28 September 1994.

82. "Report of the Secretary-General Pursuant to Resolution 947 (1994)," S/1995/222, 22 March 1995, para. 57.

4

COMPOSITION, ORGANIZATION, AND STRUCTURE OF UNPREDEP

> I welcome the recent decision of the Security Council to estab-
> lish a separate, independent UNPREDEP Command in Macedo-
> nia[1]
>
> Kiro Gligorov

The focus of this chapter is the composition, organization, and structure of UNPREDEP. It examines the civilian and military components of the mission, which underwent frequent change. A notable characteristic of the civilian component of UNPREDEP was its small size in comparison to similar peacekeeping operations, despite the growth of its functions. I shall compare and contrast the Nordic and U.S. battalions, drawing attention to their relative strengths and weaknesses. It was noted in the previous chapter that in 1992 the Nordic countries established a composite battalion for the first time to serve in Macedonia. In 1994, they went a step further by forming a new Scandinavian Company (SCANDCOY), composed of troops from Denmark, Norway, and Sweden as part of the Nordic battalion.

The U.S. decision that its troops serving with UNPREDEP would be under the operational control of the UN commander was unprecedented. The United States, however, imposed certain restrictions on the force commander's operational control over its troops, which affected their capacity to implement the mandate of the mission. In some instances, commanders of the U.S. battalion received operational orders directly from their national chain of command that differed from those of the UNPREDEP commander.

The decision of the Security Council in February 1996 to establish UN-PREDEP as an independent mission was a benchmark in the history of the operation. The second part of the chapter deals with the Macedonian government's campaign to separate the operation in Macedonia from UNPROFOR.

The government viewed an autonomous operation as a reflection of national sovereignty and independence. Ironically, however, developments in other parts of the former Yugoslavia determined the eventual achievement of the government's cherished goal.

CIVILIAN ORGANIZATION

A striking feature of the civilian component of UNPREDEP was its consistently small size throughout the evolution of the Mission. In the early days of the peacekeeping operation in Macedonia, the civil affairs section of UNPRO-FOR FYROM Command was composed of only three members headed by the civil affairs coordinator (CAC). The two civil affairs officers were responsible for liaison between UNPROFOR and the central and local authorities, as well as providing political advice to the general officer commanding (GOC). One press and information officer was in charge of the public information program and served as spokesperson. The CAC reported to the GOC and the head of Civil Affairs at UNPROFOR headquarters in Zagreb.

On 31 March 1994, the Security Council in Resolution 908 authorized a good offices mandate for the SRSG for the former Yugoslavia aimed at contributing to Macedonia's peace and stability. Consequently, the SRSG, Yasushi Akashi, appointed a delegate in Macedonia, a more senior position, who held the concurrent post of CAC. The delegate of the SRSG became the head of the civilian component of FYROM Command and reported directly to the SRSG in Zagreb. An additional civil affairs officer joined the team, thereby increasing it to five members.

As part of the restructuring of UNPROFOR in 1995, UNPROFOR FYROM Command was renamed UNPREDEP and established as one of three separate but interlinked peacekeeping operations in the former Yugoslavia. A theater headquarters known as United Nations Peace Forces headquarters (UNPF-HQ) in Zagreb, led by the SRSG, exercised overall policy direction, administration, and logistics for the three operations in Macedonia, Bosnia, and Croatia. UNPREDEP was headed by a civilian chief of mission, at the level of assistant secretary-general, who was accountable to the SRSG. The chief of mission was responsible for the efficient conduct of all activities of the mission; assurance, within his delegated authority, that the tasks of all components of the mission were implemented in accordance with the mandate and policy guidelines; diplomatic and political negotiations required to carry out the mandate; and coordination between the civilian and military components of the operation.[2]

With the establishment of UNPREDEP as an independent mission in early 1996, a significant reorganization of the civil affairs component followed, being transformed into the Office of the SRSG, but the size remained quite small, with only seven professional staff members. The SRSG's office was composed of a deputy SRSG, a special assistant to the SRSG, a Political and Humanitarian Affairs Section consisting of two officers, the spokesperson, and a legal adviser.

The twenty-six civilian police monitors were deployed as follows: two monitors at the headquarters in Skopje, and the remaining twenty-four divided into three teams of eight monitors based in Skopje, Tetovo, and Ohrid.

The administration was composed of several sections: communications, finance, procurement, personnel, transportation, engineering, general services, supply and property management, air operations, security, information technology, and transport, responsible to the chief administrative officer. It provided support to all the components of the mission and ensured accountability.

Prior to the establishment of UNPREDEP as a fully independent mission, administrative and logistical control was centralized in Zagreb and under the successive control of UNPROFOR headquarters, UNPF-HQ, and the United Nations Transition Office in the Former Yugoslavia (UNTOFY). The centralized approach to administration that existed for nearly four years had certain drawbacks. First, the mission lacked a local procurement capability; therefore, goods and supplies that could be purchased locally had to be ordered through Zagreb. This necessitated costly and time-consuming deliveries from Zagreb via Belgrade to Skopje. Second, only Zagreb had the authority to issue purchase orders for the provision of services by local vendors, which also resulted in delays. Another impediment was due to the mission's limited financial and budgetary authority. All expenditures over $5,000 had to be submitted to Zagreb for approval, as well as requests to use funds for local contracts such as leases for buildings. Invariably, there were delays in paying local vendors, whose frequent and vociferous complaints affected the public's perception of the United Nations.

MILITARY FORCE ORGANIZATION

The force commander had operational control over the two mechanized infantry battalions, NORDBAT and USBAT, whose strength at the peak of the operation was five hundred personnel each, the fifty-man Indonesian engineering platoon, and thirty-five military observers. He coordinated with the twenty-six civilian police monitors.

UNPREDEP's military headquarters was divided into seven branches: Personnel and Administration, Information and Liaison, Operations, Logistics, Engineering, Military Police, and Medical. Each was headed by a chief officer in charge with the rank of lieutenant colonel except the force provost marshal, who was a major. The branches were supervised by the chief of staff, an American colonel, who was responsible to the force commander. The chief of staff also performed an unofficial but vital role as a bridge between the headquarters and the U.S. battalion and between the force commander and U.S. Army commanders in Naples and Germany. However, the chief of staff and the other American officers were assigned to the headquarters for six months, in contrast to the Nordic personnel, who served for one year or longer. This short tenure hampered the effectiveness of the chiefs of staff, especially as all of them lacked prior experience in UN peacekeeping operations. By the time they had mastered the distinctive demands of the post, it was time to move on.

Originally, the Nordic battalion was composed of three rifle companies from Finland, Norway, and Sweden. During the second half of 1994, NORDBAT was significantly restructured as a result of two main factors. The first was the redeployment of the Swedish company in Bosnia, and the second was Norway's decision not to replace its troops at the end of their tour but to reassign them to Bosnia instead. Consequently, about 260 soldiers augmented the Finnish contingent. By the end of August, the Swedish and Norwegian personnel at NORDBAT's headquarters, who were responsible for administration and logistics, were replaced by Finns. To retain the multinational character of the Nordic battalion following the increase in the number of Finnish soldiers, a new Scandinavian Company (SCANDCOY) of some 108 Danish, Norwegian, and Swedish soldiers was created in October 1994.[3] SCANDCOY was based at Camp Valhall in Kumanovo and served as a reconnaissance and reserve unit. NORDBAT now consisted of two Finnish rifle companies, FINCOY 1 based in Tetovo and FINCOY 2 in Gjorce Petrov; SCANDCOY; and a logistics company at NORDBAT headquarters.

Following the Security Council's decision in 1997 to reduce the mission's military component by 300 of all ranks, both the Nordic and U.S. battalions were reduced to 350 from their previous strength of 500. NORDBAT was restructured to consist of a single Finnish company (FINCOY) based in Tetovo; SCANDCOY, whose base was moved to Gjorce Petrov; and the headquarters Logistics Company.

A Finnish colonel commanded NORDBAT. As the battalion was composed largely of reservists, they had other skills such as carpentry, plumbing, and masonry that could be put to good use at the observation posts. The majority of the soldiers had also participated in other UN peacekeeping operations and could draw on a wealth of experience in carrying out their duties in Macedonia. The length of their tour was another asset as the senior officers served for one year, and most of the soldiers six to eight months, extendable to twelve. About one-third of the battalion was replaced every four months, thus ensuring that there were always some personnel who were familiar with the mandate, operations, and mission area. But a major drawback of the troop rotation policy was that just when a particular section or unit was functioning cohesively, one-third of its members were preparing to leave.

The U.S. battalion was an active duty combat unit taken from the U.S. Army–Europe and led by a lieutenant colonel. During the period in which the battalion was five hundred strong, it consisted of five companies and an aviation platoon. With the reduction of its size to 350 soldiers, it was restructured to three companies, but the platoon was retained. As we have seen, the first U.S. company deployed in Macedonia in July 1993 had limited preparation for peacekeeping. However, the U.S. military learned its lessons fast. It introduced important changes aimed at improving the effectiveness of subsequent battalions. Each new battalion trained for three months in peacekeeping techniques, rules of engagement, and the use of specialized UN equipment before its deployment. Some four to six weeks before it was deployed, the commander, subcommanders, and key staff officers of the incoming battalion visited Skopje on orientation for about one week. Later, their counterparts in the outgoing battalion visited Germany to observe and evaluate the training of the incoming battalion.

In contrast to the Nordic battalion, the entire U.S. battalion rotated every six months. In 1995, the commander of UN troops in Macedonia, Norwegian Brig. Gen. Tryggve Tellefsen, praised the American peacekeepers as "vital" and "professional" but urged U.S. defense planners to deploy them, especially officers, for longer than six months: "If you [the United States] are to establish credibility in UN missions, you have to realize that you are to stay more than six months. This is not a mission fulfilled in six months."[4] The U.S. military was not eager to extend the deployment of U.S. troops because many commanders believed that participation in peacekeeping diminished the combat readiness of the troops. Another reason was that a longer deployment would have necessitated moving from a policy of "rotation on temporary duty" to that of a "permanent change of station" for the soldiers. The latter would have required higher levels of remuneration, benefits, and privileges.

The military component included thirty-five unarmed military observers who were divided into five teams based in the capital Skopje; Gjorce Petrov, a suburb outside Skopje; Kumanovo, a northern town with a large ethnic Serb population; Tetovo, a predominantly ethnic Albanian city in western Macedonia; and Ohrid, a popular tourist resort in the south. A chief military observer led the military observers.

In September 1995, an Indonesian engineering platoon was deployed as part of UNPREDEP's military component to provide an engineering capability in support of its operations. It was a sorely needed addition given the poor road conditions in the country, particularly in the mountain areas where a number of observation posts were located, and also given the fact that the battalions were not equipped to undertake major road construction. The work of the platoon was initially delayed as its equipment arrived in December, three months after its deployment and in the middle of winter when construction was not easy. After these minor initial troubles, the platoon provided "indispensable support to the two battalions through the construction of roads and repair of the main supply routes to the observation posts."[5]

COMMAND AND CONTROL

The UNPREDEP chain of command was consistent with that of traditional peacekeeping operations and had four levels of authority. The force commander reported to the SRSG, who was responsible for operations in the field; the secretary-general was responsible for the executive direction of the mission; and ultimate responsibility for the political direction of the mission was the Security Council's. However, the presence of U.S. troops as part of UNPREDEP raised particular command and control issues. When the U.S. administration decided to contribute troops to the UN's peacekeeping operation in June 1993, President Clinton indicated that

> the U.S. contingent will serve under the operational control of UNPRO-FOR Macedonia and will conduct missions as directed by the UN commander. Although UNPROFOR Macedonia is a UN peacekeeping force under Chapter VI of the Charter and has not encountered hostilities to date, our forces are fully prepared not only to fulfill their peacekeeping mission but to defend themselves if necessary.[6]

On the whole, the president's decision was not controversial as would probably have been the case had it been taken after the tragedy in Somalia three months later. In fact, the deployment of American troops in Macedonia was hardly noticed in the United States.

On 3 October, during a clash with militia loyal to the warlord General Mohammed Farah Aideed, eighteen American Army Rangers were killed, seventy-eight others were injured, and one was taken prisoner. Although the

Rangers were not under UN but rather U.S. command and control, the incident sparked strong opposition in the U.S. Congress to UN command of American troops in peace enforcement actions, particularly if the UN commander was a foreign national. Many legislators believed that a foreign commander should never direct American soldiers.

While the United States transferred operational control of its task force, a subset of command, to the UN, the president retained command. As the public version of the Presidential Decision Directive 25 (PDD-25) on multilateral peace operations of 3 May 1994 makes clear:

> The President retains and will never relinquish command authority over U.S. forces. On a case by case basis, the President will consider placing appropriate U.S. forces under the operational control of a competent UN commander for specific UN operations authorized by the Security Council. The greater the U.S. military role, the less likely it will be that the U.S. will agree to have a UN commander exercise overall operational control over U.S. forces. Any large scale participation of U.S. forces in a major peace enforcement mission that is likely to involve combat should ordinarily be conducted under U.S. command and operational control or through competent regional organizations such as NATO or ad hoc coalitions.[7]

The directive emphasized that the Clinton Administration's position on the command and control of U.S. forces was merely the continuation of established U.S. policy.

> There is nothing new about this Administration's policy regarding the command and control of U.S. forces. U.S. military personnel have participated in UN peace operations since 1948. American forces have served under the operational control of foreign commanders since the Revolutionary War, including in World War I, World War II, Operation Desert Storm and in NATO since its inception. We have done so and will continue to do so when the President determines it serves U.S. national interests.[8]

Nonetheless, the United States imposed three key restrictions on the UN-PREDEP force commander's operational control over American troops. First, the U.S. soldiers were initially prohibited from patrolling within one thousand meters of the UN Patrol Line; in March 1995, it was reduced to three hundred meters. This restriction limited the soldiers' ability to accomplish effectively the Force's mandate to monitor and report developments in the border areas between Macedonia and Serbia. Second, they were forbidden to patrol at night, which meant that any monitoring of the border after dark could be conducted only from the observation posts. Third, the American troops were not permitted to deviate from their planned route while on patrol. As a result of this rigidity, the patrols were not always able to investigate incidents in the border areas properly. Inevitably, these restrictions also created some degree of tension between the commander of the U.S. battalion and the UN commander, as well as with the Nordic battalion, which functioned without any constraints.

The restrictions on the U.S. troops reflected the paramount importance of "force protection" and the sensitivity to casualties by American society. The avoidance of casualties is a central objective of a military mission and a fundamental criterion of success.

In practical terms, the commander of the U.S. battalion had the difficult and sensitive task of serving different masters. He was required to respond on an almost daily basis to three separate chains of command: to the UN commander in Macedonia, to the commander of Joint Task Force–Provide Promise (JTF-PP) in Naples who was in charge of all U.S. military involvement in the Former Yugoslavia, and to the commanding general of the U.S. Army Europe (USAREUR) in Heidelberg. It requires uncommon qualities of tact, judgment, and resourcefulness on the part of a lieutenant colonel to balance the competing demands placed on him by a one-star Nordic general and two four-star American generals and to reconcile, if possible, his contending loyalties.

At times the UN commander believed that the U.S. battalion should perform certain functions, within the UN mandate, but the U.S. national chain of command took a different view.[9] The Nordic battalion then had to perform the designated tasks. For example, in the summer of 1994, a confrontation occurred between Macedonian and Serbian soldiers at a strategic hilltop, Cupino Brdo. Following the intervention of the UN commander, Brig. Gen. Tellefsen, the forces of both sides withdrew, and a UN buffer zone was established with an observation post to observe, monitor, and report any activities in the disputed area. The United States, however, would not allow the UN commander to deploy American peacekeepers at this observation post even though it was in the sector under the responsibility of the U.S. battalion. In March 1997, as negotiations continued in the Joint Border Commission established by Macedonia and Yugoslavia, there was a marked increase in the number of Serbian patrols crossing the UN Patrol Line. Yugoslavia was evidently staking its territorial claims. Most of the crossings occurred around Tupan Hill, an area monitored and patrolled by U.S. soldiers. Believing that there was a risk that encounters with Serb soldiers could lead to violence, the United States decided to terminate its patrols in the areas north of the administrative border, and USAREUR ordered increased force protection. As this decision effectively resulted in no UN patrols around Tupan Hill and in other areas along the border, the force commander, Swedish Brig. Gen. Bo Wranker, decided to deploy Nordic soldiers in the U.S.

battalion's sector. The pragmatism and flexibility of the UN commanders served them well in resolving the problems at Cupino Brdo and Tupan Hill.

The United States, in a precedent-setting move, placed American troops under the operational control of the UN commander in Macedonia. In a formal sense, this act symbolized a new approach by the United States toward UN peacekeeping operations. In practice, however, the United States continued the tradition of reserving key operational decisions to its national chain of command.

THE ROAD TOWARD AN INDEPENDENT MISSION

Since the early days of UNPROFOR's presence in Macedonia, the Macedonian government had been strongly in favor of a separate and independent command structure for the UN's peacekeeping operation in the country. The government believed that since Macedonia was now an independent and sovereign state, it should not be linked with the UN's missions in Bosnia and Croatia. An independent mission, led by its own SRSG and force commander, was seen as another step toward defining a Macedonia that was distinct from the other former Yugoslav republics. The government also felt that Macedonia always ranked third and last in UNPROFOR's priorities in the former Yugoslavia. However, although the Macedonian authorities made no secret of their unhappiness over FYROM command's connection with UNPROFOR during contacts with UN officials, the government refrained from submitting a formal request to the secretary-general for an independent mission for over two years. The government was aware that there was little support within the Security Council, especially among the permanent members, for a separate peacekeeping operation in Macedonia. Thus, it would have been futile for Macedonia to press its demand prematurely. Rather than risk making a diplomatic blunder, the government prudently decided to wait until the political climate was more propitious.

The anticipated political winds of change came in early 1995. On 12 January 1995, President Franjo Tudjman announced that the Croatian government would withdraw its support for UNPROFOR's continued presence in Croatia after its mandate expired on 31 March 1995.[10] "Although UNPRO-FOR has played an important role in stopping violence and major conflicts in Croatia," he stated, "it is an indisputable fact that the present character of the UNPROFOR mission does not provide conditions necessary for establishing lasting peace and order in the Republic of Croatia, a sovereign State Member of the United Nations."[11] Tudjman's decision was later endorsed by the Croatian Parliament.

This development created much uncertainty about the future of UN-PROFOR not only in Croatia but in the entire region. On 17 January, the Security Council, in a presidential statement, declared that it believed that UN-PROFOR's continued presence in Croatia was "of vital importance for regional peace and security."[12] Tudjman came under strong and ultimately effective diplomatic pressure from the United States to reverse his decision. On 12 March, Tudjman agreed to the retention of the peacekeeping operation, but the Croatian government requested that the UN forces deployed on its territory should be separated from UNPROFOR. The government of Bosnia and Herzegovina also indicated that it was in favor of restructuring UNPROFOR.

Long resentful that the UN's mission in Macedonia was linked to its two other operations in the former Yugoslavia, the Macedonian government now saw an opportunity to press for the severance of FYROM command's umbilical ties to UNPROFOR. On 13 March 1995, on the heels of the requests by Bosnia and Herzegovina and Croatia, the Macedonian government submitted a similar request to the secretary-general asking that the military, administrative, and logistical functions of the UN's presence in Macedonia be separated from UNPROFOR and placed under a separate SRSG and force commander. The reasons for the government's request were that Macedonia had not been involved in the war in the former Yugoslavia and therefore was not sustainable politically that the UN's mission in the country should be a part of UNPRO-FOR, UNPROFOR's preventive mandate in Macedonia was different from its mandates in Bosnia and Herzegovina and Croatia, and the success of the UN's first preventive deployment mission warranted greater recognition.[13]

Other considerations, however, had an impact on the government's desire for an independent mission. First, a separate mission would emphasize Macedonia's status as an independent and sovereign state. Second, an autonomous mission would necessitate direct communication with and greater attention from UN Headquarters in New York. Third, an independent operation would increase the amount of local procurement in Macedonia, thereby boosting the weak local economy.

Not surprisingly, the Macedonian government's request for an independent peacekeeping operation was of considerable local media interest. UNPRO-FOR's response to queries from the media was brief and to the point. A press release stated:

> The Government have informed this Headquarters about the letter from the foreign minister and about their reasons for making this request. Any decision concerning this request will be in the hands of the Secretary-General and of the Security Council, in mutual agreement with the authorities of the Former Yugoslav Republic of Macedonia.[14]

In his report of 22 March 1995, Secretary-General Boutros-Ghali recommended that UNPROFOR be replaced by "three separate but interlinked
peacekeeping operations: United Nations Peace Force–One in Croatia, United
Nations Peace Force–Two in Bosnia and Herzegovina, and United Nations
Peace Force–Three in the former Yugoslav Republic of Macedonia."[15] Each
operation would be led by a civilian chief of mission at the assistant secretary-
general level and would have its own military commander. The three operations
would be under the overall command and control of the SRSG and a Theater
force commander based at the United Nations Peace Forces Headquarters
(UNPF-HQ) in Zagreb. UNPF-HQ would be responsible for the coordination
of the administrative, logistical, and public informational activities of all three
operations.[16] The secretary-general's recommendations were based on the following justifications: the nature of the problems in the former Yugoslavia were
interrelated, the expense of duplicating existing structures had to be avoided,
and an integrated peacekeeping operation in the region was both cost-effective
and efficient.[17]

On 31 March 1995, by terms of its Resolutions 981 (1995), 982 (1995),
and 983 (1995), the Security Council reorganized UNPROFOR as recommended by the secretary-general. In Resolution 983(1995), the Security Council decided that "UNPROFOR within the former Yugoslav Republic of
Macedonia shall be known as the United Nations Preventive Deployment
Force (UNPREDEP)."[18] Given the unresolved dispute between Greece and
Macedonia, no reference was made to the latter's name in the operation's new
name. The two other operations were UNPROFOR in Bosnia and Herzegovina, and in Croatia, the United Nations Confidence Restoration Operation
(UNCRO). The secretary-general appointed Henryk J. Sokalski, a Polish diplo-
mat, as UNPREDEP's chief of mission.

Although Security Council Resolution 983 (1995) gave the Macedonian
government less than they had requested and hoped for, it nevertheless had
symbolic significance. For the first time there was a separate resolution on the
extension of the UN's peacekeeping operation in Macedonia, the new name of
the mission stressed its unique preventive character, and the political level of the
civilian leadership was raised. The importance of the Resolution was not lost
on either the Macedonian authorities or the local press. The government recognized that it was a benchmark on the road to their ultimate objective of gaining an independent status for the UN's mission in their country. Macedonia's
foreign minister, Stevo Crvenkovski, publicly expressed his government's "satisfaction" with Resolution 983 (1995).[19]

An article published in *Nova Makedonija* stated that the political reasons
underlying the Macedonian government's request for a separate UN mission

had been legitimized by Resolution 983 (1995). It argued that this development would have positive repercussions on the future treatment of Macedonia within the United Nations. The article stressed that while Macedonia's ultimate objective of an independent status for UNPREDEP had not yet been realized, the Resolution was an important step toward ending the country's relegation to the "tail end" of UNPROFOR's priorities in the former Yugoslavia.[20]

The Macedonian government's determination to separate UNPREDEP from the other UN missions in the region did not wane following the adoption of Resolution 983 (1995) by the Security Council. In August 1995, three months before the expiration of UNPREDEP's mandate on 30 November 1995, the government began signaling to its domestic audience and the international community its continued interest in an independent United Nations operation. The defense minister, Blagoj Handziski, a former professor of engineering, took the lead in the government's concerted public campaign. During a panel discussion on Macedonian television in August 1995, Handziski declared:

> In such a situation where the central UN Command in Zagreb is losing its role or will lose it in a few month's time, it is unacceptable to us that General Engstrom reports to General Janvier in Zagreb. We feel that the time has come for the UNPREDEP mission to cut loose from the mission in Zagreb, especially from a military standpoint. It is especially vital to establish its own military independence. The second change that is very important, politically and militarily, is in the area of logistics. In these two areas, UNPREDEP is still linked to the command in Zagreb. Logistics are important not only from a political, but also from an economic perspective.[21]

Macedonia's move for an independent mission was aided by striking events in Bosnia and Croatia in the summer of 1995. In July 1995, the Bosnian war reached new depths of depravity after the Bosnian Serbs launched a bloody assault against the UN safe area of Srebrenica. Thousands of Bosnian Muslim civilians were massacred by the Bosnian Serbs and buried in mass graves.[22] After the fall of Srebrenica, the Bosnian Serbs attacked Zepa, another UN safe area, which they captured on 25 July. Following a meeting in London that month of the foreign ministers of the Contact Group, NATO, and UNPROFOR troop-contributing nations, the warring parties, especially the Bosnian Serbs, were warned that further attacks on the safe areas would lead to NATO air strikes. On 28 August 1995, there were five mortar attacks on Sarajevo's Markale marketplace, one of which killed thirty-seven people and injured eighty-eight others. In response, NATO launched air strikes against Serb antiaircraft systems and heavy weapons around Sarajevo, as well as against ammunition supply depots and other military installations in Bosnian Serb territory.[23]

The atrocities committed at Srebrenica and Zepa galvanized the Clinton administration to mount a vigorous peace initiative led by Richard Holbrooke, assistant secretary of state for European affairs. His intense shuttle diplomacy between Sarajevo, Belgrade, Zagreb, and Washington during the summer of 1995 and a three-week negotiating marathon at Wright-Patterson Air Force Base in Dayton, Ohio, in the autumn culminated in the initialing of the General Framework Agreement by the Presidents of Bosnia and Herzegovina, Croatia, and Serbia on 21 November 1995.

The Dayton Agreement ended the Bosnian War, which had been raging for three and a half years. A new multinational Implementation Force (IFOR), composed of troops from NATO and non-NATO member states, would undertake the implementation of the military aspects of the Dayton Agreement. Consequently, UNPROFOR would be terminated upon the transfer of authority from its commander to the IFOR commander.

On 1 May 1995, two days after the Security Council authorized the deployment of UNCRO, the Croatian Army launched an attack on Western Slavonia. The military offensive continued despite calls from the Security Council for its cessation.[24] After only three days, the area was firmly under the control of the Croatian Army. The following month, the Croatian Army began a major military campaign in the Krajina, and by mid-August, the region was in its hands. Following the Croatian Army's rapid military successes in Western Slavonia and the Krajina, UNCRO's responsibilities were now limited to Eastern Slavonia, Baranja, and Western Sirmium.[25] Croatian leaders declared that they would take the area by force if negotiations for peaceful reintegration failed. From September to October 1995, the secretary-general's special envoy, Thorvald Stoltenberg, and the United States ambassador to Croatia, Peter Galbraith, conducted local negotiations. Further negotiations were undertaken at the Dayton peace talks, and on 3 November 1995, Presidents Milosevic and Tudjman agreed to revitalize local efforts to reach an agreement. The negotiations led to the signing of the Basic Agreement on the Region of Eastern Slavonia, Baranja, and Western Sirmium on 12 November 1995, which provided for the peaceful reintegration of the region into Croatia.[26] In its Resolution 1023 (1995) of 22 November 1995, the Security Council welcomed the Basic Agreement, declaring that it would consider "expeditiously" the request to establish a transitional administration and an appropriate international force. The days of UNCRO were numbered.

The dramatic changes in the regional situation during the second half of 1995 had important political and operational implications for UNPREDEP. The secretary-general's reasons for recommending in March 1995 that the

UN's peacekeeping operations in the former Yugoslavia should be "separate but interlinked" were no longer relevant. The continued operation of UNPF-HQ in Zagreb, as well as a political linkage between UNPF-HQ and UNPREDEP, especially after the termination of UNCRO and UNPROFOR, would have been both superfluous and politically untenable. An autonomous status for UN-PREDEP was now inevitable. Accordingly, in his report of 23 November 1995, the secretary-general stated that he was

> conscious of the need to revert to the Council, as soon as practicable, on the establishment of UNPREDEP on a fully independent footing, reporting directly to New York. This will require adjustments to the administrative, logistic and military support structures of the mission and thus minor adjustments to its authorized strength.[27]

In its Resolution 1027 (1995) of 30 November 1995, the Security Council welcomed the secretary-general's report and requested him "to keep the Council regularly informed of any developments on the ground and other circumstances affecting the mandate of UNPREDEP, and in particular to submit, if possible by 31 January 1996, a report on all aspects of UNPREDEP in the light of developments in the region, for review by the Council."[28] However, the Council did not give any indication of its position on the issue of an independent status for UNPREDEP. Macedonia's ambassador to the United Nations, Denko Maleski, lost no time in reminding the Security Council of his country's view that the UN's first mission with a preventive mandate should be autonomous. In a statement to the Security Council following the adoption of Resolution 1027 (1995), Ambassador Maleski said that "the Force should become a completely independent United Nations operation, reporting directly to the Secretary-General," and its "base, military command and logistics structure should be located in Skopje."[29]

Meanwhile, Kofi Annan, the special representative of the secretary-general to the former Yugoslavia and NATO, paid a visit to Macedonia on 10–11 January 1996 to meet with Macedonian government officials.[30] President Gligorov and Stojan Andov, speaker of the Macedonian Parliament, reiterated to the secretary-general's envoy that UNPREDEP should be separated from UNPF in Zagreb.[31] Annan indicated that the secretary-general would recommend to the Security Council that UNPREDEP become an autonomous mission from 1 February 1996.[32] The secretary-general's forthcoming recommendation had been foreshadowed a few weeks before Annan's visit to Skopje. In his report to the Security Council of 13 December 1995 on aspects of the implementation of the Dayton Peace Agreement on Bosnia and Herzegovina, the secretary-general had stated explicitly, "that the time has now come to wind down UNPF-

HQ in Zagreb and to make the three United Nations operations in the former Yugoslavia fully independent of one another."[33]

Thus, it was hardly surprising when Secretary-General Boutros-Ghali, in his report to the Security Council of 30 January 1996, recommended "that the mandate of UNPREDEP should not only be continued but that it should become an independent mission, reporting directly to United Nations Headquarters in New York."[34] He added that, "despite its new status, the operation would have basically the same mandate, strength and composition of troops."[35] He proposed, however, that to provide for a continuing engineering capability for UNPREDEP, its size should be increased by about fifty personnel.[36] There were also operational, financial, and administrative implications regarding the independence of UNPREDEP from UNPF-HQ in Zagreb. A force commander of UNPREDEP who would have authority over the military components of the operation had to be appointed, since overall operational control of the three operations in the former Yugoslavia had been exercised by the Theater force commander of UNPF-HQ; the financial resources for UNPREDEP, which were previously included in the budget of UNPF-HQ, had to be reallocated in a separate UNPREDEP budget;[37] UNPREDEP's communications infrastructure had to be improved, including provision of a direct satellite link with UN Headquarters in New York; independent financial, procurement, personnel, and security services had to be established; and the facilities for maintaining and repairing vehicles would require enhancement.[38]

On 1 February 1996, Ambassador Madeleine Albright, in her capacity as president of the Security Council, informed the secretary-general that the members of the Council concurred "in principle" with his recommendation that UNPREDEP should become an independent mission.[39] Twelve days later, on 13 February, the Security Council adopted Resolution 1046 (1996) authorizing an increase in the strength of UNPREDEP by fifty military personnel to enhance the operation's engineering capability; approved the establishment of the post of force commander; and requested the secretary-general to submit to the Council by 20 May 1996 "additional recommendations on the composition, strength, and mandate of UNPREDEP in the light of developments in the region."[40] Boutros-Ghali redesignated UNPREDEP's chief of mission, Henryk J. Sokalski, as his special representative for Macedonia and appointed Brig. Gen. Bo Wranker as the force commander. Wranker had served as deputy commander of the Swedish Southern Naval Command based in Karlskrona. He was analytical, witty, and convivial and encouraged close cooperation between civilian and military staff members of the mission.

UNPREDEP's independence was greeted with enthusiasm in Macedonia. In an address given at the headquarters of the Nordic battalion in late February, President Gligorov "welcomed" the Security Council's decision that UN-PREDEP would become a separate and independent peacekeeping operation. However, he noted "regretfully" that the

> causes that motivated the establishment and deployment of UNPREDEP in Macedonia have not been eliminated. In the interest of peace and stability in this region, and of course in the interest of the stability of our country, the continued presence of United Nations peacekeeping forces here will still be essential for some time ahead.[41]

On the same occasion, the SRSG, Henryk Sokalski, called the Council's decision an "important act of political justice" that had "confirmed the validity of the long-standing aspirations of our Host Country and the unique quality of the operation."[42] The Council's decision made the headlines in all the major print and electronic media in Macedonia. The headline of the daily newspaper, *Nova Makedonija,* read, "Peacekeeping Mission in Macedonia Independent,"[43] and the other major daily, *Vecher,* carried a similar headline: "UNPREDEP—Independent Mission."

CONCLUSION

This chapter has reviewed the composition and organization of UNPREDEP, command and control of the Force, and the campaign by the Macedonian government to separate the mission from those in Croatia and Bosnia. The Force combined the long and varied experience of Nordic troops in peacekeeping with the robust credibility of U.S. ground forces. It had the requisite resources and trained personnel to fulfill its mandate. The civil affairs team remained small despite the expansion of the mission's tasks. As we shall see in chapter 6, in contrast to the military component, the lack of adequate civilian personnel and resources limited the mission's ability to implement the nonmilitary aspects of a preventive mandate, such as election monitoring and economic and developmental activities. The command and control problems reflected the tensions between UN and national military chains of command in peacekeeping operations.

From its establishment in December 1992 until February 1996, the operation in Macedonia was linked structurally with the UN's peacekeeping operations in other parts of the former Yugoslavia. An independent operation led by an SRSG and with its own force commander had international symbolism for the Macedonian government. Like the presence of the blue helmets, it symbolized the independence of a small but strategic country that was considered an artificial creation by its neighbors.

NOTES

1. "Address of H. E. Kiro Gligorov, President of the Republic of Macedonia at the UNPREDEP Change of Command Ceremony," Skopje, 29 February 1996.

2. A/49/540/Add. 2, Annex VII.

3. UNPROFOR FYROM Command, Press Release, "Formation of New Company within UNPROFOR's Nordic Battalion," 20 October 1994.

4. *Stars and Stripes,* 53, 11 January 1995, 1.

5. "Report of the Secretary-General on the United Nations Preventive Deployment Force," S/1997/365, 12 May 1997, para. 3.

6. White House Press Release, "Text of a Letter from the President to the Speaker of the House of Representatives and the President Pro Tempore of the Senate," 9 July 1993, 2.

7. "The Clinton Administration's Policy on Reforming Multilateral Peace Operations," 3 May 1994, 9.

8. "The Clinton Administration's Policy on Reforming Multilateral Peace Operations," 3 May 1994, 9.

9. Secretary-General Boutros-Ghali strongly criticized the practice of some troop-contributing nations to give direct operational orders to their contingents serving in peacekeeping operations:

> Another important principle is unity of command. The experience in Somalia has underlined again the necessity for a peacekeeping operation to function as an integrated whole. That necessity is all the more imperative when the mission is operating in dangerous conditions. There must be no opening for the parties to undermine its cohesion by singling out some contingents for favorable and others for unfavorable treatment. Nor must there be any attempt by troop-contributing Governments to provide guidance, let alone give orders, to their contingents on operational matters. To do so creates division within the force, adds to the difficulties already inherent in a multinational operation and increases the risk of casualties. It can also create the impression amongst the parties that the operation is serving the policy objectives of the contributing Governments rather than the collective will of the United Nations as formulated by the Security Council. Such impressions inevitably undermine an operation's legitimacy and effectiveness.

Supplement to "An Agenda for Peace: Position Paper of the Secretary-General on the Occasion of the Fiftieth Anniversary of the United Nations," A/50/60-S/1995/1, 3 January 1995, para. 41.

10. The Security Council's decision to extend UNPROFOR's mandate until 31 March 1995 was taken in Resolution 947 (1994) of 30 September 1994.

11. Quoted in "Report of the Secretary-General on the Situation in the Occupied Territories of Croatia," A/50/648, 18 October 1995, para. 5.

12. Quoted in "Report," A/50/648, 18 October 1995, para. 6.

13. Foreign Minister Stevo Crvenkovski made the same points in an interview to the weekly *Puls,* 24 March 1995.

14. UNPROFOR HQ, Press Release, Skopje, 16 March 1995.

15. "Report," S/1995/222, 22 March 1995, para. 84.

16. "Report," S/1995/222, 22 March 1995, para. 84.

17. "Report," S/1995/222, 22 March 1995, para. 84.

18. Security Council Resolution 983(1995), 31 March 1995.

19. Statement by Stevo Crvenkovski to Makpress, as quoted in *Vecher,* 3 April 1995.

20. Zoran Petrov, "UNPREDEP Facing an Alteration in its Mandate? More Than a Political Question," *Nova Makedonija,* 19 August 1995.

21. Macedonian television, Skopje, 15 August 1995.

22. See S/1995/755, 30 August 1995. For a critical account of the UN's role, see David Rohde, *Endgame: The Betrayal and Fall of Srebrenica, Europe's Worst Massacre since World War II* (New York: Farrar, Straus & Giroux, 1997).

23. "Report of the Secretary-General Pursuant to Security Council Resolutions 981(1995), 982(1995) and 983 (1995)," S/1995/987, 23 November 1995, paras. 13–14.

24. See "Statements of the President of the Security Council," S/PRST/1995/23 and S/PRST/1995/26, 4 May 1995.

25. From 1992 until the dramatic events of the summer of 1995, UN peacekeeping troops were deployed in four United Nations Protected Areas (UNPAs), under the control of local Serb authorities: Krajina (Sectors North and South), Western Slavonia (Sector West), and Eastern Slavonia, Baranja, and Western Sirmium (Sector East).

26. "Report," S/1995/987, 23 November 1995, para. 6.

27. "Report of the Secretary-General Pursuant to Security Council Resolutions 981 (1995), 982 (1995) and 983 (1995)," S/1995/987, 23 November 1995, para. 38.

28. Security Council Resolution 1027 (1995), 30 November 1995.

29. Security Council 3602d Meeting, SC/6135 (Press Release Security Council, DPI), 30 November 1995.

30. Kofi Annan, then undersecretary-general for peacekeeping operations, served on a temporary basis as the secretary-general's special representative from 1 November 1995 to 29 February 1996. He was responsible for establishing the UN's new missions in the former Yugoslavia and ensuring a smooth transition from UNPROFOR to IFOR in Bosnia and Herzegovina.

31. "Press Statement," Cabinet of the President of the Republic of Macedonia, Skopje, 10 January 1996; and *Vecher,* 11 January 1996.

32. Statement by Kofi Annan, undersecretary-general and special representative of the secretary-general, Skopje, 11 January 1996.

33. "Report of the Secretary-General Pursuant to Security Council Resolution 1026 (1995)," S/1995/1031, 13 December 1995, para. 43.

34. "Report of the Secretary-General Pursuant to Security Council Resolution 1027 (1995)," S/1996/65, 30 January 1996, para. 20.

35. "Report," S/1996/65, 30 January 1996, para. 21.

36. The secretary-general indicated that the engineering support for UNPREDEP had been "provided on a temporary basis by a platoon of the Indonesian engineer battalion," which was an UNPF-HQ asset, and was scheduled to leave the mission area in March 1996. See "Report," S/1996/65, 30 January 1996, para. 22.

37. Letter dated 6 February 1996 from the Secretary-General Addressed to the President of the Security Council, S/1996/94, 8 February 1996.

38. "Report of the Secretary-General Pursuant to Security Council Resolution 1027 (1995)," S/1996/65, 30 January 1996, paras. 21–23.

39. "Report," S/1996/76, 1 February 1996.

40. Security Council Resolution 1046 (1996), para. 3.

41. "Address of H. E. Kiro Gligorov, President of the Republic of Macedonia at the UNPREDEP Change of Command Ceremony," Skopje, 29 February 1996.

42. "Statement by Mr. Henryk J. Sokalski at the UNPREDEP Transfer of Command Ceremony," Skopje, 29 February 1996.

43. *Nova Makedonija,* 2 February, 1996.

5

KEEPING WATCH

The United Nations . . . [has] done no more and no less than [its] job; to monitor events in and around Macedonia closely, and to lend a hand of assistance where it is useful and required.[1]

Hugo Anson

After fifty years of UN experience in peacekeeping, one of the truisms of peacekeeping is that the nature of a mandate is fundamental to the success or failure of operations. It follows, therefore, that a clear, practicable, and implementable mandate is a precondition for effective peacekeeping operations. There is an important link between the nature and content of the mandate authorized by the Security Council and its implementation.

This chapter will be concerned with UNPREDEP's implementation of its mandate to monitor and report any developments that could threaten Macedonia. The preventive mandate of the Force broke new ground, but it was implemented by traditional peacekeeping methods. Monitoring and reporting were the functions of the earliest UN observer missions. UNPREDEP's mandate was implemented primarily through the establishment of permanent and temporary observation posts on Macedonia's borders with Serbia and Kosovo, and Albania, as well as by active patrols by the Nordic and U.S. battalions, military observers, and civilian police. A major impediment to implementing the mandate was the lack of a demarcated border between Macedonia and Serbia. However, this obstacle was overcome through the creativity of the UN commanders who negotiated a "UN Patrol Line" to facilitate patrolling by the peacekeepers.

In June 1994, the Cupino Brdo border incident brought Macedonia and Serbia to the brink of conflict. The UN commander, Brig. Gen. Tellefsen, played a critical role as a mediator between the two countries, and the crisis was successfully and peacefully defused. He had a commanding presence and in-

87

spired confidence. Without the timely intervention of the UN, this incident would most likely have escalated.

The military component of UNPREDEP assumed tasks that were not foreseen when peacekeeping troops were initially deployed in 1992. However, care was taken to ensure that carrying out these additional responsibilities did not jeopardize the core mandate of the operation. While the Force embraced an important new function, humanitarian assistance, with enthusiasm, another, sanctions monitoring, was undertaken with reluctance.

The effects of sanctions against the Federal Republic of Yugoslavia and the economic embargo imposed by Greece caused considerable damage to the economy of Macedonia. The country's economic woes exacerbated political, social, and interethnic tensions. The Macedonian government called for international economic assistance on the basis of Article 50 of the Charter. The secretary-general made similar appeals, indicating that poor economic conditions can impact on preventive deployment. However, few member states responded to these appeals.

BORDER MONITORING AND REPORTING

When peacekeeping troops were deployed in Macedonia, the international border between Macedonia and Serbia was not settled and was a contentious issue between the two countries. The existing border had been an administrative one, established in the bygone era of the Socialist Federal Republic of Yugoslavia. From the outset of the deployment, the absence of a demarcated border posed a major challenge in implementing the mandate of the Force that required the blue helmets to patrol on the Macedonian side of the border. In addition, the dispute over the border carried the risk of border incidents between Macedonian and Serbian military patrols, as well as the citizens of both countries, which could escalate into conflict.

During the first eighteen months of the operation, several encounters took place between UN military personnel and Serb soldiers, with the latter alleging that UN peacekeepers had strayed into Serbian territory.[2] A typical incident occurred in June 1993, when a Nordic battalion patrol consisting of three Swedish soldiers was detained by Serb soldiers for nine hours, at the police station in Zeravina, a Serbian town close to the border with Macedonia and Bulgaria. The Serb soldiers alleged that the UNPROFOR patrol had been approximately three hundred to five hundred meters inside Serbian territory. An UNPROFOR Reserve team of sixteen soldiers and a UN helicopter were sent to the area. After negotiations between Nordic battalion officers and Serb soldiers, the

Swedish soldiers were released. In April 1994, two CIVPOL monitors and their interpreter were detained for eleven hours by the Serbian Army, after they had inadvertently entered a section of the disputed territory. An UNPROFOR reaction team of twenty-seven soldiers and civilian police was dispatched to the scene and successfully negotiated the release of the three UNPROFOR personnel.³ In addition, because of the dispute over the Macedonian-Yugoslav border, in the early months of UNPROFOR's deployment in Macedonia, some observation posts, which Serbia claimed were in disputed areas of the border, had to be relocated.

It was against this background in the summer of 1994 that the commander of UNPROFOR in Macedonia, Brig. Gen. Tryggve Tellefsen, negotiated between the Macedonian and Yugoslav military authorities a military administrative boundary known as the Northern Limit of the Area of Operations (NLAOO), to prevent further tension between UN and Serbian patrols. Although Macedonia and Yugoslavia did not recognize the NLAOO as a legitimate international border under the "gentleman's agreement," both countries accepted it as the northern limit of the UN's area of responsibility and as the basis for reporting and managing border crossing incidents. It was also agreed that should UN troops cross north of the NLAOO, such crossings should be considered "honest mistakes," and the peacekeepers were to be allowed to return south without delay. The acceptance of the NLAOO led to a significant reduction in the number protests from both Macedonia and Yugoslavia against alleged border violations.

However, after several months, it became evident that the NLAOO was unsatisfactory as it covered rugged terrain, which was difficult to patrol and to locate on maps. A revision of the NLAOO was therefore initiated by Tellefsen's successor, Finnish Brig. Gen. Juha Engström, in early 1995, which followed more practical and visible terrain features such as roads, streams, and ridges, thus allowing the UN troops to accomplish their mission more effectively. The proposed revisions were submitted to the Ministries of Defense in Skopje and Belgrade and were accepted without objections by both parties in February 1996. The new NLAOO was given the more manageable name of the UN Patrol Line and became effective one month later.

Another development, which facilitated the execution of the mandate, was the agreement by Serbia in 1995 to periodic meetings at the working level among Nordic and U.S. battalion commanders, company commanders, and their Serbian counterparts. As a result, border incidents could be resolved at a low level, expeditiously, without recourse to the highest military authorities at the Ministry of Defense in Belgrade.⁴

By January 1996, UNPREDEP had established twenty-four observation posts and thirty-three temporary observation posts along Macedonia's borders with Yugoslavia and Albania. The Nordic and U.S. battalions conducted a daily average of forty border and community patrols by foot, vehicle, and helicopter.[5] In addition, separate patrols were conducted by thirty-five military observers who were divided into five groups: one based at the headquarters in Skopje and one team each at Kumanovo, Tetovo, Gjorce Petrov, and Ohrid. They conducted an average of twelve border and community patrols daily. The Kumanovo team was composed of seven military observers who monitored the UN Patrol Line and the eastern part of the Yugoslav-Macedonian border, which covered one thousand square kilometers. The area contained about sixty towns and villages, three border crossing points, nine Macedonian Army (ARM) border posts, two ARM battalion HQs, and about twenty UN observation posts. The Tetovo team was made up of seven military observers who monitored the UN Patrol Line and the western part of the Yugoslav-Macedonian border extending to Debar on the Macedonian-Albanian border. Its area of responsibility covered 1,200 square kilometers and included approximately seventy towns and villages, two border crossing points, thirteen ARM border posts, two ARM battalion HQs, and thirteen UN observation posts. The Gjorce Petrov team had seven military observers who monitored the western part of the Macedonian-Yugoslav border to the Janzince border crossing and the corresponding portion of the UN Patrol Line. The area was about one thousand square kilometers and included three ARM border posts, twelve UN observation posts, about seventy villages, and one border crossing. The Ohrid team monitored the southwestern Macedonian-Albanian border from Debar, which covered 1,500 square kilometers. The area included about 110 towns and villages, two border crossing points, eleven ARM border posts, and one ARM battalion HQ. Given the negative attitude of ethnic Albanian leaders to the deployment of UN peacekeeping troops in this area, there were no observation posts there, and the military observers and monitors constituted the United Nations presence along that section of the Macedonian-Albanian border. In addition, the military observers investigated any incident along the UN Patrol Line or those that involved the Macedonian military and periodically manned temporary observation posts.[6]

CIVPOL's patrols were conducted by twenty-six monitors, who were divided into three teams based at its headquarters in Skopje, Tetovo, and Ohrid. The monitors on the Skopje team covered an area of 2,725 square kilometers, which included 240 villages and seven border crossing points. On average the team conducted fifty border patrols and thirty-five village patrols monthly. The Tetovo team was responsible for an area of 1,865 square kilometers, which included 180 villages and one border crossing point. The monitors conducted an average of fifteen border patrols and sixty village patrols monthly.[7] The Ohrid team covered an area of 2,600 square kilometers, which included 270 villages and four border crossing points. The team conducted, on average, thirty-six border patrols and forty village patrols monthly. The police monitors also co-operated with the local law enforcement authorities and investigated numerous complaints of alleged assaults by local police against ethnic Albanians.[8] During the village patrols, they obtained information on humanitarian needs, which were made available to national and international aid agencies.

The effectiveness of CIVPOL was, however, limited by the small number of monitors. It was only possible for the monitors to work in a one-shift system during the day, from eight in the morning to four in the afternoon. Some of the border incidents, which CIVPOL could have monitored, occurred in the evening and at night when no monitors were on duty, a fact that was not lost on the local border police.

In the spring of 1996, UNPREDEP launched a Road Safety Campaign for schoolchildren, in cooperation with the Macedonian police and Ministry of Education. The aim of the campaign was to promote safety on the roads and highlight the dangers of traffic. It was conducted by teams of CIVPOL monitors and Macedonian police. During a period of three weeks, the campaign involved three thousand children, aged seven to fourteen, in forty-two schools across the country.[9]

The operational problems faced by the Force as a result of the absence of a demarcated border between Macedonia and Serbia illustrated the difficulty of implementing mandates of the Security Council in the field. The Force was able to cope with the challenge through the skill of its commanders and the co-operation of the Macedonian and Serbian authorities. It applied enduring techniques of peacekeeping such as border and community patrols to meet the unique demands of a preventive operation. The visible and active patrolling was a cornerstone of the deterrence strategy of UNPREDEP. It also contributed to the reduction of tension in ethnic communities.

THE CUPINO BRDO INCIDENT

An important test of the peacekeeping operation occurred in the summer of 1994, at Cupino Brdo (Hill 1703), a strategic hill on the northern corner of the border between Macedonia and Serbia.[10] Intense fighting had occurred in the area during World War II among Macedonian, Serbian, German, and Bulgarian forces. As a result, it has symbolic importance for Macedonians and Serbs, and a memorial on the hill commemorates the battle fought there on 14 June 1944.[11] The monument is approximately 250 meters south of the disputed border. In early June 1994, about twelve Serb soldiers occupied the hilltop, which

Macedonia claimed was within its territory. It is not easy to know why the Serbs occupied Cupino Brdo. The UN commander in Macedonia, Brig. Gen. Tellefsen, believed that it was probably a deliberate move authorized by the Yugoslav General Staff. It is possible that this was an attempt by Serbia to test the resolve of Macedonia, especially to see whether the Macedonian government would take action to recover what Macedonia considered its territory. Second, Serbia may have wanted to test the reaction of UNPROFOR FYROM Command to its occupation of Macedonian territory. Third, in April 1994 the 140 Swedish troops serving with UNPROFOR in Macedonia had been redeployed to Bosnia and had been replaced by 180 U.S. soldiers. The Serbs may have interpreted the increase in the number of U.S. soldiers serving in Macedonia, as a signal that aggressive action by UNPROFOR FYROM Command would now be taken against them. Finally, Cupino Brdo was both a strategically attractive and unprotected target. Macedonian border guards very rarely patrolled Cupino Brdo because the absence of proper roads made accessibility to the area difficult. The nearest Macedonian border stations were in Ogut and Slatinje, which were approximately six kilometers from the area. Given the area's strategic importance and the absence of regular Macedonian border patrols, UNPROFOR had established a temporary observation post there, which was occupied regularly by the Swedish company before it was taken over by the U.S. battalion in August 1993. However, because the United States restricted its soldiers from patrolling within one thousand meters of the UN Patrol Line, there had ceased to be a UN presence on the hilltop.

In response to Serbia's occupation of Cupino Brdo, Macedonia dispatched about thirty troops to the area and placed another hundred on standby for possible deployment. Tension increased when the Macedonian government denied permission to Serbs who wished to visit the Cupino Brdo Monument in commemoration of the fiftieth anniversary of the June 1944 battle. After a Macedonian soldier was detained and later released by the Serbs near Cupino Brdo in mid-June 1994, the Macedonian authorities threatened military action to eject the Serbs from the hill if they did not leave voluntarily.

In view of the rising tension between Macedonia and Serbia, Brig. Gen. Tellefsen met Lt. Gen. Blagoje Kovacevic, deputy chief of the Serbian General Staff, in Belgrade on 1 July 1994. The generals were not strangers to each other—this was their third meeting since Brig. Gen. Tellefsen assumed command of UN troops in Macedonia in January 1994. Following discussions between Tellefsen and Kovacevic, the Serbs agreed to withdraw their soldiers up to a distance of one thousand meters from Cupino Brdo under UN monitoring if the Macedonians did likewise. FYROM Command communicated this proposal to the General Staff of Macedonia, which readily accepted the terms.

During the meeting, Brig. Gen. Tellefsen gave Lt. Gen. Kovacevic a map show-ing a proposed trace of the UN Patrol Line, which would serve as the northern limit of the mission's area of operations. Tellefsen hoped that if the Yugoslav and Macedonian authorities agreed to the trace, the number of border incidents would decrease significantly.

On 2 July 1994, Macedonia and Serbia withdrew their respective soldiers five hundred meters from the hilltop. Meanwhile, a temporary observation post was established on Cupino Brdo to observe, report, and maintain a UN pres-ence in the disputed area to deter Serbian and Macedonian troops from reoc-cupying Hill 1703.

On 10 July 1994, Brig. Gen. Tellefsen organized a meeting between Col. Gen. Dragoljub Bocinov, chief of the Macedonian General Staff, and Lt. Gen. Kovacevic of the Serbian General Staff, at Cupino Brdo, aimed at reaching a final agreement on resolving the dispute. As Serbia and Macedonia had not rec-ognized each other, their military representatives would not meet one another face to face. Consequently, Tellefsen engaged in "shuttle diplomacy by military vehicle" in driving rain on the windswept hill of Cupino Brdo. The "proxim-ity talks" resulted in an agreement to establish a buffer zone around Cupino Brdo, under UN control, that would be off limits to Macedonian and Serb sol-diers. An observation post was established at Cupino Brdo. Given the restric-tions imposed by the United States on the deployment of and patrolling by U.S. troops serving with the United Nations in sensitive areas on the Macedonian-Serbian border, it was agreed that only Nordic troops would be stationed at Cu-pino Brdo, although it was in the U.S. battalion's area of operation.[12] Another breakthrough occurred at the meeting on Cupino Brdo when Lt. Gen. Ko-vacevic confirmed to Brig. Gen. Tellefsen that the Serbian authorities had ap-proved the trace of the UN Patrol Line, which had already been accepted by the Macedonian General Staff. The Yugoslav General Staff also agreed that if any UN soldiers crossed the UN Patrol Line inadvertently, they would be al-lowed back into Macedonian territory promptly.

The tense stand-off between the Serbian and Macedonian forces was suc-cessfully defused by the timely and effective intervention of Brig. Gen. Tellef-sen. There were certain reasons for the success of his mediation. First, Tellefsen enjoyed the confidence of both the Macedonian and Serbian General Staff. He had established contacts between FYROM Command and the Serbian General Staff during two visits to Belgrade prior to events at Cupino Brdo, and his re-lationship with Lt. Gen. Kovacevic was especially helpful in resolving the crisis. Second, throughout the negotiations, Tellefsen observed the principles of neu-trality and impartiality that are keys to successful peacekeeping. Third, the Macedonian authorities favored a peaceful outcome because they wished to avoid an escalation of the crisis. Finally, the Serbs were also willing to find a negotiated solution to the Cupino Brdo incident as a way of improving their tarnished international image.

On the whole, the buffer zone on Cupino Brdo was respected by both Macedonian and Serb soldiers. However, on 8 May 1995, nine Serb soldiers penetrated the sensitive buffer zone and aimed their rifles and a recoilless anti-tank gun at the UNPREDEP troops manning the observation post on the hill. The UNPREDEP troops confronted the Serb soldiers, insisting that they leave the area. After some initial reluctance, the Serb soldiers complied, and the incident was over within an hour. The immediate and firm response of UNPREDEP troops was an important deterrence to further breaches of the buffer zone.

The Cupino Brdo incident demonstrated in a compelling way the benefits of preventive deployment. First, since the peacekeeping troops had been deployed before the onset of conflict, they were in a position to intervene when the incident erupted and before the dynamics of escalation made it difficult or impossible to stop. Second, UNPREDEP as a neutral force did not favor the Macedonians over the Serbs or vice versa. It provided a face-saving mechanism for both sides to pull back from open confrontation. Third, the UN buffer zone freed Macedonia of the financial and military burden of having to deploy its own troops at Cupino Brdo.

SANCTIONS MONITORING

The international community viewed sanctions as an important tool to end the war in Bosnia-Herzegovina. On 30 May 1992, acting under Chapter VII of the UN Charter, the Security Council adopted Resolution 757 (1992), imposing mandatory and comprehensive sanctions against the Federal Republic of Yugoslavia (Serbia and Montenegro) for interference in the war and aiding the Bosnian Serbs. The Resolution imposed a binding blockade on all economic, diplomatic, scientific, cultural ,and sports exchanges with Serbia and Montenegro.[13]

Beginning in October 1992, in response to requests from the neighboring countries of Yugoslavia for international assistance in enforcing UN sanctions, the EC and the CSCE jointly established Sanctions Assistance Missions (SAMs) in Albania, Bulgaria, Croatia, Hungary, Macedonia, Rumania, and Ukraine. The SAMs reported directly to a communications center (SAMCOMM) established by the European Commission in Brussels. SAMCOMM was responsible for coordinating the work of the SAMs and providing technical support to the EU/CSCE sanctions coordinator. The SAMs were composed of customs officers from CSCE member states, whose duties consisted of verifying customs documents for goods to be exported to Yugoslavia, inspecting and sealing vessels on the Danube, verifying and monitoring the use of copies of UN authorizations, advising local customs authorities on effective enforcement measures, and assisting the national authorities with their investigations of companies suspected of sanctions violations. The Macedonia Sanctions Assistance Mission (MACSAM) was the largest of the seven SAMs.[14] But as one analyst has observed, "Lacking adequate enforcement capabilities, however, this extensive monitoring neither cut off the flow of goods nor prevented their inevitable reallocation to the ruling elite and military in Serbia."[15]

After the failure of the Bosnian Serbs to accept the Vance–Owen Peace Plan for Bosnia and Herzegovina, the Security Council decided by terms of Resolution 820 (1993) of 17 April 1993, to strengthen the sanctions regime imposed against Yugoslavia. Resolution 820 (1993), inter alia, prohibited the transportation "of all commodities and products across the land borders or to or from the ports of the Federal Republic of Yugoslavia (Serbia and Montenegro)." The only exceptions were medical supplies, foodstuffs, and other essential humanitarian supplies authorized by the United Nations Sanctions Committee. States neighboring Yugoslavia were also to prevent the passage of all road and rail traffic into and out of Yugoslavia, except at a limited number of border crossing points; all states were to impound all Yugoslav ships, aircraft, trains, and trucks found outside the country; and all financial transactions between Yugoslavia and other countries were prohibited, with the exceptions of telecommunications, postal and legal services, as well as for humanitarian or "other exceptional purposes."

As a result of informal arrangements between the UN and the CSCE and EC, it was agreed that UNPROFOR would monitor the traffic at selected road and railway crossings at Macedonia's border with Yugoslavia. UNPROFOR was reluctant to become actively involved in the implementation of sanctions for three main reasons. First, none of the relevant Security Council Resolutions included a mandate for UNPROFOR in Macedonia, to monitor or enforce UN sanctions against Yugoslavia. Second, since Macedonia's compliance with tougher sanctions was bound to contribute to economic hardship in the country, monitoring by UNPROFOR could prompt a hostile domestic public reaction toward the operation, resulting in security problems for UN troops and other UNPROFOR personnel. Third, the Macedonian government had the duty and responsibility to implement the sanctions, and there was a risk that the authorities might interpret UNPROFOR's involvement as relieving them of their obligations. Such a development would set an undesirable precedent for the enforcement of UN sanctions in the future.

Of the three reservations of UNPROFOR concerning the monitoring of sanctions, the fear that this could spark negative or even dangerous public reactions to the Force had the most serious operational implications. The sanctions enriched a tiny minority but increased the economic difficulties of the majority of Macedonians. Fortunately for UNPROFOR, its fears in this regard were never realized. It would be unwise to conclude that hesitations about assuming responsibilities not included in a peacekeeping operation's mandate are usually misplaced. The fact that Macedonians did not blame UNPROFOR for their privations or turn against the Force does not mean that people elsewhere would have reacted in a similar manner.

Despite the misgivings of UNPROFOR officials about the appropriateness of monitoring sanctions, on 30 April 1993, four days after Resolution 820 took effect, Macedonia Command, in cooperation with MACSAM, assumed its new responsibilities. The soldiers stationed at the observation posts at the four official border crossing points between Macedonia and Serbia, Jazince, Blace, Tabanovce, and Pelince monitored and recorded all bus, truck, and rail traffic over a twenty-four-hour period, every day of the week. They then sent the reports to the operations branches of their company and battalion, which forwarded them to Macedonia Command Headquarters. The reports from the observation posts were analyzed by civil affairs officers and forwarded to UN headquarters in New York weekly. UNPROFOR and MACSAM collaborated closely by exchanging information, statistics, and reports. While MACSAM, like UNPROFOR, monitored the two main road crossing points at Blace and Tabanovce, MACSAM depended on UNPROFOR to observe the two other border crossing points at Jazince and Pelince.

Although the UN troops had no authority to stop and search the vehicles and trains, the substantial traffic suggested regular and massive sanctions violations. On average, two thousand trucks, five hundred railway wagons, and four hundred buses crossed the Serbian-Macedonian border in both directions weekly. Given the country's high unemployment rate, smuggling was an attractive and lucrative business. Moreover, the meandering and porous border between both countries facilitated smuggling. Private enterprises and organized crime also violated the sanctions because it was financially profitable. According to the cargo manifests of trucks and trains crossing the border to and from Serbia, large quantities of building materials, machinery, chemicals, and textiles were transported from Macedonia into Serbia, in violation of UN sanctions. Mountain villagers living on Macedonia's border with Serbia also found the financial rewards of sanctions busting irresistible, and they routinely led around 150 donkeys daily through the forbidding mountains into Serbia. Typically, each donkey carried plastic containers filled with gasoline, and the smugglers earned around $400 per load, more than the average monthly salary.[16]

The Macedonian government consistently maintained that without effective economic assistance from the international community to help Macedonia implement the UN sanctions, the violations would continue because the UN sanctions, and the unilateral trade embargo that Greece had imposed against landlocked Macedonia in February 1994, were strangling the country on its northern and southern borders. According to official estimates by the Macedonian government, the cost to the Macedonian economy of sanctions against Yugoslavia and the Greek blockade amounted to approximately U.S.$4 billion.[17] The Macedonian satirical weekly, *Osten*, captured the negative attitude of Macedonians toward the UN embargo and the Greek blockade in a cartoon depicting a school teacher saying to her class. "The termination of the embargo and the blockade will be our third Ilinden!"[18] This was an emotive reference to the Ilinden Uprising of 2 August 1903 (St. Elijah's Day), when Macedonians rebelled against Ottoman rule, and 2 August 1944, when the First Session of the Anti-Fascist Assembly of National Liberation of Macedonia (ASNOM) was held in the monastery of St. Prohor Pchinski, and delegates decided on the establishment of a Macedonian republic within the new Yugoslav Federation.

For the Macedonian authorities, then, tacitly condoning violations of the sanctions was a matter of economic and therefore political survival. They feared that the economic adversity, which would be caused by strict compliance, could lead to political and social unrest. Therefore, while the government maintained a formal commitment to observe UN sanctions, its will to take practical measures to ensure compliance was both inconsistent and half-hearted. The number of customs officers was increased from about 109 in December 1992 to approximately 249 in May 1993, but they often turned a blind eye to sanctions violations. On 24 June 1993, the government issued a decree making the violation of sanctions a criminal offence punishable with heavy fines of up to $25,000, but no one was ever prosecuted under the decree. In August 1993, after the urging of the European Union and the CSCE, President Gligorov decided that all oil shipments to Serbia would be stopped, and early the next month, the minister of internal affairs issued a directive to the customs and border authorities to enforce strictly the provisions of Resolution 820 (1993). Commercial traffic was to be allowed only through the Blace and Tabanovce border crossing points, while the two other official border crossings, Jazince and Pelince, were restricted to private cars and pedestrians. Consequently, the number of trucks crossing the Macedonian-Serbian border decreased significantly from 5,472 during the last week of August 1993, to 349 during the first week of October 1993. However, as noted earlier, the number of trucks crossing the border in both directions rose again, and sanctions violations continued on a large scale.

Serbia had a vested interest in ensuring that sanctions violations continued unabated. Following the move by the Macedonian government to implement the UN sanctions strictly, it came under sustained pressure from Belgrade to change course and revert to the mutually beneficial status quo. On 6 September 1993, Serbian Prime Minister Nikola Sainovic paid an urgent visit to Skopje with the issue of sanctions at the top of his agenda. Born in Bor, a major copper mining center in southeastern Serbia, he had served as a provincial Communist Party leader from 1978 to 1982, and later as minister for mining. Sainovic proposed that Macedonia continue to allow oil and other products into Serbia, in exchange for which Serbia would supply Macedonia with wheat, as the latter's grain reserves had been depleted because of a severe drought that summer. He also threatened that Serbia would cut off its coal and electricity supplies to Macedonia during the winter if strict enforcement of sanctions was maintained. The Serbian press launched a hostile propaganda campaign against Skopje, charging that the Macedonian government had capitulated to political pressure from the United States by instituting the new measures of compliance.

Three weeks later, on 30 September, President Gligorov addressed the General Assembly in New York. It was a milestone for him as it was the first time that Macedonia was participating in the Assembly's Annual Session. The issue of sanctions was a central theme of his speech. Gligorov emphasized that Macedonia's compliance with sanctions had that year alone, reduced its gross national product by 50 percent, and substantially decreased its external trade as a result of higher transportation costs. He maintained that the country's survival, as well as democratic and economic development, were "fundamentally dependent" on international assistance. He argued that without help from the international community, there was a strong possibility that social tensions would intensify and the economy collapse, resulting in a new crisis in the region. Gligorov then appealed to the United Nations for "concrete forms of assistance" on the basis of Article 50 of the Charter, which states:

> If preventive or enforcement measures against any state are taken by the Security Council, any other state, whether a Member of the United Nations or not, which finds itself confronted with special economic problems arising from the carrying out of those measures shall have the right to consult the Security Council with regard to a solution of those problems.

Pressing the point, Gligorov declared, "It is inconceivable to expect a small country to bear the damages of an international action . . . on its own, without solidarity and timely assistance. In accordance with . . . preventive measures, assistance should be provided now, not subsequent to . . . likely social clashes which may grow into new conflicts."[19] Finally, Gligorov indicated that the

Macedonian delegation would put forward concrete proposals regarding compensation for damages and the particular problems facing landlocked countries. Ten days before his speech to the General Assembly, President Gligorov in talks with the delegate of the SRSG, Hugo Anson, had also "as a matter of priority, emphasized the need of Macedonia, apart from being helped politically, to be helped economically and financially, in order to overcome the difficulties which have arisen as a result of the Greek embargo as well as the consequences of the international sanctions against the Federal Republic of Yugoslavia."[20]

The importance of providing Macedonia with adequate and effective international support to help it cope with the adverse effects of sanctions against Serbia and Greece's draconian economic embargo was a recurring theme in Boutros-Ghali's reports to the Security Council.[21] For example, the secretary-general stated:

> The Former Yugoslav Republic of Macedonia continues, however, to labor under the combined constraints of the economic blockade imposed by Greece and the effects of sanctions against the Federal Republic of Yugoslavia (Serbia and Montenegro). . . . The Council may . . . wish to call, in the context of Article 50 of the Charter, for increased international economic support which would play a key role in contributing to future peace and stability there.[22]

In Skopje, the delegate of the SRSG, Hugo Anson, reiterated Boutros-Ghali's call for increased economic assistance to Macedonia. In an interview with the weekly magazine *Puls,* Anson said:

> As you are probably aware, I have frequent contacts with the international media, diplomats, economic experts, and other visitors. . . . I always stress to these visitors that it is not enough to deploy troops here. The international community must give more economic support to this country as well. Macedonia has received a lot of promises for help, but so far there has not been enough action. These visitors ask what kind of help is meant. We are always precise: help such as economic assistance through the World Bank, through the IMF. Help for international projects like the East-West railway, roads, hospitals, the airport and other kinds of infrastructure.[23]

The appeals by Gligorov and Boutros-Ghali were echoed by the cochairmen of the ICFY, Lord Owen and Thorvald Stoltenberg. They observed that while the preventive deployment of UN troops in Macedonia had played an "important part" in stabilizing the political situation in the country, there was "a need for more economic preventive action."[24] In an official telegram to EU foreign ministers in July 1994, Lord Owen recommended that the UN should adopt a resolution addressing the closure of the Macedonia-Serbia border as a way of compelling Milosevic to pressurize the Bosnian Serbs. He also appealed for financial compensation for Macedonia:

> The latest figures for traffic across the border show 1,018 trucks and 148 railway wagons going north in one week, and 1,173 trucks and 351 railway wagons going south. This is an intolerable situation. We know that President Gligorov's freedom to act is circumscribed by the continuing weakness of his economy. Without the black market dealing it would be an even worse situation. He has to be granted generous financial support immediately, and the vehicle to use is Article 50 of the UN Charter, and a Security Council Resolution taken under Chapter VII, which will automatically bind all European Union states. There will also have to be a simultaneous strengthening of the UN presence in Macedonia. Any other action on sanctions, be it further attempts to free Serbian assets or demands on the neighboring governments, will not be taken seriously either by those governments or by the rest of the world.[25]

The Sanctions Committee established by Security Council Resolution 724 (1991) set up a Working Group to consider appeals for help on the basis of Article 50.[26] On 18 June 1993, the Security Council adopted Resolution 843 (1993), confirming that the Sanctions Committee was "entrusted with the task of examining requests for assistance under the provisions of Article 50 of the Charter of the United Nations." It welcomed the establishment of the Committee's Working Group and invited the Committee "as it completes the examination of each request, to make recommendations to the President of the Security Council for appropriate action."

Encouraged by Resolution 843, the Macedonian government took its case to the Sanctions Committee. In a statement to the Working Group on 30 November 1993, Macedonia's permanent representative, Denko Maleski, outlined the severe economic consequences of sanctions for his country. He reminded the Working Group that as early as June 1992, the Macedonian government sent a letter to the secretary-general pointing out that sanctions would hurt the country's economy badly and requesting assistance under Article 50. Sanctions had cost Macedonia $2.3 billion in industry, agriculture, trade, tourism, communications, and construction. Ambassador Maleski urged the Security Council "to call for immediate assistance" for Macedonia, concluding, "It is not, as I hope I have made clear, only a question of economy. It is also a very important political question; the survival of a democratic process is at stake."[27] The Sanctions Committee recommended that the Security Council adopt a resolution appealing to all states and the international financial institutions to provide immediate financial assistance to Macedonia to mitigate the adverse impact on its economy of sanctions.[28]

The General Assembly added its voice and authority to the matter, but ultimately with little impact. In December 1993, the Assembly adopted Resolution 48/210 that appealed to all states and invited the competent organs and specialized agencies of the UN system, including the international financial institutions and the regional development banks, to fulfill the recommendations of the Sanctions Committee. The resolution also requested the secretary-general to submit a report on what had been done to alleviate the economic problems confronting states as a result of sanctions against Serbia and Montenegro. One year later, the General Assembly recognized "the urgent need for a concerted response from the international community to deal in a more effective manner with the special economic problems of the affected States in view of their magnitude and the adverse impact of the sanctions on those States."[29]

However, as late as January 1996, the secretary-general observed that "in spite of several resolutions adopted by the General Assembly . . . and by the Security Council . . . few Member States have responded to the appeals to provide immediate technical, financial and material assistance to mitigate the adverse impact on the economy of States affected by compliance with the sanctions against the Federal Republic of Yugoslavia."[30] Macedonia unquestionably had an international duty to comply with the sanctions, which had been imposed on Yugoslavia by the Security Council, and under international law, the performance of that duty could not be conditioned on compensation. Resolutions of the Security Council are binding on UN member states, and under Article 25 of the Charter, "the Members of the United Nations agree to accept and carry out the decisions of the Security Council in accordance with the present Charter." But given the perilous economic circumstances the country was facing, it was politically unrealistic to expect that the Macedonian authorities would scrupulously enforce the UN sanctions without adequate international financial assistance.

Following the initialing of the Dayton Agreement in November 1995, the Security Council suspended indefinitely the economic sanctions it had imposed against Yugoslavia. However, the Security Council stipulated that economic sanctions would be automatically reimposed if Yugoslavia failed formally to sign the peace agreement on the expected date.[31] Thus, UNPREDEP continued the monitoring of cross border traffic between Macedonia and Yugoslavia until the signing of the Dayton Peace Agreement in Paris on 14 December 1995, after which it was no longer required.

In sum, the United Nations had deployed peacekeeping troops as a preventive measure to support Macedonia's security. At the same time, punitive international sanctions against its neighbor, Yugoslavia, were threatening Macedonia's internal stability. The lack of prompt and effective international assistance to compensate Macedonia for the considerable economic damage caused by sanctions increased the hardship of many ordinary people and interethnic tensions. As the international community has discovered repeatedly, sanctions are blunt instruments with unintended effects and uncertain consequences. This basic contradiction in international action toward Macedonia undermined the effectiveness of the UN's preventive strategy.

HUMANITARIAN ASSISTANCE

There was no specific mention of humanitarian assistance in UNPREDEP's mandate. However, through a combination of humanitarian concern, moral duty, and pragmatic considerations, the mission felt compelled to assist in alleviating humanitarian needs. Given the poverty in many areas in Macedonia, the mission believed it had a moral responsibility to assist in providing humanitarian assistance, within its limited resources. Humanitarian assistance was also viewed as a means to enhance the UN's image in the country, support "force protection," and strengthen the operation's links with the local population. As the UNPREDEP force commander Brig. Gen. Bo Wranker remarked:

> Humanitarian aid provided by the military troops is a peacekeeping tool or technique that enhances the security of the Force and to a large degree the execution of the mandate.... The cost of providing humanitarian aid will always pay off . . . in decreasing the tensions between the local population and the members of the Force.[32]

In June 1993, on the recommendation of Civil Affairs, the CIVPOL monitors were authorized to start a village visitation program aimed at providing reports on the humanitarian situation. The initial program included all of the three hundred to four hundred villages that were then in the area of operation, and the first reports revealed an acute humanitarian need in the villages. Most of the villages, particularly those in the mountains, lacked electricity, sewage facilities, basic health care, running water, and paved roads, which made them inaccessible during the long winter months. Many of the villagers lacked adequate food, clothing, and heating in the winter.

Civil Affairs established an informal Humanitarian Committee composed of international agencies, the IFRC, and NGOs to monitor and coordinate humanitarian activities. The IFRC later assumed the central role within the Humanitarian Committee because of its links with the Macedonian Red Cross, which has branches in every municipality in Macedonia. The mission also preferred the IFRC to take the lead because it wanted to avoid a possible charge by the Macedonian authorities that it was interfering in the country's internal matters. As a result of the information provided by the CIVPOL monitors, about one thousand people in the remotest and poorest villages received food and health kits in the autumn of 1993.[33]

In July 1993, the UNPROFOR force commander, Lt. Gen. Jean Cot of France, visited Macedonia and was struck by the degree of poverty in the country.[34] Consequently, the UN commander in Macedonia, Brig. Gen. Thomsen, authorized the military component to provide logistical support for the delivery of humanitarian supplies and to aid in medical emergencies and evacuations. It would also initiate "good works" projects, in cooperation with local aid agencies. However, since humanitarian support operations were not explicitly covered in the mandate, they were not to jeopardize the Force's main responsibility to monitor and report any developments that might increase tension or threaten peace and stability.

The soldiers manning UNPREDEP observation posts in the mountainous regions regularly provided basic medical and transportation assistance, as well as search and rescue help to local villagers. In March 1993, UNPROFOR personnel assisted rescue efforts following the crash of a Macedonian airliner shortly after take-off at Skopje airport. Medical assistance was also provided by the Nordic battalion, and a UN helicopter evacuated injured passengers to Skopje's military hospital.[35] Following another tragic airplane crash in Ohrid in November 1993, UNPROFOR personnel again participated in the rescue operation. A medical team was sent by helicopter to Ohrid from Skopje, and another helicopter with a second medical team was placed on standby.[36] In January 1994, UNPROFOR responded to an emergency request from Col. Gen. Bocinov, chief of staff of the Macedonian Army, to rescue six Macedonians, three soldiers, and three police officers who were stranded in the mountains. The helicopter rescue mission was successfully accomplished, despite inclement weather, bad visibility, and treacherous terrain.[37]

In January and February 1994, Catholic Relief Services (CRS), in cooperation with the IFRC and UNPROFOR, organized a humanitarian assistance program for remote mountain villages. The goal of the program was to avert a decline in food security caused by a severe drought, national economic problems, and a potentially harsh winter.[38] The villages selected were drawn from CIVPOL reports and according to the following criteria: the degree of poverty; remoteness and isolation during winter; the percentage of inhabitants who were disabled, elderly, and/or women and children; high unemployment; and the level of assistance received from the Macedonian Red Cross, the Macedonian

Social Welfare Centers, or other relief organizations.[39] CRS, the IFRC, and UNPROFOR developed a joint coordination plan whereby, CRS purchased seventy metric tons of wheat flour that were divided in rations of seventy-five kilograms; the IFRC provided two hundred baby parcels; and UNPROFOR provided the logistical support for transporting, delivering, and distributing the commodities to 4,358 villagers in thirty-eight villages.[40]

The Humanitarian Assistance Program had positive results: it brought immediate relief to thousands of individuals in need; it brought the needs of the villagers to the attention of other international aid agencies and the Macedonian welfare system; and it strengthened the collaboration among CRS, the IFRC, and UNPROFOR by laying a foundation of experience on which they could build in future emergencies.[41] The report by Catholic Relief Services on the Humanitarian Assistance Program stressed the significant role played by UNPROFOR: "UNPROFOR personnel were efficient, cooperative and reliable, and much of the credit for smooth implementation of the project goes to the soldiers charged with the actual deliveries."[42]

In addition, UNPREDEP personnel took part in several blood donation campaigns to benefit the Macedonian Red Cross. In February 1995, Macedonia Command presented gifts to nearly one hundred students from twenty schools in the Skopje area, which had been donated on the mission's request, by two Danish companies, Lego and STIMOROL. The donations were transported free of charge from Copenhagen to Zagreb by Scandinavian Airlines and from Zagreb to Skopje by UN aircraft.[43] On the initiative of UNPREDEP, the Finnish Red Cross donated a significant amount of winter clothing for 120 socially and economically disadvantaged families in Macedonia in February 1996. With the assistance of the Macedonian Red Cross, UNPREDEP troops distributed the donations in villages located in the Nordic battalion's area of operations.[44] The U.S. battalion "adopted" an orphanage in Skopje, providing the children with clothes, repairing the building, and constructing a timber trestle footbridge. UNPREDEP troops also helped to construct and repair roads, telecommunications facilities, and water distribution systems in different parts of the country.

The humanitarian assistance provided by the peacekeeping troops benefited thousands of Macedonians of all ethnic groups during years of economic crisis. However, these efforts were a palliative and could not address the fundamental causes of economic and social problems. Through the peace-building initiatives of UNPREDEP, an attempt would be made to link humanitarian aid and sustainable development activities as part of a comprehensive preventive strategy.

CONCLUSION

This review of the role played by the UN troops reveals key lessons for the use of preventive deployment as an instrument in international efforts to promote peace and security. First, even a relatively small force can have a major impact in enhancing the security and stability of a weak state in a region plagued by violence and strife. Preventive deployment can and does make a difference. Second, trip wire troops serve as an early warning mechanism to the UN and can alert the international community to potentially destabilizing developments. Third, the peacekeeping force was able to fulfill its mandate in the field because of adequate human and material resources. Fourth, humanitarian assistance and civic action by trip wire troops can serve preventive humanitarian and military objectives.

NOTES

1. Statement of Hugo Anson, delegate of the SRSG, prior to his departure from Macedonia in 1995. Quoted in *MILS News*, 26 May 1995.

2. "Report of the Secretary-General Pursuant to Security Council Resolution 795 (1992)", S/26099, 13 July 1993, para. 12.

3. UNPROFOR FYROM Command, press release, SP0072, Skopje, 6 April 1994.

4. This development was due to the efforts of Brig. Gen. Juha Engström, who served as commander UNPROFOR FYROM Command and UNPREDEP from 15 February 1995 to 29 February 1996. The first meeting between UNPREDEP peacekeepers and FRY border troops at the battalion level took place on 22 September 1995.

5. "Report", S/1996/65, 30 January 1996, para.5.

6. UNPREDEP, *UNMO Briefing Summary,* Skopje, 17 May 1996.

7. As the Tetovo team had to monitor only one border crossing, it conducted a greater number of village patrols than both the Skopje and Ohrid teams.

8. "Report," S/26099, 13 July 1993, paras. 15–17.

9. *METRO,* English ed., No. 7, Skopje, April 1996, 2. The campaign was dubbed the "Teddy Bear" campaign by the local media because thousands of Macedonian children received plastic reflector bears sporting the UN blue beret.

10. I am indebted to Major H. Gaarder who served as deputy chief military information and liaison officer, UNPROFOR FYROM Command from 20 January 1994 to 1 April 1995 for his recollections of the Cupino Brdo incident.

11. The inscription on the monument reads:

> This memorial tablet, dedicated to the guards of our united peoples' history, tells of the immortal acts of the Third Macedonian Assault Brigade, the Sixth Southmorava Brigade and

the Kosovo Battalion which jointly defeated the more powerful and numerous Bulgarian Fascistic Army Units in this place on June 14, 1944. May the glory of the fallen fighters, whose famous acts became an indicator of our heroic history, be eternal.

It was erected by the Veterans Associations of the municipalities of Kriva Palanka, Macedonia, and Trgoviste, Federal Republic of Yugoslavia.

12. In June 1995, the U.S. battalion assumed control of the observation post at Cupino Brdo.

13. The Resolution was adopted by a vote of thirteen in favor, zero against, and two abstentions (China and Zimbabwe).

14. Richardt Vork, "Information Note: UN Sanctions against Serbia and Montenegro: EU/CSCE Sanctions Assistance Missions and SAMCOMM" (Brussels: European Commission, 20 April 1995). According to Vork, in April 1995, MACSAM had sixty-five staff deployed or pledged.

15. John Stremlau, *Sharpening International Sanctions: Toward a Stronger Role for the United Nations*, a report to the Carnegie Commission on Preventing Deadly Conflict (New York: Carnegie Corporation, November 1996), 29.

16. Elizabeth Williamson, "Smuggling Lessens Contact Group Lure," *Daily News,* 13 March 1995, 5.

17. "Report of the Secretary-General Pursuant to Security Council Resolution 1027 (1995)," S/1996/65, 30 January 1996, para.16.

18. *Osten,* 29 July 1994.

19. "Address of the President of the Republic of Macedonia at the 48th Session of the General Assembly of the United Nations," New York, 30 September, 1993.

20. Cabinet of the President of the Republic of Macedonia, *Press Statement,* 20 September 1994.

21. The secretary-general's emphasis on this issue was consistent with what he had written in *An Agenda for Peace* (New York: United Nations, 1992), 24:

> In circumstances when peacemaking requires the imposition of sanctions under Article 41 of the Charter, it is important that States confronted with special economic problems not only have the right to consult the Security Council regarding such problems, as Article 50 provides, but also have a realistic possibility of having their difficulties addressed. I recommend that the Security Council devise a set of measures involving the financial institutions and other components of the United Nations system that can be put in place to insulate States from such difficulties. Such measures would be a matter of equity and a means of encouraging States to cooperate with decisions of the Council.

In his *Supplement to An Agenda for Peace,* A/50/60-S/1995/1, 3 January 1995, para. 73, Boutros-Ghali reiterated that

> there is an urgent need for action to respond to the expectations raised by Article 50 of the Charter. Sanctions are a measure taken collectively by the United Nations to maintain or restore international peace and security. The costs involved in their application, like other such

costs (e.g. for peacemaking and peacekeeping activities), should be borne equitably by all Member States and not exclusively by the few who have the misfortune to be neighbors or major economic partners of the target country.

He reported (para. 74) that on the instructions of the Security Council, he had sought the views of the heads of the international financial institutions about this matter. "In their replies, the latter acknowledged the collateral effects of sanctions and expressed the desire to help countries in such situations, but they proposed that this should be done under existing mandates for the support of countries facing external shocks and consequent balance-of-payment difficulties. They did not agree that special provisions should be made."

22. "Report of the Secretary-General Pursuant to Resolution 947 (1994)," S/1995/222, 22 March 1995, para. 81.

23. *Puls,* 25 November 1994.

24. "Biannual report of the Co-Chairmen of the Steering Committee on the Activities of the International Conference on the Former Yugoslavia," S/1994/1454, 29 December 1994, para. 25.

25. Quoted in David Owen, *Balkan Odyssey* (New York: Harcourt Brace, 1995), 288.

26. Resolution 724 (1991) was adopted on 15 December 1991. The Council, inter alia, endorsed the secretary-general's offer to send to Yugoslavia a small group of personnel to prepare for possible deployment of a peacekeeping operation, and decided to establish a committee to ensure that the general and complete embargo imposed by Resolution 713 (1991) of 25 September 1991 was effectively implemented.

27. "Report," S/26040/Add. 2, Attachment III, 14 December 1993, 19-20.

28. "Report," S/26040/Add. 2, Annex II, 14 December 1993, 12.

29. General Assembly Resolution 49/21 2 December 1994.

30. "Report of the Secretary-General Pursuant to Security Council Resolution 1027 (1995)," S/1996/65, 30 January 1996, para. 17.

31. Security Council Resolution 1022(1995), 22 November 1995.

32. Bo Wranker, "Preventive Diplomacy: Military Component," paper presented at the International Workshop on an Agenda for Preventive Diplomacy: Theory and Practice, Skopje, 16–19 October 1996.

33. I am grateful to Mark Penn, former civil affairs officer of UNPROFOR FYROM Command, for his insights into the mission's early humanitarian activities.

34. General Jean Cot served as force commander of UNPROFOR in former Yugoslavia from 1993 to 1994.

35. UNPROFOR, press statement, SP0017, Skopje, 5 March 1993.

36. UNPROFOR FYROM Command, press release, SP0055, Skopje, 21 November 1993.

37. UNPROFOR FYROM Command, press release, SP0062, Skopje, 11 January 1994.

38. Catholic Relief Services/Macedonia, "Summary Report on Humanitarian Assistance to Remote Mountain Villages, 1994," 1.

39. CRS/Macedonia, "Summary Report," 3.
40. CRS/Macedonia, "Summary Report," 3.
41. CRS/Macedonia, "Summary Report," 7-8.
42. CRS/Macedonia, "Summary Report," 7.
43. UNPROFOR FYROM Command, press release, Skopje, 22 February 1995.
44. *Vecher,* 13 February 1996.

6

THE GOOD OFFICES FUNCTION

> The Security Council . . . encourages the Special Representative
> of the Secretary-General for the Former Yugoslavia, in coopera-
> tion with the authorities of the former Yugoslav Republic of
> Macedonia, to use his good offices as appropriate to contribute to
> the maintenance of peace and stability in that Republic.
>
> Security Council Resolution 908 (1994)

As we have seen, when UN troops were initially deployed on the borders of Macedonia, the most pressing concern was the danger of external attack and the spillover of violence. While the Macedonian government believed that the threats to Macedonia were solely external, the United Nations recognized that it was dangerous to ignore internal threats. Therefore, the Security Council insisted on the deployment of UN civilian police monitors to monitor the Macedonian border police as there had been incidents in which Albanians attempting to cross the border illegally had been shot by border guards. These incidents had led to increased interethnic tension. During the first year of the UN's presence, it became increasingly apparent that internal tensions, particularly between ethnic Macedonians and Albanians, were mounting. It was this concern about the possibility of domestic conflict that prompted the Security Council to authorize a good offices mandate for the special representative of the secretary-general aimed at contributing to the maintenance of the republic's peace and stability.

The government was not enthusiastic about the good offices mandate. It viewed "good offices" as a menacing formula for the UN to interfere in the country's internal affairs. The government also believed that the implementation of international standards on the treatment of ethnic minorities, which was advocated by regional and international organizations, would contribute to the disintegration rather than the consolidation of the Macedonian state. Nonetheless, the Macedonian government resigned itself to the good offices mandate as the price it had to pay for the political legitimization and security provided by UNPREDEP.

Ethnic Albanian political parties, however, took a different view of the good offices mandate. They welcomed a greater role for the UN in the republic's internal affairs in the belief that the organization would serve as an objective and impartial broker in their campaign for full equality. In addition, they viewed good offices as a positive step toward the internationalization of the "Albanian question" in Macedonia.

The attitude of the ethnic Macedonian opposition parties was more ambiguous. When the good offices mandate was authorized, they shared the government's apprehension that it would give the mission the authority to raise uncomfortable questions concerning interethnic relations. But following their boycott of the 1994 presidential and parliamentary elections, VMRO-DPMNE and the Democratic Party believed that through its good offices, UNPREDEP could serve as an important channel of communication between the government and the extraparliamentary opposition. They also hoped that through the good offices function UNPREDEP would encourage the government to hold early parliamentary elections. In the final analysis, both ethnic Albanian and nationalist Macedonian opposition parties had much higher expectations of the good offices function than were realistically attainable.

On the basis of the mandate granted to the special representative of the secretary-general by Resolution 908, FYROM Command monitored the 1994 presidential and parliamentary elections and helped to defuse the eruption of the crisis surrounding the Albanian-language University of Tetovo. The mission also took practical steps to improve dialogue among political parties, to promote mutual understanding between ethnic communities, and to monitor the observance of human rights.

THE AUTHORIZATION OF GOOD OFFICES

During the first fifteen months of the peacekeeping operation, the mandate of the Civil Affairs component was limited to performing "liaison functions between UNPROFOR and the central and local authorities, as well as to provide political advice to the Commander."[1] Civil Affairs was also responsible for the mission's public information program. However, in his report to the Security Council of 16 March 1994, Secretary-General Boutros-Ghali struck a cautionary note. He stressed that "UNPROFOR has no mandate in relation to the internal situation in the former Yugoslav Republic of Macedonia, which could prove to be more detrimental to the stability of the country than external aggression."[2] The Security Council heeded his warning. A fortnight later, on 31 March 1994, the Council adopted Resolution 908 (1994), which "encouraged the Special Representative of the Secretary-General for the Former Yugoslavia, in cooperation with the authorities of the former Yugoslav Republic of Macedonia, to use his good offices as appropriate to contribute to the maintenance of peace and stability in that Republic."[3]

A key determinant of the successful use of good offices is the margin of discretion provided in the authorizing resolution. As Thomas M. Franck and Georg Nolte explain, "Good offices are informal, loosely structured, and, to a large extent, depend on the flexibility, sensitivity, and imaginativeness of the good officer. The successful good officer thus usually demands the authority to operate within a wide margin of discretion."[4] Resolution 908 gave some degree of discretion to the SRSG as to how to perform his good offices functions, for the term *as appropriate* was open to interpretation. However, in light of the need for the United Nations to respect the sovereignty of the state, the Security Council also imposed an important constraint by specifying that good offices had to be undertaken "in cooperation with the authorities of the former Yugoslav Republic of Macedonia." This also reflected a practical reality: that the use of good offices would be impossible without the cooperation of the Macedonian authorities.

Special Representative of the Secretary-General for the Former Yugoslavia Yasushi Akashi faced a crucial choice concerning the implementation of good offices: "to delegate or not to delegate."[5] As SRSG, he led the largest and arguably the most complex peacekeeping operation in the UN's history. In March 1994, the strength of the military personnel of UNPROFOR was 30,655, including 580 United Nations military observers. The civilian component included 679 civilian police, 1,075 international civilian staff, and 1,574 local staff.[6] The diversity and scope of the problems that the SRSG had to deal with in the former Yugoslavia, especially in Bosnia and Croatia, were gargantuan. Akashi decided to delegate, and appointed Hugo Anson as delegate of the SRSG in Macedonia.[7] Anson, an Englishman and an Oxford graduate, was on secondment to the UN Secretariat from the World Trade Organization. He had served with UN peacekeeping operations in Namibia, Angola, and Croatia. He was dynamic, principled, and straightforward. Franck and Nolte observe that "to delegate is sometimes advantageous: more often it is simply unavoidable." The decision to delegate the good offices task was unavoidable, but in the long run it also proved to be advantageous.

Security Council Resolution 908 (1994) raised the UN's political profile in Macedonia through the good offices mandate given to the SRSG. It also resulted in an integrated political and military command with the delegate of the SRSG and the commander cooperating as heads of their respective components. Hugo Anson believed that the SRSG's good offices mandate in Macedonia should be interpreted cautiously and dynamically rather than cautiously and restrictively. With regard to interethnic relations, he believed that the UN had to resist the temptation to view Macedonia as an ethnic tinderbox about to explode at any moment, because this "imminent catastrophe" approach could become a self-fulfilling prophecy. Anson and the Civil Affairs team maintained regular contacts with the government, members of parliament, political parties, local leaders, and nongovernmental organizations. The delegate of the SRSG encouraged the government and major political parties to seek centrist political solutions to internal problems, made specific proposals to increase international economic assistance to Macedonia, and regularly explained to the local and international media the political and economic situation in and around Macedonia and what the UN was doing to assist.

The Macedonian government viewed Security Council Resolution 908 (1994) with a certain degree of apprehension. It was concerned that the good offices mandate would lead to what it considered undue interference by the UN in sensitive internal matters, especially interethnic relations. The fact that the Resolution stipulated that the good offices function would be implemented in cooperation with the authorities of the host country lessened, but did not dispel the government's anxiety. The government also feared that the SRSG's delegate would act as a "colonial governor," an undesirable prospect for the newly independent and sovereign state.[8] In short, the UN was welcome to "look out," but its decision to "look in" was quite another matter. Nevertheless, while the good offices mandate was unpalatable to the government, it reckoned that tolerating it was the price it had to pay for a continuation of the deployment of UN troops along its borders.

MONITORING THE 1994 PRESIDENTIAL AND PARLIAMENTARY ELECTIONS

At a reception in honor of Macedonia's independence day held on 8 September 1994, Stojan Andov, the speaker of the National Assembly and leader of the Liberal Party, announced that the first and second rounds of Macedonia's first parliamentary and presidential elections since its independence would be held on 16 and 30 October 1994. Andov had served as Yugoslavia's ambassador to Iraq in the 1980s and was widely regarded as a possible successor to President Gligorov. The day before his announcement, Parliament, after a rancorous debate, had appointed the State Elections Commission and electoral commissions for all 120 constituencies.[9] The opposition parties resented the government's decision to hold the first round of elections on the first possible constitutional date. They maintained, with some justification, that the government had set an early election date to make it difficult for the opposition to organize and campaign effectively, as well as to avoid the possible negative electoral consequences of a worsening economic situation.

Political parties mushroomed during the campaign and 37 of them contested the elections. Three parties belonging to the ruling coalition, the Social Democratic Union of Macedonia (SDSM), the Liberal Party, and the Socialist Party, ran on a joint platform as the "Alliance for Macedonia." However, the two main opposition parties, VMRO-DPMNE, which had the largest number of seats in parliament, and the Democratic Party, were unable to form a coalition. The Democratic Party was reluctant to enter an alliance with the right-wing nationalist VMRO-DPMNE, as this would have compromised the Democratic Party's centrist political image. Macedonian voters faced a choice of striking clarity between the two presidential contenders: the incumbent, Kiro Gligorov of the Alliance for Macedonia, and Ljubisha Georgievski, a flamboyant theater director, of VMRO-DPMNE. The rival candidates held contrasting views on interethnic relations, nationalism, and the economy.[10]

A key issue during the election campaign was interethnic relations, particularly between Macedonians and Albanians. Early in the campaign, it became apparent that VMRO-DPMNE intended to play the nationalist card of an alleged threat to the Macedonian nation from ethnic Albanian extremists. In an incendiary speech to the party's convention on 14 September 1994, Ljubisha Georgievski attacked the idea of a multiethnic state. He argued that "multinationalism" was a threat to Macedonian unity, as it would lead to the federalization of the country and ultimately to war. According to him, there was no future for a multiethnic state in the Balkans. In what became his campaign slogan, Georgievski declared that "Macedonia is for Macedonians."[11] Georgievski was evidently using the term *Macedonian* in an ethnic rather than a civic sense. A hard-liner on interethnic issues, he made it clear that if he were elected president, ethnic Albanians would be kept firmly in their place.

To prevent the exacerbation of interethnic tensions during the campaign, the delegate of the SRSG, Hugo Anson, encouraged political leaders to sign a Declaration setting a code of conduct for the elections, as well as principles for interethnic cooperation. The Declaration committed the leaders of political parties to ensuring that the elections were free and fair, and to respect the results. The signatories pledged that their respective party members and supporters would refrain from activities and language that could encourage interethnic and religious hatred or intolerance. The Declaration further stated that all citizens of the country "no matter what their ethnic origin, have equal rights and equal obligations."[12] It was signed by twelve political parties, including the SDSM and the Liberal Party, two of the five major parties. VMRO-DPMNE and the Democratic Party did not sign the Declaration, their major objection being that they could not commit themselves to respecting the results of the elections when they had serious doubts that the elections would be free and fair.[13] Although the leadership of the largest ethnic Albanian party, the moderate PDP, had supported the Declaration when it was first proposed by Anson, they also decided not to sign it. That decision stemmed from the fact that the PDP had threatened to boycott the elections if the government prevented about 145,000 ethnic Albanians from voting on the grounds that they were without citizenship.[14]

The Declaration was an important initiative and the result of a creative interpretation of the UN's good offices function by Anson. However, the refusal of the two major opposition parties, VMRO-DPMNE and the Democratic Party, as well as the influential PDP to sign the Declaration reduced its political significance.

Given the delicate state of interethnic relations in the country, an election boycott by ethnic Albanians carried the risk of political and social instability. It was also unlikely that ethnic Albanians would have accepted the legitimacy of any newly elected government. Anson held a number of meetings with the government and ethnic Albanian leaders aimed at resolving the differences. The government also held talks with the CSCE and the ICFY's Working Group on Ethnic and National Communities and Minorities. UNPROFOR, the CSCE, and the ICFY all encouraged the PDP to take part in the elections, and the government to take practical measures to address the concerns of the ethnic Albanians. In a spirit of grudging, but determined compromise, the government decided that ethnic Albanians who had the right to citizenship, but lacked citizenship documents, would be included in the voters' lists.

On 13 October, just three days before the first round of the presidential and parliamentary elections, the PDP withdrew its threat to boycott the elections. Several factors contributed to that decision. First, it was the result of the concerted efforts of the government and the PDP to settle their differences on the issue of citizenship. Both sides realized that it was in their self-interest to do so and prevent a boycott of the elections by Macedonian Albanians. For the government, participation in the elections by ethnic Albanians was important for internal stability and international legitimacy. For the PDP, continued representation in Parliament and in the government was essential if ethnic Albanians were going to fulfill their aspirations for full equality. Second, the interventions by Anson; the head of the CSCE Mission, U.S. Ambassador Norman Anderson; and the chairman of the ICFY's Working Group, German Ambassador Geert Ahrens, had a positive impact on both the PDP and the government. Significantly, all three international representatives spoke with one voice and conveyed the same message to both camps. Third, the radical ethnic Albanian Party for Democratic Prosperity of Albanians in Macedonia (PDPA), which was a splinter group of the PDP and its main political rival in the ethnic Albanian community, had announced that it would participate in the elections. A boycott by the PDP would have left the field clear for the PDPA to make electoral gains and increase its political influence among ethnic Albanians at the expense of the PDP. Fourth, President Sali Berisha of Albania had appealed to ethnic Albanians to take part in the elections. According to Berisha, the elections were of "extreme importance" for Macedonian Albanians, for it would help them "consolidate their rights" and contribute to Macedonia's "overall stability."[15]

The outcome of the presidential election was never in doubt, for President Gligorov enjoyed wide popularity as the "Father of the Nation." In what was Macedonia's first direct election for the presidency, Gligorov was reelected in the first round, defeating his opponent, Ljubisha Georgievski. Voter turnout was very high: 77.76 percent. Gligorov won 67.43 percent of the total number of votes cast and 52.44 percent of the registered voters, while Georgievski won 18.61 percent and 14.47 percent respectively. Only ten members of Parliament were elected in the first round. The two main opposition parties, the nationalist VMRO-DPMNE and the Democratic Party, alleged that the first round of elections were fraudulent, manipulated and rigged by the Alliance for Macedonia. The opposition parties maintained that there had been massive irregularities concerning citizenship documents, identification cards, electoral lists, voting invitations, and delineation of some constituencies. At a protest rally held in Skopje's main square on 19 October 1994, the opposition leaders made five demands which they later sent in a letter to the speaker of Parliament, Stoyan Andov: the authorities should annul the first round of elections, the authorities should create the necessary conditions for free and fair elections, the government should resign and a "caretaker" government appointed, the State Elections Commission should resign, and parliamentary and presidential elections held separately. VMRO-DPMNE and the Democratic Party stated that if those demands were not met by the evening of 22 October, both parties would boycott the second round. The demands of the two opposition parties were rejected by Andov on the grounds that Parliament lacked the authority to fulfill them.[16]

Notwithstanding the allegations of the opposition parties, observers from the parliamentary assemblies of the CSCE and the Council of Europe who monitored the first round concluded that the electoral campaign and the first round had generally been well conducted, despite some major irregularities such as unreliable electoral lists.[17] They urged the government and the State

Elections Commission to correct "the more blatant irregularities" before the second round of voting, and stressed the "vital importance" of having national and international observers during the second round.[18]

The head of the CSCE's Mission in Skopje, Ambassador Norman Anderson, and Anson strongly urged the leaders of VMRO-DPMNE and the Democratic Party, as well as all other political parties and citizens to participate fully in the second round. The CSCE and the UN held the view that any irregularities in the first round were not of a scale to justify any calls for a boycott.[19] Their appeals were to no avail, and VMRO-DPMNE and the Democratic Party carried out their threatened boycott of the second round of elections. Supporters of the ruling coalition maintained that VMRO-DPMNE and the Democratic Party boycotted the second round because they did poorly in the first and did not wish to concede their electoral defeat. Nevertheless, though vanquished at the polls, VMRO-DPMNE and the Democratic Party represented a voice that no real democracy could afford to ignore.

Following the first round of elections on 16 October, Andov had invited the UN to monitor the second and decisive round of elections on 30 October, together with observers from the CSCE, the Council of Europe and some non-governmental organizations.[20] Andov believed that election monitoring was consistent with the UN's role in Macedonia and the good offices mandate given to the SRSG by the Security Council.

The government understood clearly the significance of credible elections for internal stability and its own international standing. International monitoring of the presidential and parliamentary elections was supported by practically all political parties as a means of ensuring transparency. The government's willingness to invite the UN to monitor the elections on the basis of the good offices mandate, which it resented, was the result of practical political considerations of self-interest. In this instance, the government saw a useful role for the good offices function that it had not expected when it was authorized by the Security Council.

Within UNPROFOR, there was strong support for a positive response to the request of the Macedonian authorities. Given that the rationale of the good offices mandate was to assist the Macedonian authorities in maintaining peace and stability in their country, official monitoring of the elections was seen as contributing to that end. However, since the request had been made rather late, it was not possible for the UN to dispatch any monitors from New York to observe the elections.

The five members of the UNPROFOR Civil Affairs team in Macedonia joined about fifty other international monitors to observe the second round of voting on 30 October. The UNPROFOR observers visited forty polling stations in the capital Skopje, as well as in other key towns of Kumanovo, Prilep, and Tetovo. They contributed their observations to the central CSCE coordinators. The following day, the United Nations and the CSCE issued a joint statement saying that the impression of the observers was that the second round of elections had been conducted in a generally orderly, peaceful, and regular manner, although the statement pointed out that the elections were held "in the framework of outdated laws"; these laws were in some cases "imprecise and open to loose interpretation by the election commissions and judiciary."[21]

As a result of the boycott of the second round of the parliamentary elections by the two main ethnic Macedonian opposition parties, the ruling Alliance for Macedonia won an overwhelming majority of seats in the new Parliament.[22] With more than a two-thirds majority, it did not need a coalition partner to form a new government. However, when Prime Minister Branko Crvenkovski, announced the new government on 16 December 1994, four PDP MPs were appointed as ministers in the new cabinet. Three were appointed to the Ministries of Development, Labor and Social Policy, and Culture; and one was appointed as minister without portfolio.[23] The Alliance for Macedonia realized that a failure to include Macedonian Albanians in the government would have sent the wrong message to the ethnic Albanian community and threatened the country's stability.[24] The government was also encouraged to include ethnic Albanians in the new cabinet by the cochairmen of the Steering Committee of the ICFY, Lord David Owen and Thorvald Stoltenberg, the chairman of the ICFY's Working Group on Ethnic and National Communities and Minorities, Ambassador Geert Ahrens, as well as by the delegate of the SRSG, Hugo Anson. In the words of the ICFY, the "absence of minority representation in the government could endanger the constructive approach in interethnic relations" in the country.[25]

For the ruling coalition, its overwhelming parliamentary majority was a mixed blessing. First, good government is encouraged by an effective opposition, and the lack of a parliamentary opposition contributed to complacency. Second, because the composition of Parliament did not reflect the entire spectrum of political opinion in the country, the government had to engage in political chess to anticipate the activities of the extraparliamentary opposition. Furthermore, the ethnic Macedonian opposition parties were not subject to the institutional constraints of a legislature. And like all opposition parties, whether parliamentary or extraparliamentary, they had the luxury of not having to adapt their ideological campaign rhetoric to the practical realities of governing. Third, the government could no longer justify its inability to address important national issues, including interethnic problems, by claiming as it had in the past that its capacity to act was restricted by a nationalist and uncompromising parliamentary opposition.

The monitoring of the elections by the mission's civil affairs officers high-lights the importance of the nonmilitary aspects of a preventive operation in promoting stability within a state. While the electoral process was imperfect, the elections were vital for the consolidation of democracy in Macedonia. The UN observers' experience in the country and knowledge of its political and ethnic cross-currents were distinct advantages in monitoring the elections. But their small number limited the role the operation could play in election supervision.

THE UNIVERSITY OF TETOVO CRISIS

A serious conflict between the Macedonian authorities and ethnic Albanians arose over the decision on 4 June 1994 of a group of ethnic Albanian academics to establish an Albanian-language university in Tetovo, a predominantly ethnic Albanian city of three hundred thousand people in western Macedonia. As has been observed:

> Education is one of the most hotly contested issues between majorities and minorities in Eastern Europe. . . . As the postcommunist era commences, these minorities focus much of their political energies on the reform of pre-viously discriminatory educational policies, for they view education as their primary avenue for social and economic advancement, the "great equalizer" that can raise their standing relative to other ethnic groups.[26]

The University of Tetovo was not the first contentious Albanian-language institution of higher learning in the former Yugoslavia. Kosovar Albanians had founded an underground university in Pristina after Milosevic stripped Kosovo of broad autonomy in 1989. As the first step toward founding the University of Tetovo, a Council for the Foundation of an Albanian University was formed under the direction of three ethnic Albanian intellectuals, Fadil Sulejmani, Murtezani Ismaili, and Agni Dika.

According to the Council, the main purpose of the university was to provide adequate training to a sufficient number of teachers responsible for teaching in Albanian primary and secondary schools. The Council maintained that the Pedagogical Faculty in Skopje was inadequate since it had only a two-year curriculum and its courses were not offered in Albanian. The Council stressed that the university was also necessary because very few ethnic Albanian students were admitted to the country's Universities of Sts. Cyril and Methodius in Skopje and St. Climent of Ohrid in Bitola; and ethnic Albanian students no longer had the opportunity of studying at the University of Pristina in Kosovo, as it had been closed by the Serbian authorities in 1990.[27] According to the

Council, ethnic Albanians had a constitutional right to higher education in their mother tongue. It announced that the university would have six faculties: philosophy, philology, natural sciences, and mathematics, economy, law, arts.

The Tetovo University project was supported by all the ethnic Albanian political parties and the Albanian-language press. Some of this support was undoubtedly based on the desire for greater educational opportunity, but much also flowed from a more generalized resentment against pervasive discrimination against ethnic Albanians. Ethnic Albanian political leaders were eager to nail their colors to the Tetovo University mast. The leader of the PDP, Abdurahman Aliti, said unambiguously, "We support the initiative,"[28] while the People's Democratic Party (NDP), blamed the Macedonian-language media for portraying the university initiative as a "Satanic" cause.[29] Enthusiastic endorsements were received from the municipal assemblies of Tetovo, Gostivar, and Debar, three towns with large ethnic Albanian populations. During the session in which the Tetovo Assembly formally decided to support the project, an ethnic Albanian councilor argued that the university "will be an affirmation of Macedonia as a democratic country."[30] But in what was to become a recurring pattern, the ethnic Macedonian councilors walked out of the session after expressing their opposition to the university initiative.[31] An article in the Albanian-language daily *Flaka e Vëllazërimit*, asked rhetorically, "How can a state succeed when one part of its population is educated, while the other is semi-literate? Does Macedonia have a greater interest in having [ethnic] Albanian children selling cigarettes on the streets than in working with computers"?[32]

On 25 October 1994, the Council submitted a formal request to the government for authorization to establish the university within the framework of the country's educational system. It indicated that the administration of the university would be bilingual: in both Macedonian and Albanian.[33] The timing of the request was not opportune as it came between the two main rounds of the presidential and parliamentary elections. Not surprisingly, the attention of government leaders was focused on winning the elections and establishing a new government. In November 1994, the Ministry of Education issued two brief statements saying that the initiative to open an Albanian-language university had "no legal grounds" and that "neither the Constitution, nor existing laws, leave space for establishing higher education institutions in the languages of the minorities." The statements added that minorities should be educated within the two national universities in Skopje and Bitola.[34] Apart from those two statements, the government maintained a deafening silence on the matter. But behind the scenes, the police began mobilizing to stop the university project. Sulejmani and some of his colleagues were summoned by the police for "informative talks" and spent several hours in custody.[35]

The Council was undeterred and made clear that it intended to press ahead with the establishment of the university. Sulejmani, a former professor at the University of Pristina, was by then the key leader of the initiative. He turned up the rhetorical heat with his public pronouncements, telling a press conference in Skopje in November 1994 that after waiting for fifty years, Macedonian Albanians refused to remain in "educational darkness." He stated that the Macedonian authorities were against knowledge in general and against ethnic Albanian intellectuals in particular and were continuing "the old tradition of discrimination and pressure against any Albanian education, science and culture." Sulejmani continued, "If the government shows no greater understanding, [for the University of Tetovo] we will be forced to work out of the state's institutions, and the responsibility for all consequences of that will be born solely by the government."[36] A few weeks later, in an interview published in *Nova Makedonija,* Sulejmani declared, "If the Macedonian government refuses to help us, it should at least not obstruct us. Otherwise, everything will go to hell."[37] Meanwhile, the opening ceremony of the university was set for 17 December 1994.

While Sulejmani's strident remarks aggravated the already tense interethnic atmosphere, the prolonged silence of the government did not help matters either. At best, it suggested that the government lacked a coherent strategy to deal with this brewing problem in a constructive manner and at worst, it conveyed an impression of indifference. On 12 December, however, five days before the University of Tetovo was to open, the government broke its silence following a cabinet meeting at which the project was discussed. The government decided that the establishment of Tetovo University was unconstitutional and illegal. It announced that it would take "all measures within its competence" to suspend the university's illegal activities.[38]

The constitutional and legal questions were not clear-cut. The right to education is recognized in Article 44 of the Macedonian Constitution, which also states that "education is accessible to everyone under equal conditions."[39] With regard to higher education, Article 45 provides, "Citizens have a right to establish private schools at all levels of education, with the exception of primary education, under conditions determined by law."[40] Article 46 guarantees the "autonomy of universities" and declares that "the conditions of establishment, performance and termination of the activities of a university are regulated by law."[41]

Since the adoption of Macedonia's new constitution in 1991, no new law on higher education had been enacted by Parliament. Consequently, higher education in the country was still regulated by the Law on Professional or "Streamed" Education of the Socialist Republic of Macedonia, adopted in

1985. According to Article 18 of that law, a university could be established only by "social or public" organizations or associations. Private universities were not included or envisaged in the law. Thus, there was an apparent inconsistency between the constitution and the 1985 law regarding the establishment of private universities. According to the law, the other conditions required for establishing a university included, a long-term need of professional education that could not be provided by existing educational institutions; that the university was in accordance with the educational plans of the Republic; and that the necessary faculty, equipment, and facilities would be provided.[42]

With respect to the language to be used in instruction, Article 48 of the Macedonian Constitution provides that "members of the nationalities have the right to instruction in their language in primary and secondary education, as determined by law."[43] No reference is made to the language to be used in higher education. Thus, the use of the language of a national minority in higher education is neither provided for nor expressly prohibited in the Constitution. And since Article 8 of the Constitution states that "anything that is not prohibited by the Constitution or by law is permitted in the Republic of Macedonia,"[44] the use of the language of an ethnic minority in higher education was not necessarily a violation of the Constitution. However, Article 11 of the 1985 Law on Professional Education states that higher education will be conducted in the Macedonian language and that ethnic minorities could use their mother tongue in secondary school.[45]

Tetovo University evoked the hostility of ethnic Macedonians as much as it inspired the loyalty of ethnic Albanians. The government's opposition to Tetovo University was strongly supported by ethnic Macedonians and the Macedonian-language media. They regarded the University of Tetovo as a clear and present danger; a direct threat to the security and territorial integrity of the state, as well as the interests of the majority of its citizens. On 13 December 1994, ethnic Macedonian students at Sts. Cyril and Methodius University staged a rally in front of the Parliament building against the University of Tetovo. One of the student protesters said on Radio Skopje, "We believe that there is no justified reason for establishing such a university. . . . They [ethnic Albanians], have just too many rights. We cannot have them at the same level with us."[46] The nationalist Macedonian Association of Ethnologists condemned the university initiative and argued that it was ostensibly an educational project, but its real purpose was the ultimate creation of a Greater Albania, the fulfillment of the dream of "Ilirida."[47] Nearly one hundred ethnic Macedonian intellectuals signed a memorandum condemning the University of Tetovo as an attempt to create a parallel higher educational system and the first step toward federalization of the country.[48]

The government and the Council were clearly on a collision course. Both sides viewed compromise and accommodation as tantamount to surrender. On 14 December, police raided the university's headquarters in Tetovo, confiscated documents, damaged part of the building, and sealed it. They also damaged the roof and fence surrounding a building, which was to house the university's science laboratory. Three members of the Council, including Sulejmani and Milaim Fejziu, president of the Forum for Human Rights in Gostivar, were arrested, interrogated, and released after about twelve hours.[49] Following this incident, Agni Dika, a Council member, reiterated the Council's resolve and rebuked the Macedonian authorities: "They can tear down all the buildings they want, but we will still open the University on 17 December. What this state knows how to do best is harass and oppress non-Macedonian nationalities in the country."[50]

On 17 December, the university's organizers and more than three hundred Macedonian Albanians assembled in front of the Tetovo Assembly Hall to mark the establishment of the university. They were prevented from entering the building by police in riot gear. In light of the government's determined and implacable opposition to Tetovo University, the organizers had shrewdly held the formal foundation ceremony secretly in the early hours of 17 December, at the headquarters of the PDP in Tetovo. It had been attended by the leaders of all ethnic Albanian political parties in Macedonia, ethnic Albanian government ministers and representatives of the municipal assemblies in western Macedonia. The thirty-seven-year-old minister of interior and law professor, Ljubomir Frckoski, dismissed the ceremony in Tetovo as a "private party" and the university as a "still-born baby," but his assessment would prove premature.[51] In a jubilant editorial, the Albanian-language daily, *Flaka e Vëllazërimit,* opined, "The wish that Macedonian Albanians have had for a long time, to establish a higher educational institution in their mother tongue, has finally become a reality. The founding of a University in Tetovo is without doubt, a noble and humane act."[52] Meanwhile, the Albanian Foreign Ministry publicly expressed its concern about the use of force to suppress what it regarded as the legitimate right of Macedonian Albanians to higher education. Predictably, this statement provoked a sharp response from the Macedonian Foreign Ministry criticizing Albania for interfering in Macedonia's internal affairs.

At a meeting of the university Council on 8 January 1995, Sulejmani was elected as rector of the university. Two provosts, faculty deans, and a twenty-five-member senate were also appointed. For several weeks the university had been actively recruiting students, and by January 1995 about five hundred had passed the entrance exams.[53] Financing of the university came from ethnic Albanians in Macedonia, Kosovo, Albania, and the Diaspora. On 31 January 1995, the Skopje District Court rejected Tetovo University's application for registration as a legal institution.[54]

On 15 February 1995, nearly two thousand people attended a rally in Tetovo to mark the start of lectures at the university. Sulejmani warned the authorities not to continue their attempts to prevent the university from functioning, and if they did, "200,000 [ethnic] Albanians were ready to defend it."[55] The rally was attended by former U.S. Congressman Joseph Dioguardi, an Albanian-American, who strongly supported the university in a speech that was predictably well received by the crowd. Although tensions were running high, no major incident occurred. Later, the Macedonian government spokesperson, Guner Ismail, reiterated the government's position: the University of Tetovo was an "impudent violation of the constitution" and a "political" project. With regard to the involvement of former U.S. Congressman Dioguardi, Ismail was dismissive: "His attempts to be involved in politics in this region probably result from his inability to perform well as a politician back home."[56] Dioguardi had lost his reelection bid.

Matters came to a head on 17 February, when the police intervened to stop classes, which were being held in Mala Recica, just outside Tetovo. Abduseljan Emini, an ethnic Albanian man in his early thirties, was killed and twenty-eight people, including nine police officers, were wounded during a violent confrontation between Macedonian police and ethnic Albanians. The Tetovo University cause had gained its first martyr. Sulejmani and four of his associates, Miliam Fejziu, Musli Halimi, Arben Rusi, and Nevzat Halili, were arrested. The following day, some ten thousand people attended the funeral of the victim, which was held peacefully. On 19 February, about thirty Muslim graves were desecrated in Kumanovo, an event that was likely related to the disturbances at Tetovo. In the tense interethnic climate, the Students Council of Skopje's Sts. Cyril and Methodius University held a protest rally against Tetovo University in front of the parliament building on 23 February.[57]

During the Tetovo University crisis, UNPROFOR faced a choice either to support the university and incur the wrath of the Macedonian government as well as ethnic Macedonians or to oppose the project and alienate ethnic Albanians as a result. Adopting either position would have had far reaching consequences for the peacekeeping operation in Macedonia, which had so far enjoyed the strong support of the Macedonian government, and all ethnic groups in the country. UNPROFOR had to steer between the Scylla of government opposition to Tetovo University and the Charybdis of ethnic Albanian support for it. Therefore, UNPROFOR chose the middle course, which was to express neither support for nor opposition to the project.[58] And if UNPROFOR were to play a constructive role in encouraging moderation and dialogue between the opposing camps, it had to be perceived as an impartial broker. Consequently, UNPROFOR maintained that minorities had the same rights as members of majority ethnic groups, including the right to strive for better educational opportunities, and they also had the same obligations to the state as all other citizens. But since UNPROFOR's mandate in Macedonia was based on the Security Council's commitment to ensuring respect for the sovereignty and territorial integrity of the country, it expressed "reservations about any project which might lead toward separation, rather than further integration, of the ethnic groups in Macedonia."[59]

In playing the role of an impartial broker, UNPROFOR's strategy was to blend quiet diplomacy with public interventions, but with a distinct emphasis on the former. In the period leading up to the events of 17 February, the delegate of the SRSG, Hugo Anson, held several meetings with government and ethnic Albanian leaders to urge compromise solutions to the problem. In response to queries from the media regarding UNPROFOR's position on the disturbances at Tetovo in February 1995, Anson issued a statement urging "all parties to continue on the path of dialogue, goodwill, compromise and restraint. . . . [and] to act strictly within the Constitution and laws" of Macedonia. The statement appealed to all Macedonians "to think of themselves first and foremost as citizens and only afterwards as members of various ethnic groups."[60]

The developments at Tetovo reflected a marked deterioration of relations between the government and ethnic Albanians and raised fears that an ethnic confrontation was imminent. Further polarization between the ethnic groups also threatened the successful termination of the UN's first peacekeeping mission with a preventive mandate. The events surrounding Tetovo University prompted a visit to Macedonia by the SRSG, Yasushi Akashi, on 7 March 1995. It was his third trip to the country since his appointment as SRSG for the former Yugoslavia in December 1993.[61] The timing of the visit in the wake of the incident of 17 February conveyed an important symbolic message of the UN's interest in a stable Macedonia, and was a timely reminder that the Security Council in Resolution 908 of 31 March 1994 had authorized the SRSG "to use his good offices as appropriate to contribute to the maintenance of peace and stability in that republic." Akashi met President Gligorov, Prime Minister Branko Crvenkovski, and other members of the government. The SRSG stressed the importance of solving political and ethnic differences through dialogue, tolerance and moderation. The head of Civil Affairs of UNPROFOR, Michel Moussalli, who accompanied Akashi to Macedonia, remained in Skopje for an extra day and met with a broad spectrum of political parties, including the leaders of the main ethnic Albanian parties. He underlined the message of conciliation that Akashi had conveyed the previous day.

The public and private interventions of UNPROFOR, especially following the February 1995 incident at Tetovo, helped to defuse the situation, and
pull both the Macedonian government and ethnic Albanians from the brink of
open confrontation. In his report of 22 March 1995, Boutros-Ghali records:

> UNPROFOR, acting within the good offices mandate given to my Special
> Representative by Resolution 908 (1994) and in full Cooperation with the
> FYROM authorities . . . has made a modest but important contribution to help-
> ing the authorities and various ethnic groups to maintain peace and stability and
> build a workable future. It is encouraging to note . . . that both the Government
> and ethnic Albanian leaders have expressed appreciation to UNPROFOR for
> what they have termed its clear, objective, appropriate and helpful actions.[62]

The Tetovo University issue was, however, far from over. What had been
achieved was a temporary cease-fire. Following the disturbances at Tetovo in
February, the PDPA and NDP began a boycott of Parliament, which lasted four
months, in protest against the government's opposition to Tetovo University.[63]
Sulejmani was charged under Article 206 of the Penal Code with inciting the
Albanians in Macedonia to civil disobedience, while his four colleagues were
charged under Article 205 with participation in a mob that prevented the police
from discharging their duties during the demonstration at Tetovo on 17 February. On 26 April 1995, the opening day of Sulejmani's trial at the District Court
in Tetovo, several thousand ethnic Albanians took part in a protest rally calling
for his release.[64] The trials of all five defendants were politicized, were not in
conformity with international standards, and contained many violations of due
process.[65] They were all found guilty and received sentences ranging from two
and a half years in prison, in the case of Sulejmani, to six months.[66] By early June,
however, the defendants had been released on bail, pending their appeals.[67]

Predictably, the sentences were harshly criticized by all ethnic Albanian
parties as politically motivated and the penalties of a kangaroo court. A large
demonstration was held by ethnic Albanians in Gostivar against the prison sentences. The protesters condemned the trials and maintained that they had
clearly demonstrated that the authorities were opposed to the educational rights
of Macedonian Albanians.

Following the Tetovo trials, the government demonstrated restraint and
took no action against the university. At the start of Tetovo University's second
academic year in October 1995, Sulejmani claimed that it had 1,259 students,
one hundred professors, six faculties, seventeen classrooms, three laboratories,
and a library.[68] He stated that "narrow-minded forces" had tried to prevent the
university's work and suppress the desire of ethnic Albanians for education.
Sulejmani expressed optimism that the government would alter its "Bolshevist"
tendencies and end its discrimination against ethnic Albanians.[69]

The public controversy surrounding Tetovo University resurfaced two months later, following a special ceremony commemorating its first anniversary, attended by ethnic Albanian MPs and the mayors of various municipalities with large ethnic Albanian populations. The event and the presence of Minister of Culture Eshtref Aliu, an ethnic Albanian, were strongly criticized by the media as well as the nonparliamentary nationalist parties, VMRO-DPMNE and the Democratic Party. They were also critical of the authorities for not taking more forceful measures against the university.[70]

During the first five months of 1996, Tetovo University was not a dominant issue on the political scene. The university continued to function, and the authorities, while still maintaining that it was illegal, turned a blind eye to it. The truce was broken in May 1996 when President Gligorov, in an interview with the German newspaper *Frankfurter Allegemeine Zeitung,* branded the leaders of Tetovo University as "Albanian separatists."[71] All ethnic Albanian political parties condemned Gligorov's statement. The PDP, a member of the ruling coalition, stated that it was "a serious provocation [to] the Albanians in Macedonia," the National Democratic Party (NDP) called it "irresponsible, badly-judged and completely anti-Albanian," and the PDPA characterized it as "a danger to all Macedonian citizens, peace in the country and the region."[72] The Tetovo University Council sent a detailed letter to the editor in chief "setting the record straight" about the university. After dismissing Gligorov's remarks concerning Tetovo University as "pure misinformation," the letter outlined the history of the University and the government's actions against it. It reiterated that Macedonian Albanians were "determined to acquire education and nurture their culture; to support the University of Tetovo; . . . and would never give up their sacred and civilized intention."[73] Ethnic Albanian political leaders claimed that Gligorov's statement was prompted by Macedonia's improved relations with Serbia following the establishment of diplomatic relations the previous month and was aimed at demonstrating support for Belgrade in the wake of a series of terrorist attacks in Kosovo.[74]

The interethnic temperature increased when the Skopje District Court on 19 June, reduced the sentences of the Tetovo University leaders.[75] The supporters of the university had hoped that the sentences would be dropped completely. In response, the PDPA and NDP, with the support of the university and several ethnic Albanian community organizations, initiated a three-pronged strategy protesting the prison sentences and the continued refusal by the authorities to legalize the university. The first strand was public rallies and demonstrations; the second, a boycott of Parliament; and the third, petitions to diplomatic missions and international organizations.

The first protest rally, attended by more than ten thousand ethnic Albanians, was held in Tetovo on 4 July.[76] The rally, whose motto was "We Demand Protection," was peaceful and orderly. The organizers sent a letter to the United Nations, OSCE, Council of Europe, the U.S. State Department, and Amnesty International, appealing for help in improving the political status of ethnic Albanians, legalizing Tetovo University and incorporating it in the country's educational system, and securing the release of the "political prisoners," especially the university rector, Fadil Sulejmani.[77] Subsequent demonstrations were held throughout the month in Gostivar, Skopje, Debar, Kumanovo, Kicevo, and Struga. The strong arm of the law, while clearly visible during the protests, was not flexed.

On 18 July, the PDPA and NDP walked out of Parliament, in protest against Parliament's refusal to address the university issue and the imprisonment of the leadership of the university. In their letter to the speaker of Parliament, Tito Petkovski, they stated that they bore "no responsibility for a possible crisis of the political system [or] permanent danger to peace and stability in Macedonia [and] the Balkans."[78]

Four days later, on 22 July, Sulejmani and Fejziu began their prison sentences following a protest rally outside Tetovo prison by more than three thousand supporters.[79] It was the only demonstration that threatened public order, and one police car as well as shop windows were damaged. Using a megaphone, Sulejmani addressed the protesters, thanking them for their support of Tetovo University. He called the university "the greatest victory of the Albanians in Macedonia," and threatened that anyone who tried "to harm Tetovo University will burn." Fejziu declared that he and Sulejmani were "proud" to go to prison for their commitment to the university and told the demonstrators that it was their "duty to protect and finance Tetovo University."[80]

On 26 July, over one thousand ethnic Albanians participated in a demonstration in front of the U.S. Embassy and UNPREDEP headquarters. It coincided with the arrival of the first U.S. ambassador to Macedonia, Christopher Hill. The protesters carried banners in Albanian and English that read, "Release Fadil," "We will give our lives for the University and Fadil," "The Macedonian government is a killer," "We want education," and "UN Help Us."[81] A group representing the protesters delivered two petitions to the U.S. Embassy and UNPREDEP demanding the release of the Tetovo University leaders and the legalization of the university. The organizers had planned to demonstrate in front of the OSCE mission as well, but the protesters dispersed after visiting UNPREDEP Headquarters because the organizers feared they would not be able to control the crowd marching through the center of the city. However, a small delegation delivered similar petitions to the OSCE mission.

Ethnic Macedonians did not look favorably upon the protests. The nationalist Movement for All-Macedonian Action-Conservative Party warned the authorities that if nothing was done about the rallies in western Macedonia, ethnic Macedonians in the area would be "forced to organize their own protection by themselves."[82] Ethnic Macedonians were particularly resentful of the demonstrators' waving of the Albanian flag, singing of the Albanian national anthem, use of the term "Slavo-Macedonians," and the acronym FYROM instead of the constitutional name of the state, the Republic of Macedonia. They viewed such acts as provocative and evidence of disloyalty to the Macedonian state on the part of ethnic Albanians.

The Albanian Parliament entered the fray by adopting a Resolution on 31 July, requesting the Macedonian government to respect the right of Macedonian Albanians to higher education in their mother tongue, and calling for the release of the leaders of Tetovo University. The Resolution went on to say that respect for the rights of Albanians in Macedonia was a precondition for cordial relations between Skopje and Tirana.[83] In response, the Macedonian ambassador to Tirana submitted a protest note to the Albanian foreign ministry denouncing the resolution as interference in the internal affairs of Macedonia. It stressed that the action of the Albanian Parliament was not conducive to the development of good neighborly relations and threatened stability in the region. It was ironic that the note further stated that Macedonia "expects Albania to apply international standards . . . when it comes to the rights of [its] minorities, including the Macedonian minority."[84] If Albania lacked the right to raise the issue of ethnic Albanians in Macedonia, then surely the same principle applied to Macedonia with respect to ethnic Macedonians in Albania.

Following the imprisonment of Sulejmani and his colleagues, the SRSG, Henryk Sokalski, and the head of the OSCE Mission, Danish ambassador Christian Faber-Rod, jointly met President Gligorov on 29 July to express their concern and to offer the good offices of both organizations in the search for a compromise political solution to the university dispute.[85] They also requested Gligorov to use his presidential prerogative and release the imprisoned leaders as soon as possible.[86] The press release concerning the meeting, issued by the President's Office, stated that interethnic relations had been assessed as "positive," including the PDP's participation in the coalition government and the government's policy of increasing the number of ethnic Albanian students at the two state universities in Skopje and Bitola. The statement concluded by saying that it had been agreed that the "positive results" on the interethnic front should be given greater publicity.[87]

The ethnic Albanian parties reacted indignantly to the press release. They deduced, correctly, that it reflected the views of the government rather than those of UNPREDEP or the OSCE. The PDPA declared that President Gligorov had once again confirmed his "inability to comprehend social developments." It added that the "idyllic" portrayal of interethnic relations simply "did not correspond with reality," especially when thousands of ethnic Albanians had been demonstrating around the country.[88] Echoing the PDPA, the president of the PDP, Abdurahman Aliti, said on Radio Tirana that Gligorov's assessment of interethnic relations "had nothing to do with the reality in the country."[89]

On 6 August, the pro-government *Nova Makedonija* published an extensive article on the Tetovo University issue. Having reviewed the intervention of Sokalski and Faber-Rod, as well as the Resolution adopted by the Albanian Parliament, it concluded that the "various advisory statements or ultimatums could only be interpreted as attempts to put pressure on the Macedonian authorities and the Macedonian President . . . and disrespected the decisions of the independent Macedonian judiciary."[90] While the article openly accused the Albanian Parliament of interference in the country's internal affairs, the imputation of political interference by UNPREDEP and the OSCE was latent.

The action by Sokalski and Faber-Rod had no effect on the authorities. The president did not take up their offer of mediation nor did he release the prisoners.[91] The government was becoming increasingly sensitive to the role of international organizations in trying to improve the country's troubled interethnic relations. There was a growing belief in its ranks that external mediators should not be involved in resolving internal problems. Moreover, the government had been criticized by the extraparliamentary nationalist parties, VMRO-DPMNE and the Democratic Party, for what they viewed as its over readiness to comply with the dictates of international institutions. A presidential acceptance of mediation by UNPREDEP and the OSCE would not have been welcomed by the government, and the nationalist parties would very likely have condemned the move. Similarly, the authorities did not release the prisoners because they believed that such action would be interpreted as a sign of weakness and capitulation to the pressure of militant ethnic Albanians and international organizations.

Tetovo University, which for two years had been an invidious issue between ethnic Macedonians and ethnic Albanians, also widened the split between the moderate government-affiliated PDP, on one hand, and the radical PDPA and NDP, on the other. While all the ethnic Albanian parties supported Tetovo University and its legalization, the radicals and moderates differed over strategy. The PDP, in contrast to the PDPA and NDP, was opposed to protests and demonstrations as a means of pressuring the authorities. Although the PDP on more than one occasion publicly threatened to leave the government and boycott Parliament over Tetovo University, those threats were never carried out.

As a result, the PDP became suspect to the true believers. Shortly before his imprisonment, Sulejmani had launched a scathing attack on the PDP, accusing it of betrayal and of not supporting the university.[92]

The University of Tetovo has continued to function. Its classes are held in private houses, apartments, basements and garages. It is tolerated by the Macedonian government, if not officially recognized. After hundreds of the intelligentsia of Pristina fled to Tetovo in the wake of the Kosovo crisis in early 1999, the University of Tetovo welcomed the Professors and students from the underground university in Pristina.[93]

The Tetovo University issue reflected a fundamental tension between ethnic Macedonians and Albanians. Ethnic Macedonians fear that their fissiparous new state would disintegrate if special consideration is accorded to ethnic Albanians. Ethnic Albanians believe that they have a right to full equality and to develop their national identity. The government's massive majority after the 1994 elections raised expectations among ethnic Albanians that with no parliamentary opposition to contend with it would take concrete measures to address ethnic issues. The ethnic Albanian parties regarded Tetovo University as a litmus test of the government's commitment to accommodate the needs of ethnic Albanians. The government underestimated the seriousness of the educational problems facing the ethnic Albanian community and the potency of the university issue. Moreover, when the government took action, it was as a result of pressure and agitation.

The Tetovo University affair illustrates both the potential and limits of peacekeeping operations in resolving internal ethnic problems. On the one hand, UNPREDEP helped to contain the dispute and to prevent it from igniting a violent ethnic confrontation. On the other hand, lacking leverage, the mission was unable to get the Macedonian government and the ethnic Albanians to find a permanent solution to the dispute.

PROMOTING DIALOGUE

As it became clear in early January 1996 that the Security Council would soon decide to establish UNPREDEP as an independent mission reporting directly to UN headquarters in New York, the SRSG, Henryk Sokalski, initiated a series of informal monthly luncheons at UNPREDEP headquarters with the participation of the leaders of the twelve major political parties representing the various ethnic groups in Macedonia. The luncheon meetings had three main objectives. The first was to promote dialogue among the various political forces in the country, especially as the two main ethnic Macedonian opposition parties, VMRO-DPMNE and the Democratic Party, were not represented in Parliament following their boycott of the 1994 presidential and parliamentary elections, and tensions were growing between the government and the opposition ethnic Albanian PDPA and NDP. As Winston Churchill famously observed, "to jaw-jaw is better than to war-war." The second goal was to strengthen UNPREDEP's relations with the political parties and its understanding of the internal situation. Finally, the meetings were to serve as a channel for keeping the political leaders informed of UNPREDEP's activities and its role in helping to maintain peace and stability in the country.

At an early stage in the meetings, the participants focused on whether certain issues constituted a basic national consensus, which all political leaders could support irrespective of ideology or ethnic affiliation. The parties mentioned in general terms, respect for Macedonia's sovereignty and territorial integrity, development of democracy, respect for human rights, and commitment to a free market economy. Encouraged by the discussions, Sokalski began bilateral consultations with the parties on a "Joint Declaration on the Fundamental Consensus for Macedonia," which he believed would have a positive impact on the political climate in the country. The following principles were considered the ingredients of such a consensus: the inviolability of the country's sovereignty and territorial integrity; the development of democracy, pluralism, and democratic institutions in multiethnic realities and a civil society of equal opportunity; maintenance of the country's internal and external stability; membership in collective security arrangements, notably in NATO; respect for human rights, based on international standards and principles of social justice; commitment to free market economy and entrepreneurship; integration into the European Union and other European regional institutions; furtherance of good relations with the neighboring countries; and preservation of a healthy environment.[94]

Whether the draft declaration would be acceptable to the political parties became clear in July 1996 when they gave their responses to it. The SDSM, the senior partner of the governing coalition, commended the draft, especially as it embodied elements contained in the Macedonian Constitution. Nevertheless, it stressed that the fact that the draft had been initiated by the chief of mission of an international organization would not be viewed kindly by the local population who were sensitive to perceived interference in the country's internal affairs. Furthermore, Macedonians would blame the signatories, particularly the SDSM, for resorting to an external mediator to forge such an important agreement. Consequently, the SDSM would not sign the draft. The ethnic Albanian PDP and NDP said they would support the draft as long as the two references to interethnic relations were retained. The extraparliamentary opposition VMRO-DPMNE opposed the draft on the following grounds: it would have no practical impact as the ruling coalition would simply disregard its provisions; it was impossible to support democracy, because the government had rigged the 1994 presidential and parliamentary elections and were opposed to a referendum on early elections; and the clauses on interethnic relations were too general and subject to various interpretations. Similarly, the Democratic Party was skeptical about the value of the draft, maintaining that political declarations and agreements signed by the government were more honored in the breach than the observance. The Liberal Party supported the draft but stated that it should focus more on individual rights and less on collective and ethnic rights.

As the parties had either opposed the draft or given it qualified support, the initiative could not proceed. Despite the failure to reach an agreed text among the political parties, the process stimulated an unprecedented interparty dialogue, and the meetings continued to provide the only opportunity available to the political leaders to meet in a non-partisan setting and freely exchange views.[95] As the secretary-general reported to the Security Council, UNPREDEP had "maintained an active dialogue with all political forces and ethnic groups in the country in order to promote internal peace and stability. As a result, UNPREDEP has been recognized as a significant instrument for facilitating dialogue, restraint and practical compromise between different segments of society."[96]

Similar monthly working luncheons for the leaders of all the registered youth organizations in the country began in March 1997. The catalyst for this initiative was the events surrounding the Pedagogical Faculty at the University in Skopje. Since early February hundreds of ethnic Macedonian university and high school students had been protesting against a law permitting the use of Albanian as a language of tuition at the faculty. The law was a compromise between the demands of ethnic Albanians for the legalization of Tetovo University, and the government's position that the Macedonian Constitution allows teaching in minority languages only at primary and secondary school levels. In a chilling echo of Nazi Germany, the protesters chanted "Shkiptars [Albanians] to the gas chambers!"[97] They demanded the resignation of the minister of education, Sofija Todorova, threw eggs and stones at the education ministry, the main government building, and Parliament, and about twenty of them set up a tent in a park near Parliament and went on a hunger strike.[98] There was little doubt that many of the younger generation had imbibed the suspicions and prejudices of the old. It was hoped that the informal meetings under the auspices of UNPREDEP would encourage dialogue and tolerance, thereby assisting in the maintenance of internal peace and stability. In May 1997, UNPREDEP organized a symposium on "Youth as Bridge-Builders in Multi-Ethnic Communities: The Meaning of International Educational and Linguistic Standards," which was cosponsored by eleven youth organizations of various ethnic and political hues.[99]

Human Rights Watch accused the UN and the OSCE of supporting the Gligorov regime and of tolerating human rights violations in Macedonia to maintain stability: "In the name of stability, however, both the UN and the OSCE tend to defend the status quo in Macedonia and downplay human rights violations within the country. Only gentle criticism is directed against a friendly government that is seen as a stabilizing force."[100] However, it cannot fairly be said that the UN has played down the violations of human rights that take place in Macedonia. In fact, as noted earlier, since the establishment of a peacekeeping operation in Macedonia in 1992, the UN has been increasingly concerned about human rights violations and the threat they pose to the country's stability. The authorization of a good offices function in 1994 stemmed from the concern of the Security Council about the internal dangers to Macedonia's stability.

Secretary-General Annan and his predecessor, Boutros-Ghali, highlighted human rights issues in the republic in their periodic reports on UNPREDEP to the Security Council. In May 1996, Boutros-Ghali stressed the dangers of interethnic problems: "Although the new government includes five ministers and a number of other senior officials of ethnic Albanian origin, interethnic tensions remain a threat to the country's social fabric, its integration and its long-term stability."[101] Four months later, he underlined the seriousness of the Tetovo University issue:

> A new and disturbing rise in [interethnic] tensions has been generated by the ethnic Albanians' insistence upon, and the Government's consistent refusal to recognize as legal, the establishment and functioning of the Albanian-language "Tetovo University." The situation has been further aggravated by the imprisonment of some of the organizers of the University. The over-politicization of the issue on both sides has added to its complexity.[102]

By November 1996, most observers were in agreement that the presence of UNPREDEP had contributed to the security and stability of Macedonia, and raised the political price of any possible external attack. The Secretary-General suggested directly that the most likely source of instability was domestic political tensions:

> The original purpose of deploying a preventive United Nations mission in the former Yugoslav Republic of Macedonia was to prevent conflicts elsewhere in the former Yugoslavia from spilling over or threatening that country. Recent developments in the region, and the enhanced international standing of the former Yugoslav Republic of Macedonia, have made such a

scenario more remote. Moreover . . . it has become increasingly evident that the primary threat to the country's stability may come from internal political tensions. UNPREDEP has accordingly devoted considerable attention to strengthening dialogue between the political forces and has assisted in monitoring human rights and interethnic relations.[103]

In his first report on UNPREDEP as secretary-general, Kofi Annan noted "a number of worrisome developments" in the area of interethnic relations. Ethnic Macedonian students and the opposition had organized demonstrations in protest against the law on instruction in the languages of ethnic minorities and displayed slogans, which reflected "intolerance and xenophobia." Ethnic Albanians had also criticized the law for failing to legalize Tetovo University. At the same time, some radical ethnic Albanian leaders had called for federalization of the country. The secretary-general observed, "Those developments have tested the country's fragile communal mosaic and have underscored the fact that, unless they are tackled in earnest by all concerned, interethnic relations may ultimately prove to be a significant destabilizing factor in the former Yugoslav Republic of Macedonia."[104]

One of the complaints of the Albanian community is that the state symbols, such as the national flag and anthem, are those of the ethnic Macedonian people. In early 1997, the mayors of the predominantly ethnic Albanian towns of Gostivar and Tetovo began displaying the Albanian national flag in front of their town halls. In June 1997, the Macedonian Constitutional Court decided that displaying the flags of ethnic minorities was unconstitutional, but the mayors defied the ruling. In the early hours of 9 July, a day after Parliament adopted a compromise law on the use of flags of national minorities, special police forces stormed both town halls and removed the flags. The law allowed the nationalities to choose their own flag and to use it for their private celebrations and during cultural, sports and other events. It listed buildings in and in front of which flags of the nationalities may not be displayed, including those of the president, Parliament, government, local government, and public service institutions and enterprises. In his report to the Security Council in August 1997, the secretary-general stated:

> During clashes with the police, three demonstrators died in Gostivar and many were wounded in what appeared to be an excessive use of force by government special police forces. In the wake of the Gostivar events, a number of demonstrators were called by the police for "informative talks," a practice restricted by the new law on criminal procedures. Some of the demonstrators complained of brutal methods of interrogation.[105]

The allegation that the UN attempted to preserve the status quo and played down violations of human rights reveals a misunderstanding of the role of UNPREDEP and the nature of its mandate. UNPREDEP was present in Macedonia at the request and with the consent of the Macedonian government. It was not an occupying force or an enforcement operation under Chapter VII of the Charter. It could not coerce the Macedonian authorities or operate by fiat. While the good offices function provided a basis to raise questions of human rights, it was never welcomed by the Macedonian government, and the Security Council stipulated that good offices had to be exercised in cooperation with the authorities. UNPREDEP therefore had to walk a tightrope in not condoning the human rights violations of the government, while at the same time using its good offices to encourage the government to address the human rights concerns of all its citizens.

PEACE BUILDING

Over the years, the focus of the reports of the secretary-general on UNPREDEP shifted from external military threats to internal nonmilitary threats to Macedonia's peace and stability. The reports stressed the importance of promoting internal political dialogue, strengthening interethnic relations, and improving social and economic conditions. In the words of former Secretary-General Boutros-Ghali, "only sustained efforts to resolve underlying socioeconomic, cultural and humanitarian problems can place an achieved peace on a durable foundation."[106] The Security Council in a Presidential Statement in February 1995 declared:

> The Security Council endorses the view expressed by the Secretary-General concerning the crucial importance of economic and social development as a secure basis for lasting peace. Social and economic development can be as valuable in preventing conflicts as in healing the wounds after conflicts have occurred. The Council urges States to support the efforts of the United Nations system with regard to preventive and post-conflict peace-building activities and, in this context, to provide necessary assistance for the economic and social development of countries, especially those which have suffered or are suffering from conflicts.[107]

The views of the Security Council and the secretary-general were strongly supported by the SRSG, Henryk Sokalski, who believed that a preventive operation should have a peace-building component, or in his words, "a human dimension."[108] His enthusiasm came from professional experience. Prior to his appointment as chief of mission of UNPREDEP in 1995, he had served for a decade as director for social development in the Center for Social Development and Humanitarian Affairs, at the UN office in Vienna, and as the UN coordinator for the International Year of the Family in 1994.

The endeavor by UNPREDEP to concentrate on social and economic development confronted three formidable obstacles. First, UNPREDEP had no discretionary funds for programs in this area and consequently would have to rely on extrabudgetary resources and voluntary contributions. Second, it lacked civilian personnel with the necessary professional expertise to formulate and implement development programs. Third, the Macedonian authorities and some Security Council members believed that such activities constituted peace building rather than peacekeeping and therefore it was more appropriate that they should be undertaken by the United Nations Development Program and other development agencies, rather than a peacekeeping operation authorized by the Security Council.

Despite these problems, UNPREDEP managed to initiate a number of projects including training programs for social welfare workers; training police officers in crime prevention, drug trafficking, and narcotics control; and workshops and seminars in social development. A small family business incubator project was launched with $50,000 from the Voluntary Fund of the International Year of the Family to enable a modest number of families to gain economic independence and get off social welfare. As part of the project, twelve families received interest free credit up to a maximum of $5,000 to be repaid after three years to start their own businesses. In 1996, Secretary-General Boutros-Ghali noted that these projects "have had important results in building confidence between the people of the host country and the mission. They have also paved the way for any successor arrangements that may be put in place once the preventive deployment operation in the country comes to an end."[109]

At the initiative of UNPREDEP, an independent intersectoral mission on Developmental Social Issues, funded by the Finnish government, visited Macedonia in May and June 1996 to evaluate the level of social development programs and services and suggest measures for their upgrading according to the Plan of Action prescribed by the UN Summit for Social Development in 1995; outline policy directions for the future; and propose model programs and projects for international assistance.[110] It made ten policy recommendations, which it believed would contribute to job creation, reduction of poverty, and social integration. The recommendations stemmed from "the three-faceted commitment to ensure development in accordance with best professional practice and international standards, to meet the continuing humanitarian needs of the populations and to ensure ethnic harmony."[111]

The mission also identified ten model projects costing some U.S.$6 million "as examples of small-scale initiatives that could be undertaken either by the government or by appropriate district authorities or nongovernmental organizations, if funds were made available by bilateral or multilateral aid agencies."[112] They were as follows: establishment of a social policy and social care think tank within the Ministry of Labor and Social Policy; training the trainers in social policy, social work, and social development; enhancing professional practice in social welfare institutions; improving early childhood home-based education; welfare for the elderly; community development in the Roma district; nonviolent conflict resolution; incubator for non-governmental organizations; microcredit assistance for women; and care in the community.[113]

UNPREDEP disseminated the mission's report to the relevant ministries in Skopje, foreign governments, including the troop-contributing nations, regional organizations, UN specialized agencies, and NGOs, with the aim of raising funds for the projects. The initial response was disappointing, and a Pledging Meeting that was to be held in Skopje in April 1997 had to be canceled. By the end of the year, however, some countries had decided to fund certain projects on a bilateral basis and other international donors were providing financial assistance. The National Research Development Center for Welfare and Health in Helsinki provided $50,000 for the preparatory work for the think tank; the Danish government offered $200,000 for community development in the Roma district and other low income multiethnic neighborhoods; the Swiss government supported training in nonviolent conflict resolution for schoolchildren and teacher-training programs; Japan offered a grant of some $167,000 from the trust fund of the former SRSG for former Yugoslavia, Yasushi Akashi, to be used for two projects aimed at promoting cultural tolerance and understanding among the youth; the local UNICEF office provided support for early childhood home-based education; and the Open Society Institute in Skopje, with assistance from Switzerland, undertook a project to assist NGOs in economically depressed regions of the country to develop their capacity for income generation activities. In two and a half years, UNPREDEP managed to raise some U.S.$6 million, in cash and in kind for social integration projects.[114]

The inclusion of social and economic activities as part of the strategy of a preventive operation has conceptual and practical merit. These programs address the underlying roots of problems threatening domestic stability and exacerbating ethnic tensions. Equally important, they may strengthen local capacities for conflict prevention, mediation, and resolution. UNPREDEP's peace-building efforts reinforced its military, political, and diplomatic action and enhanced local support for the operation. They bridged the humanitarian assistance provided by the Nordic and U.S. battalions and medium- and long-range development programs. UNPREDEP also filled a critical gap in international development assistance to Macedonia as the United Nations Development Program (UNDP), the lead agency for UN development activities, due to budgetary constraints, did not open an office in Skopje until June 1998.

PUBLIC INFORMATION

An effective public information program is a vital component of a peacekeeping operation. As Ingrid A. Lehmann observes, "The United Nations has a message, and it thus has a responsibility no less serious than any other aspect of its operations, to see that message accurately transmitted."[115] A peacekeeping operation has four main audiences: the host country, the neighboring states, the troop-contributing countries, and the wider international community. The General Assembly in Resolution A/RES/48/42, adopted on 10 December 1993:

> [Recognized] that public information on peacekeeping operations, particularly an understanding of their mandates, is important, and [called] for significant enhancement of the press and public information function for peacekeeping missions and in particular for rapid deployment at the start of a peacekeeping operation of a robust and professional media outreach program in the area of the operation commensurate with the scope and needs of the missions.[116]

In the same vein as the General Assembly, former Secretary-General Boutros-Ghali noted:

> An additional lesson from recent experience is that peacekeeping operations, especially those operating in difficult circumstances, need an effective information capacity. This is to enable them to explain their mandate to the population and, by providing a credible and impartial source of information, to counter misinformation disseminated about them, even by the parties themselves.[117]

The critical role of public information in peacekeeping was recognized by the exploratory mission to Macedonia in December 1992, when it recommended that from the establishment of a UN presence in the country, "a strong public information program" would need to be implemented "to ensure that the role of the United Nations presence is fully understood by the population."[118] There were three particular reasons for stressing the importance of public information in the context of Macedonia. First, the UN's operation in the country was the first preventive peacekeeping mission, and its unique preventive character had to be explained effectively. Second, given the sensitive internal political situation, especially interethnic relations, there was a risk that the UN's presence might create misperceptions or engender unrealistic expectations regarding its potential role in those matters. Third, the Macedonian authorities had not mounted a substantive public information campaign to prepare their citizens for the arrival of the UN peacekeepers. While the peacekeepers were not deployed in a hostile environment, it was still necessary to prepare Macedonians for the sudden presence of a few hundred blue helmets in their midst. The public information program was implemented by the UNPREDEP Press and Information office, in cooperation with the Public Affairs Officers of the Nordic and U.S. battalions. The primary emphasis was on close collaboration with Macedonia's print and electronic media, which generally had a positive attitude toward the UN. Less than one month after the arrival of the peacekeepers, the civil affairs coordinator and the press and information officer had agreed on a strategy with Macedonian Television and Radio aimed at ensuring that Macedonians had a clear understanding of the reasons for UNPROFOR's presence and the nature of the deployment. It had the following elements: the news and current affairs programs would provide regular coverage of UNPROFOR's activities in the course of their normal work, there would be a weekly UNPROFOR segment including a panel or phone-in program with an UNPROFOR spokesperson, and UNPROFOR and Macedonian Television and Radio would produce a series of three or four short public service announcements describing the deployment and the operation's different components. All programs were to be broadcast on both Macedonian and Albanian services.

During the first five months of the deployment, the Press and Information Office coproduced more than twenty-five radio and television reports about the UNPROFOR mission, compiled weekly news bulletins that were broadcast by three regional stations, and produced daily translations of the Macedonian press that were distributed throughout UNPROFOR. The mission's officials also gave regular interviews with the print media, and press releases were issued on various aspects of the mission. Programs subsequently produced by UN Television (UNTV) on Macedonia were broadcast on Macedonian Television. The U.S. battalion produced programs on the Nordic and U.S. battalions, which were broadcast on the independent A1 Television Station every fortnight. In his first report following the deployment, Secretary-General Boutros-Ghali observed , "Some initial concerns over UNPROFOR's presence on the part of the Albanian sectors of the population have to a large extent been overcome through direct meetings with local officials and representatives of these groups and also through the information program."[119]

In April 1994, UNPROFOR, with the cooperation of the Ministry of Defense, organized a photographic exhibition in the gallery at the Army Hall in Skopje. The eighty photographs covered the activities of UNPROFOR in the former Yugoslavia since its establishment in February 1992. In addition to the exhibits, a collection of videos produced by UNTV on UNPROFOR and its personnel were available for viewing by visitors. The two-week exhibition generated much public interest and received favorable reviews in the local media.[120]

The major challenge regarding the international dimension of the public information strategy was attracting the interest of the foreign media in the UN's peacekeeping operation in Macedonia. While the Macedonian media had a natural interest in the UN's mission in their country and were generally receptive to information on its activities, the situation was radically different with the international media. The international media were more interested in the conflict in other parts of the former Yugoslavia, especially the war in Bosnia and Herzegovina. The fact that Macedonia was the only former Yugoslav Republic that has seceded peacefully and had not suffered the tragedy of war was, evidently, not an interesting media story. There was a marked failure to recognize the real external and internal threats to the country's stability. The UN's unprecedented preventive deployment mission, which had been rather effective, did not generate much enthusiasm among the international media or capture their imagination. Moreover, few international media correspondents were based in Skopje. Most were located in Athens, Thessaloniki, Belgrade, or Zagreb and paid short and infrequent visits to Macedonia.

CORRECTING MISPERCEPTIONS

In its Resolution 947 (1994) of 30 September 1994, the Security Council decided to extend UNPROFOR's mandate for a further period of six months, terminating on 31 March 1995. As is customary, the secretary-general submitted a report to the Council in March 1995, to assist it in its deliberations on the mandate and future of UNPROFOR. As has been discussed already, the report was of special significance to Macedonia, because in it, the secretary-general recommended that UNPROFOR be replaced by "three separate but interlinked peacekeeping operations," which was an important step toward the realization of the goal of the Macedonian authorities for an independent peacekeeping operation in their country. Nevertheless, certain aspects of the report concerning Macedonia unleashed a torrent of criticism from the Macedonian government and media. The report also prompted a formal letter of protest from the Macedonian foreign minister, Stevo Crvenkovski, to Secretary-General Boutros-Ghali.

According to the government, the analysis of the situation in the country was neither objective nor balanced. The government's strongest objections concerned three issues. First was the presidential and parliamentary elections that had been held in October 1994. The secretary-general's report noted that the opposition parties "which boycotted the elections held influence over a significant portion of the electorate; as they now recognize neither the Parliament nor the President, a situation exists which is not conducive to constructive political dialogue."[121] The government maintained that such a statement questioned the legitimacy of the democratically elected president and government and could be used by the extraparliamentary opposition parties, VMRO-DPMNE and the Democratic Party, to destabilize the country.

The second issue of concern was the National Census conducted in the summer of 1994. The report observed that "despite verification by international observers of the veracity of the results and the proper conduct of the census, ethnic Albanian leaders have disputed the results."[122] In the view of the Macedonian authorities, this was an unnecessary "political statement" that would buttress the unfounded challenges of the census results by ethnic Albanians.

Third was the unresolved border dispute between Macedonia and Serbia. With regard to this problem, the secretary-general stressed that there had "been no decisive move toward establishing a clear international border between the former Yugoslav Republic of Macedonia and the Federal Republic of Yugoslavia (Serbia and Montenegro)." He added that "the potential for confrontation still exists in the absence of a mutually recognized international border and it remains of primary importance that a joint border commission begin work to resolve this long-outstanding issue."[123] In the view of the Macedonian government, this statement both challenged the validity of the country's borders, which it considered a dangerous exercise within the context of the Balkan region, and wrongly suggested that there was a territorial dispute between both countries. The government maintained that the border dispute between Macedonia and Serbia involved only minor differences over demarcation. President Gligorov declared that he was "startled" by the report's portrayal of the border issue and described it as "absurd."[124]

The government was also concerned about three other issues in the secretary-general's report, though it regarded them of lesser importance. First, the government was irked that the report had not acknowledged its efforts to resolve interethnic problems through compromise. Second, it objected to the fact that the secretary-general had referred to "the trade embargo imposed by Greece in February 1994" but had not stipulated that the embargo was an illegal and unilateral measure. Third, in the government's view, Boutros-Ghali did not stress strongly enough that the initiative to establish the Albanian-language University of Tetovo was a political rather than an educational venture.[125]

On the whole, the government's objections were strongly supported by the local media. The following comment by the government-controlled Macedonian Television was characteristic of the media's response: "Macedonian diplomacy will have to keep an eye on the activities of Boutros-Ghali's cabinet."[126] The press also blamed Macedonia's permanent representative to the United Nations, Denko Maleski, for not being more energetic in trying to ensure that a more balanced report on Macedonia was produced and argued that he should be held to account for the "inefficiency" of Macedonia's permanent mission in New York.[127]

The government's negative reaction played into the hands of the opposition parties, VMRO-DPMNE and the Democratic Party. Having boycotted the elections, both parties had lost a voice in Parliament and feared that they were becoming marginalized. Therefore, they seized with alacrity the opportunity to make political capital out of the controversy surrounding the report. VMRO-DPMNE and the Democratic Party held separate press conferences during which they emphatically endorsed the secretary-general's report on Macedonia. The leader of the Democratic Party, Petar Goshev, declared that the report had given an objective assessment of the power of the opposition and the absence of constructive political dialogue in the country.[128]

The response of the Macedonian government to Boutros-Ghali's report, like a Balkan storm, came as a surprise to UNPROFOR officials. It was a reminder that a degree of unpredictability is a natural aspect of peacekeeping. Moreover, there was a risk that the relations between UNPROFOR and the host government could deteriorate as a result. Therefore, a public information campaign, led by the delegate of the SRSG, Hugo Anson, was initiated to correct the misperceptions of the report and reassure the Macedonian authorities. Early in his career, Anson had worked with Reuters and was adept at dealing with the media. On 30 March 1995, he was interviewed by the director of Macedonian Television, Sasho Ordanoski, regarding the report. Ordanoski, thirty years old, had established a reputation as a young talented and independent journalist before taking the helm at the state television. A year later he would be dismissed from his post for giving a televised political commentary on tensions within the governing coalition. The strains within the coalition ultimately resulted in the Liberal Party leaving the government.

Based on prior agreement between UNPROFOR and Macedonian Television, Anson's interview was broadcast without editing on the main evening news that day. He emphasized that the secretary-general had made clear in his report that international observers, including UNPROFOR, had monitored the 1994 presidential and parliamentary elections and concluded that they had been conducted in a generally regular manner. Furthermore, the conduct and outcome of the elections had been accepted by the international community. With respect to the census, Anson pointed out that the secretary-general's report also mentioned that although ethnic Albanian leaders had disputed the results, international observers had verified the veracity of the results and the proper conduct of the census. The fact that the secretary-general had reported that the opposition parties and some ethnic Albanian leaders had expressed contrary views had to be reported, but doing so did not imply that they carried the secretary-general's endorsement. With regard to the particularly sensitive Macedonian-Serbian border issue, Anson emphasized that the report had rightly highlighted the necessity of resolving this crucial outstanding bilateral problem. Finally, he reiterated that the Security Council was committed to ensuring respect for Macedonia's sovereignty and territorial integrity and that the United Nations was mindful of the efforts of the authorities to resolve interethnic problems through dialogue and compromise. Anson made the same points in other interviews with the independent A1 TV station, on radio, and in the major print media. The timing and content of the interviews assuaged the Macedonian government and defused the tensions with UNPROFOR.

In the long run, the secretary-general's assessment was proved right. In the spring of 1996, VMRO-DPMNE and the Democratic Party collected over 150,000 signatures for the calling of a referendum on the holding of early elections. The campaign did not destabilize the country and was a valuable exercise in the workings of democracy. Although Parliament and the Constitutional Court concluded that there was no constitutional basis for calling a referendum, this was a Pyrrhic victory for the government. In the parliamentary elections held in the autumn of 1998, the coalition of VMRO-DPMNE and the Democratic Alternative won the largest number of seats resulting in a change of government. Although the 1994 census was recognized as fair and impartial, the results have never been accepted by ethnic Albanian political parties. The nondelineation of the border between Macedonia and Serbia proved to be an intractable bilateral problem. The Macedonian government acknowledged its importance when it later stipulated the demarcation of the common border as a precondition for the withdrawal of UNPREDEP. The Joint Border Commission established in the spring of 1996 has made little progress to date in demarcating the border.

The Macedonian government's response to the report dramatized the importance that every host government attaches to the views of the secretary-general on the internal political situation. The secretary-general's duty to provide an independent and objective report to the Security Council may not be fully appreciated by the national authorities. If the secretary-general's assessment is at odds with that of the government, this difference may lead to difficulties for a peacekeeping operation.

CONCLUSION

In sum, the experience of UNPREDEP illuminates the vital link between deterring external aggression and promoting internal stability in effective preven-

20

tive action. The deployment of UN troops was of considerable importance for the security of Macedonia. But the blue helmets could not address domestic threats to the country's stability. Therefore, the civilian functions were as important as the military tasks in fulfilling the mission's preventive mandate.

The social and developmental projects were important not solely in economic terms. They were also explicitly political in their objectives and were aimed at preventing internal conflict. As was noted in the previous chapter, one of the lessons from UNPREDEP is that adequate resources are essential for success in a preventive mission. UNPREDEP, unfortunately, was not provided with financial or human resources to undertake peace-building activities.

NOTES

1. "Report," S/24923, 9 December 1992, para. 28.

2. "Report of the Secretary-General Pursuant to Resolution 871 (1993)," S/1994/300, 16 March 1994, para.37.

3. Security Council Resolution 908 (1994), 31 March 1994, para. 12.

4. Thomas M. Franck and Georg Nolte, "The Good Offices Function of the UN Secretary-General," in *United Nations, Divided World: The UN's Roles in International Relations*, 2d ed., ed. Adam Roberts and Benedict Kingsbury (Oxford: Clarendon, 1993), 174.

5. Franck and Nolte, "The Good Offices Function of the UN Secretary-General,"176.

6. UN Department of Public Information, *The United Nations and the Situation in the Former Yugoslavia*, Reference Paper, 15 March 1994, 26.

7. Hugo Anson served as delegate of the special representative of the secretary-general and civil affairs coordinator, from 1994 to 1995.

8. G. Mihajlovski, "Lost in the Center of the Earth," *Vecher*, 1 and 2 April, 1995.

9. *MILS News*, 9 September 1994.

10. Two other candidates were nominated: George Atanasovski, a Macedonian businessman living in the United States (Independent), and Halil Shaban (Democratic Party of Turks). However, the State Election Commission rejected their nominations on the grounds that they had failed to collect the ten thousand signatures required.

11. *MILS News*, 16 September 1994.

12. Declaration by Political Parties, Skopje, 6 October 1994.

13. *MILS News*, 7 October 1994.

14. Interview with Abdurahman Aliti, president of the PDP, Tetovo, 13 April 1996.

15. *MILS News*, 14 October 1994.

16. *MILS News*, 24 October 1994.

17. See CSCE Parliamentary Assembly, "Statement on the First Round of the Presidential and Parliamentary Elections," Skopje, 17 October 1994; and Council of Europe Parliamentary Assembly, "Parliamentary Elections in the Former Yugoslav Republic of Macedonia: A Step toward parliamentary Democracy," Skopje, 17 October 1994.

18. CSCE Parliamentary Assembly, "Statement," 2.

19. "Joint CSCE and United Nations Statement to the Press," Skopje, 20 October 1994.

20. The first call for UNPROFOR to join in observing the elections came from the small, extraparliamentary Republican Party at a press conference on 25 September, 1994, *MILS News,* 26 September 1994.

21. The United Nations and the Conference on Security and Cooperation in Europe, "Statement on the Second Round of Parliamentary Elections in the Former Yugoslav Republic of Macedonia," Skopje, 31 October 1994.

22. After the second round of elections, the Alliance for Macedonia had won 89 out of the total parliamentary seats, as follows: Social Democratic Union for Macedonia (SDSM), 57; the Liberal Party (LP), 27; and the Socialist Party (SP), 5. The ethnic Albanian Party for Democratic Prosperity (PDP) won 8 seats; the ethnic Albanian Albanian People's Democratic Party (NDP), 3 seats; the Party for Full Emancipation of Romas, 1 seat; the Social Democratic Party of Macedonia, 1 seat; the Democratic Party of Macedonia (in Tetovo), 1 seat; the Democratic Party of Turks in Macedonia and the Party for Democratic Action-Islamic Way, 1 seat; and independents, 5 seats. The results of voting in the remaining eleven constituencies were declared invalid due to irregularities, and those seats were recontested on 13 November. The third round was also monitored by the CSCE and the UNPROFOR Civil Affairs team. The Alliance for Macedonia won six extra seats; the PDP, two; the NDP, one; and independents, two.

23. In the new government, the Social Democratic Union of Macedonia (SDSM) had nine ministers; the Liberal Party, four; and the Socialist Party (SP), two.

24. In an interview on Macedonian Television on 6 February 1997, Prime Minister Branko Crvenkovski stated:

> We [the Alliance for Macedonia] took 89 seats in the Parliament at the last elections in 1994, that is two-thirds of the MPs, by which we could pass any law. Nevertheless, we decided to establish a coalition with the PDP. Our motive lay in the fact that inter-ethnic relations are vital for Macedonia's stability. We concluded that the PDP, as a representative of the Albanians in Macedonia should be involved both in the Legislative and Executive branches, in order to be able to influence and share responsibility for the important events going on in Macedonia. It has proved to be a stabilizing factor.

25. "Report," S/1994/1454, 29 December 1994, para. 32.

26. Robert W. Mickey and Adam Smith Albion, "Success in the Balkans? A Case Study of Ethnic Relations in the Republic of Macedonia," in *Minorities: The New Europe's Old Issue,* ed. Ian M. Cuthbertson and Jane Leibowitz (New York: Institute for EastWest Studies, 1993), 70.

27. OSCE Spillover Mission to Skopje, *Mission Reports June 1994 to August 1995,* Report No. 57, 2–21 November 1994, 81.

28. As quoted in *MILS News,* 13 December 1994.

29. As quoted in *MILS News,* 13 December 1994.

30. *Flaka e Vëllazërimit,* 5 November 1994.

31. *Flaka e Vëllazërimit,* 5 November 1994.

32. *Flaka e Vëllazërimit,* 17 November 1994.

33. *MILS News,* 14 November 1994. The Macedonian government, however, denied receiving any such request from the Council.

34. *MILS News,* 4 and 17 November 1994.

35. *MILS News,* 14 November 1994.

36. *MILS News,* 14 November 1994.

37. As quoted in *MILS News,* 2 December 1994.

38. *MILS News,* 13 December 1994.

39. *Constitution of the Republic of Macedonia* (Skopje: 1991), 16.

40. *Constitution,* 16.

41. *Constitution,* 16.

42. *The Official Gazette of the Socialist Republic of Macedonia*16 (22 May 1985).

43. *Constitution,* 17.

44. *Constitution,* 7.

45. The languages of ethnic minorities could also be used in primary education, which was regulated by a separate law.

46. As quoted in *MILS News,* 14 December 1994.

47. *MILS News,* 28 November 1994. In 1992 a group of ethnic Albanian nationalists declared the establishment of an autonomous Republic of Ilirida, but it existed only in theory and was not a reality.

48. *MILS News,* 14 December 1994.

49. *MILS News,* 15 December 1994.

50. *MILS News,* 15 November 1994.

51. Macedonian Information Center (MIC), *Infomac Service,* Skopje, 19 December 1994.

52. *Flaka e Vëllazërimit,* 19 December 1994.

53. *MILS News,* 9 January 1995.

54. *MILS News,* 1 February 1995.

55. *MILS News,* 16 February 1995.

56. *MILS News,* 16 February 1995.

57. *MILS News,* 23 February 1995.

58. In contrast to UNPROFOR's neutrality toward Tetovo University, the special rapporteur of the Commission on Human Rights on the situation of human rights in the territory of the former Yugoslavia, Tadeusz Mazowiecki, urged "the Government to give favorable consideration to the initiative aiming at the promotion of the educational system at the university level." See "Tenth Periodic Report on the Situation of Human Rights in the Territory of the Former Yugoslavia," A/50/69, S/1995/79, 26 January 1995, Para. 110(a).

59. UNPROFOR FYROM Command, "Statement to the Press by Mr. Hugo Anson, Delegate of the Special Representative of the Secretary-General," Skopje, 13 December 1994.

60. UNPROFOR FYROM Command, "Statement to the Press," Skopje, 18 February 1995.

61. During his term of office as special representative of the secretary-general for the former Yugoslavia, from December 1993 to October 1995, Yasushi Akashi visited Macedonia four times: on 14 January 1994, 19 May 1994, 7 March 1995, and 19 October 1995.

62. "Report of the Secretary-General Pursuant to Resolution 947 (1994)," S/1995/222, 22 March 1995, para.80.

63. The PDPA and NDP resumed participation in Parliament in June 1995. The parties stated that their boycott had achieved its goal as Tetovo University was being allowed to function without government interference. It is probable, however, that their boycott was also ended because according to Article 65 of the Macedonian Constitution, MPs who are absent from Parliament "for longer than six months for no justifiable reason" can lose their seats by a two-thirds majority vote of all MPs. Given the government's massive majority in Parliament, and its opposition to Tetovo University, the PDPA and NDP MPs could have been voted out of Parliament.

64. The demonstration was organized by all the ethnic Albanian political parties (with the exception of the PDP) and the Association of Albanian Women in Macedonia. The exclusion of the PDP was the start of a strategy by its rivals, particularly the PDPA and NDP, to use the Tetovo University issue to discredit the PDP in the eyes of ethnic Albanians.

65. For a description of the due process violations, see Human Rights Watch, *A Threat to "Stability": Human Rights Violations in Macedonia* (New York: Human Rights Watch, 1996), 47-49.

66. The other sentences were as follows: Nevzat Halili, eighteen months; Arben Rusi, eight months; Musli Halimi, eight months; and Milaim Fejziu, six months.

67. The bail amounts were as follows: Fadil Sulejmani, DM100,000; Nevzat Halili, DM70,000; Arben Rusi, DM50,000, Musli Halimi, DM50,000; Milaim Fejziu was not required to pay bail.

68. *MILS News,* 18 and 30 October 1995.

69. *MILS News,* 30 October 1995.

70. Aliu dismissed the criticisms leveled against him, saying that "as a professor, an Albanian and as a human being, he could attend whatever he liked." *MILS News,* 20 December 1995.

71. *MILS News,* 6 May 1996.

72. *MILS News,* 7 May 1996.

73. Council of the University of Tetovo, "University of Tetovo founded to provide Higher Education not to score a political goal, Albanians are as scholarly inclined as Macedonians, they are not separatists," 17 May 1996.

74. On 22 April 1996, five people were killed and another five wounded in terrorist attacks in Kosovo. The Kosovo Liberation Army claimed responsibility for the attacks in a statement on the BBC Albanian-language program. However, Ibrahim Rugova, the head of the Democratic League of Kosovo continued to insist that the attacks had been instigated by Serbs to provoke a conflict for political ends. Vojislav Seselj, leader of the Serbian Radical Party, told a press conference that the Serbian regime was incapable of

solving the Kosovo problem and demanded to be appointed governor of Kosovo and Metohija. He boasted that he could "pacify and solve the Kosovo problem in two years." *MILS News,* 6 May 1996.

75. Fadil Sulejmani's sentence was reduced from two and a half years to one year, Nevzat Halili's from eighteen months to twelve, Arben Rusi's from eight months to four, Musli Halimi from eight months to three, and Milaim Fejziu from six months to four.

76. *OMRI Daily Digest,* Part II, No.130, 8 July 1996.

77. *MILS News,* 5 July 1996.

78. MIC, *Infomac-Daily News Service,* Skopje, 19 July 1996.

79. *Dnevnik,* 23 July 1996. Arben Rusi turned himself in on 19 July. Nevzat Halili and Musli Halimi had their sentences postponed for "family reasons." They started serving their terms on 26 August 1996.

80. *Flaka e Vëllazërimit,* 23 July 1996, in MIC, *Review of the Albanian Press in Macedonia,* Vol. III, No.14/96, 12-13.

81. Personal notes taken by the author, Skopje, 26 July 1996.

82. *MILS News,* 18 July 1996.

83. MIC, *Infomac—Daily News Service,* Skopje, 1 August 1996.

84. MIC, *Infomac—Daily News Service,* Skopje, 7 August 1996. The Albanian Foreign Ministry responded to the criticisms by stating that its policy toward Macedonia was characterized by goodwill but stressed that "it is our inevitable obligation to be concerned about the rights of the Albanians wherever they live." In addition, it appealed to the Macedonian government to increase the participation of ethnic Albanians in public life, pointing out that the treatment of ethnic Albanians had a direct impact on the relations between the two countries. *OMRI Daily Digest* 53, Part II, 8 August 1996.

85. *Nova Makedonija,* 31 July 1996.

86. Interview by Henryk Sokalski in *Flaka e Vëllazërimit,* 3 August 1996.

87. Cabinet of the President of the Republic of Macedonia, press release, Skopje, 30 July 1996. Also reported in *Nova Makedonija,* 31 July 1996.

88. *Nova Makedonija,* 1 August 1996.

89. *Nova Makedonija,* 3 August 1996.

90. Panta Dzambazoski, "Advice and Ultimatums on Illegal University!" *Nova Makedonija,* 6 August 1996.

91. Fadil Sulejmani was released on 31 January 1997, two months prior to the expiration of his one-year sentence.

92. *Flaka e Vëllazërimit,* 30 June 1996.

93. Barry Bearak, "Uprooted and Idle, Kosovo's Cultured Pace Sidewalks of Their Haven," *New York Times,* 26 April 1999, A12.

94. Henryk J. Sokalski, "UNPREDEP: A Challenge of Preventive Action," paper presented at the NATO Seminar on Conflict Prevention in Skopje, 15–17 October 1997.

95. In October 1997, President Gligorov initiated a dialogue with the leaders of eleven of the most important political parties. On 23 October, a joint statement was issued endorsing the three foreign policy priorities of the country: integration into the

European Union, membership in NATO, and promoting relations with its neighbors. However, in his State of the Nation Address to Parliament on 16 December, the president noted that his dialogue with political parties had revealed that the time was not yet ripe for reaching a consensus on internal problems.

96. "Report of the Secretary-General on the United Nations Preventive Deployment Force Pursuant to Security Council Resolution 1046 (1996)," S/1996/373, 23 May 1996, para. 7.

97. "Hope, and Danger, for ethnic Albanians," *The Economist,* 29 March 1997, 40.

98. *MILS News,* 20 February 1997.

99. For details of the symposium, see *Youth as Bridge Builders in Multi-Ethnic Communities: The Meaning of International Educational and Linguistic Standards,* report of a seminar coorganized by the Macedonian youth structures and associations in cooperation with the United Nations Preventive Deployment Force, Skopje, 20 May 1997.

100. *A Threat to "Stability,"* 3.

101. "Report of the Secretary-General Pursuant to Security Council Resolution 1046 (1996)," S/1996/373, 23 May 1996, para.23.

102. "Report of the Secretary-General Pursuant to Security Council Resolution 1058 (1996)," S/1996/819, 30 September 1996, para.5.

103. "Report of the Secretary-General on the United Nations Preventive Deployment Force Pursuant to Security Council Resolution 1058 (1996)," S/1996/961, 19 November 1996, para. 22.

104. "Report of the Secretary-General on the United Nations Preventive Deployment Force," S/1997/365, 12 May 1997, para. 23.

105. "Report of the Secretary-General on the United Nations Preventive Deployment Force Pursuant to Security Council Resolution 1110 (1997)," S/1997/631, 11 August 1997, para. 16.

106. Boutros Boutros-Ghali, "Supplement to *An Agenda for Peace*," A/50/60-S/1995/1, 3 January 1995, para. 22.

107. Statement by the President of the Security Council, S/PRST/1995/9, 22 February 1995.

108. See Henryk J. Sokalski, "Preventive Diplomacy: The Need for a Multi-dimensional Approach," paper presented at the International Workshop on "An Agenda for Preventive Diplomacy: Theory and Practice," Skopje, 16–19 October 1996.

109. "Report of the Secretary-General on the United Nations Preventive Deployment Force Pursuant to Security Council Resolution 1058 (1996)," S/1996/961, 19 November 1996, para.8.

110. See Bob Deacon, *Action for Social Change: A New Facet of Preventive Peacekeeping: The Case of UNPREDEP,* Report of the Intersectoral Mission on Developmental Social Issues (Helsinki: National Research and Development Center for Welfare and Health, 1996), 8.

111. *Action for Social Change,* 51. For details of the ten recommendations concerning government policy, see chap. 7.

112. *Action for Social Change,* 57.

113. *Action for Social Change,* chap. 8.

114. "Report of the Secretary-General on the United Nations Preventive Deployment Force Pursuant to Security Council Resolution 1110 (1997)," S/1997/911, 20 November 1997, para. 6.

115. Ingrid A. Lehmann, *Peacekeeping and Public Information: Caught in the Crossfire* (London: Cass, 1999), 152-53.

116. General Assembly Resolution A/RES/98/42, 10 December 1993, para. 55.

117. Boutros Boutros-Ghali, "Supplement to *An Agenda for Peace*," A/50/60-S/1995/1, 3 January 1995, para. 46.

118. "Report," S/24923, 9 December 1992, Annex, para.28.

119. "Report of the Secretary-General Pursuant to Security Council Resolution 795 (1992)," S/26099, 13 July 1993, para. 22.

120. UNPROFOR FYROM Command, press release, SP0078, Skopje, 16 April 1994.

121. "Report," S/1995/222, 22 March 1995, para. 40.

122. "Report," S/1995/222, 22 March 1995, para. 41.

123. "Report," S/1995/222, 22 March 1995, para. 44.

124. *MILS News,* 10 April 1995.

125. *MILS News,* 31 March 1995.

126. As quoted in *MILS News*, 31 March 1995.

127. *MILS News,* 3 April 1995.

128. *MILS News,* 3 April 1995.

7

WITHDRAWING A WINNING TEAM

> We believe that it is right and justified to raise the question of shutting down UNPREDEP. If we act out of inertia and transform this operation into something inviolable by maintaining it, we run the risk of wiping out all the operation's earlier positive achievements and, indeed, of calling into question the unique experience of preventive peacekeeping.[1]
>
> Sergey Lavrov

Deciding on the timing of a withdrawal of a UN preventive mission from the field is as difficult and as critical as knowing when to begin a deployment. The effectiveness of UNPREDEP in implementing its mandate raised unavoidable questions about its termination. When can a preventive mission declare victory and leave the host country? Had the threats to Macedonia's security and stability ended? This chapter will be concerned principally with the Security Council's attempts to answer these questions and the views of the Macedonian authorities on the operation's withdrawal.

In the aftermath of the Dayton Agreement, the main bone of contention was the position of some members of the Security Council, notably Russia, that the preventive deployment could be implemented more cheaply by United Nations military observers. Other Council members, notably the United States, as well as other troop-contributing governments and the host country insisted that the two infantry battalions were still required. The secretary-general's assessment was that military observers would be an inadequate replacement for the UN troops.

There was also conflict over the mandate of the mission, especially its social and developmental projects. Some member states believed that UNPREDEP had been transformed into a mission dealing with internal political and

151

interethnic issues and economic development. In their view, the operation's military functions had become tangential. They asserted that the peace-building activities should be undertaken by UN development agencies, which would implement them more effectively.

The Macedonian government and the opposition parties argued strenuously that the presence of UNPREDEP was still needed to maintain national and regional stability and to consolidate the gains it had already achieved. They stressed that the conditions that had led to the preventive deployment of UN troops in the country still prevailed.

When the end of the operation came, it was sudden, and the circumstances that precipitated it could not have been predicted. The decision reflected a diplomatic dispute between China, a permanent member of the Security Council, and the new Macedonian government.

RUSSIA RAISES OBJECTIONS

The Security Council and the Macedonian authorities understood when UN peacekeepers were deployed in Macedonia in 1992 that they would not remain in the country indefinitely. However, the precise timing of their withdrawal and the conditions that would prompt it were unknown and unspecified. This was due largely to the fact that the fate of the operation was linked with developments in the turbulent and explosive Balkan region. As Secretary-General Boutros-Ghali noted in 1994:

> In the former Yugoslav Republic of Macedonia, UNPROFOR's presence has demonstrated the value of preventive deployment. But its mission can be judged effective only if it ends successfully. That success will depend on external developments, which UNPROFOR does not control. Unresolved disputes between Greece and the former Yugoslav Republic of Macedonia over its name, state symbols, and constitution have blocked the latter's full membership in international organizations, while external threats to its economic stability and border security persist, including through the continuing economic blockade by Greece and the non-recognition by the Federal Republic of Yugoslavia (Serbia and Montenegro) of the former Yugoslav Republic of Macedonia's international borders.[2]

As positive changes in the regional landscape began to occur, the question of when UNPREDEP should be terminated came to the fore. By November 1995, three of the four neighboring countries, Albania, Bulgaria, and Greece, had officially recognized the Macedonian state. Though recognition by the Federal Republic of Yugoslavia was not yet a reality, "externally there [was] little evidence to indicate any imminent military threat to the country's territorial integrity."[3] An interim accord had been signed between Greece and Macedonia, following which the former had ended its economic blockade of the latter. Macedonia had also established full diplomatic relations with many other states, including the United States, had gained admission to the OSCE and the Council of Europe, and was participating in NATO's Partnership for Peace Program. The Dayton Agreement ending the Bosnian war had been concluded, as had the Basic Agreement on Eastern Slavonia, Baranja, and Western Sirmium, which provided for the region's peaceful reintegration into Croatia.

On the domestic front, however, the situation was less optimistic, and "internal threats to the country's stability [had] not ceased."[4] The most serious of these threats remained the tension between ethnic Macedonians and Albanians. The dispute over Tetovo University had further strained relations between both communities. The ethnic Albanian NDP had sent a letter to the Council of Europe requesting that Macedonia should not be admitted until the rights of its citizens of Albanian origin were respected. In addition, the extraparliamentary opposition parties, VMRO-DPMNE and the Democratic Party, were still challenging the results of the 1994 elections and demanding early parliamentary elections. After weighing the internal and external developments, Boutros-Ghali in his report to the Security Council rendered this judgment:

So far, the fundamental objective of the operation, that the conflict in the former Yugoslavia be prevented from spreading, has been achieved. However, the Government of the former Yugoslav Republic of Macedonia is of the opinion, which I share, that the causes that led to the establishment of the United Nations preventive deployment operation have not ceased to exist. The continued presence of UNPREDEP, with basically the same mandate, strength and troop composition, is vital to the maintenance of peace and stability in the country. . . . In any event, the mandate of UNPREDEP should be renewed for a further 12-month period irrespective of developments elsewhere in the theatre.[5]

Russia, however, believed that in light of the geopolitical changes in the region and the UN's financial crisis, UNPREDEP should be substantially reconfigured. It proposed that the infantry contingents should be withdrawn and replaced by UN military observers, thereby reducing the cost of the operation. Russia's position reflected a growing concern among many of the UN's member states, especially those in the developing world. In the post–Cold War era, it seemed that the Security Council cared more about problems in Europe than about those in other parts of the world which were equally or considerably more serious. Moreover, at a time when the UN was in dire financial straits it seemed that its scarce resources were being used to deal with European conflicts while those in Africa, Asia, and Latin America were being ignored. The other members of the Security Council took a different view. They believed that internal and external threats to Macedonia warranted the continuation of UNPREDEP and that it would be premature to change its mandate or structure.

Notwithstanding these disagreements, on 30 November, the Security Council unanimously adopted Resolution 1027 (1995) extending the mandate of UNPREDEP for six months, rather than one year, as the secretary-general had recommended. While "reaffirming its commitment to the independence, sovereignty and territorial integrity" of Macedonia, the Council recalled "its concern about possible developments which could undermine confidence and stability in the former Yugoslav Republic of Macedonia or threaten its territory." The Council requested the secretary-general to keep it regularly informed of developments in the country and other circumstances affecting UNPREDEP's mandate and to report, if possible by 31 January 1996, on all aspects of the operation.

The Macedonian media reacted negatively to Russian objections to UNPREDEP's presence. There was a flurry of articles in the Macedonian press suggesting that Russia had ulterior motives for wanting a reorganization of UNPREDEP. For example, *Nova Makedonija* wrote that Russia favored UNPREDEP's "termination" because it was opposed to NATO's expansion, which was firmly supported by Macedonia, as well as the presence of U.S. troops in the country. The paper observed that "Russia still cannot digest the idea of an American presence in the Balkans."[6] In general, the media coverage emphasized that though the Cold War may have ended, the old competition for spheres of influence among the Great Powers had not vanished.

In accordance with Resolution 1027 (1995), Secretary-General Boutros Ghali reviewed the UNPREDEP mission in early 1996. He again highlighted interethnic problems and the tensions between the extra-parliamentary opposition parties and the ruling coalition as major threats to Macedonia's stability. The tensions and suspicions had increased following an assassination attempt on President Gligorov on 3 October 1995. The secretary-general observed that "the absence of an effective parliamentary opposition adds to the political controversy, as does the lack of a viable dialogue on the country's future among the various political forces."[7] He noted that despite the government's efforts the economy remained "precarious," as industrial production continued to decline, and about 50 percent of the workforce was unemployed.[8]

Boutros-Ghali indicated that the Macedonian government had made it clear that in its view, three conditions had to be met before the mission was ended:

mutual recognition and normalization of relations with the Federal Republic of Yugoslavia and the commencement of negotiations on the demarcation of the border between the two States; the full implementation of the peace agreement in the Republic of Bosnia and Herzegovina, including its arms control and confidence-building measures; and the attainment of sufficient national indigenous defensive capability.[9]

The government also believed "that any hint of a possible early termination of the mission may be seen as a weakening of the resolve of the international community to promote stability in the area."[10]

While noting that UNPREDEP had played an important role in preventing the conflict in other parts of the former Yugoslavia from spreading to Macedonia, alleviating the country's security concerns and substituting for its minimal deterrent capacity, the secretary-general observed: "There are few indicators for measuring the full success of such an operation unless, following its withdrawal, peace and stability continue to hold, threats and tensions, so far contained, disappear from the horizon or channels and institutions for diffusing them are built or consolidated."[11] Given that existing tensions had not completely disappeared and the danger of fragmentation was a real possibility, he believed "that the continuation of the UNPREDEP mission [was] an important contribution to the maintenance of peace and stability in the region."[12]

On 8 April, the day on which Macedonia and Yugoslavia signed an agreement normalizing relations, the Macedonian government again made its views known on the question of whether UNPREDEP's mandate was still required.[13] It argued that the mandate should be extended for another year for four reasons:

(a) The sensitive phase of implementation of the Dayton Agreement, which is, in any case, exposed to risks and complications;
(b) The potential regional threats, especially Kosovo in the immediate proximity of the former Yugoslav Republic of Macedonia, and the nondemarcation of the border line with the Federal Republic of Yugoslavia;
(c) Inadequate defensive capabilities while the country's efforts to join collective security arrangements remain ongoing;
(d) The positive role of UNPREDEP in the process of establishing democratic structures and policies of good neighborliness.[14]

Prior to the expiry of UNPREDEP's mandate on 30 May 1996, the secretary-general submitted a further report on the composition, strength, and mandate of the mission to the Security Council. He stressed that "like all peacekeeping operations at this time of financial crisis, UNPREDEP must be rigorously examined to see whether its mandate is still required and, if so, whether that mandate can be executed with fewer resources."[15] As Russia believed that UNPREDEP should be restructured, Boutros-Ghali had asked the mission to evaluate the operational implications of replacing the troops with military observers. Its evaluation indicated that at least 250 military observers would be required to replace the Nordic and U.S. battalions, but it was clear "that even this number would be a poor substitute for the accurate reporting system now provided by the two infantry battalions."[16]

Two options were possible with regard to the location of an operation composed solely of military observers. The first would require the military observers to live within daily driving distance of the border areas. But because of the travel time involved, even in good weather conditions the efficiency of the military observers would be only 25 to 30 percent of the infantry units that were living at the observation posts at the border. The challenges of border patrolling would also necessitate a decrease in the military observers' community patrols and meetings with the local and military authorities. Thus, a greater number than the estimated 250 military observers would be required if those activities were to be maintained.[17] The second option would be for the military observers to man and live at some of the observation posts. While patrolling would increase because daily travel to and from the observation posts would be unnecessary, only a small area could be monitored with fewer observation posts. In addition, since the observation posts had a minimum of seven or eight soldiers, it would be "imperative to maintain or establish a robust multifunctional element to support [the smaller number of military observers] in supply management, facility and vehicle maintenance, and administration."[18] The secretary-general pointed out that "while it is therefore technically and operationally feasible to replace the current formed units with United Nations military observers, there would be severe disadvantages with regard to the UNPREDEP core function of monitoring the border and only modest savings."[19]

With regard to the civilian component of the operation, Boutros-Ghali reported that it was "small" when compared to that of similar missions, "notwithstanding the growing importance of its good offices mandate and its efforts to promote institution-building and reconciliation among conflict-prone communities."[20] As there was no UN resident coordinator or humanitarian coordinator in Skopje, the SRSG was responsible for the coordination of all UN activities as well as coordination with other international organizations such as the OSCE. The regular visits of the twenty-six UN civilian police to villages inhabited by ethnic minorities and their daily patrols had increased confidence in the local communities. Despite limited resources the small public information unit had maintained an intensive information campaign to inform the local media about UNPREDEP's role. The UNPREDEP administration had been confronting the "difficult task" of discharging its ongoing programs, while restructuring for an independent operation. The secretary-general concluded that "the strength and composition of the civilian component is, at the present point, appropriate for the tasks at hand."[21]

The secretary-general conceded that while threats to the country's stability still existed, they had diminished and were much less than they had been in November 1992 when he had recommended a preventive deployment. But he stated that it was "too soon to be confident that stability has been established in the region."[22] Boutros-Ghali continued:

> Full implementation of the General Framework Agreement for Peace in Bosnia and Herzegovina is far from being assured; the former Yugoslav Republic of Macedonia's border with the Federal Republic of Yugoslavia, where much of the UNPREDEP patrolling takes place, has yet to be demarcated; the dispute between the former Yugoslav Republic of Macedonia and Greece has not yet been completely resolved; and internal tensions of an interethnic nature persist. It is to be hoped that all these potential threats to the country's stability and security will diminish during the coming months. But for the moment I believe that it would be imprudent to withdraw UNPREDEP.[23]

He recommended to the Security Council that the mandate of the Force be extended for a further six months, to 30 November 1996.

Most of the delegates at the Security Council's meeting on UNPREDEP's mandate echoed the secretary-general's analysis and conclusions. They stressed the following points: UNPREDEP had been effective in preventing the spread of conflict to Macedonia and was one of the UN's success stories; although the Dayton Agreement had restored some measure of stability to the region, the peace process was still fragile; internal threats to the country's stability persisted; and changing UNPREDEP's mandate or extending it for a shorter period than six months would be premature and unwise. Addressing the question of whether the operation could be justified at a time of retrenchment within the UN, U.S. Permanent Representative Madeleine Albright remarked: "the continuation of UNPREDEP—at least for the period contemplated by this resolution—provides a measure of insurance that is well worth the costs."[24] The German delegate captured the prevailing mood of the Security Council:

> Germany will be among the first to welcome a situation in which peace and stability have been secured in the region in such a manner that UNPREDEP can be sent home, with its mission fully accomplished. But, unfortunately, we have not yet reached this point. With UNPREDEP, peace and security in the area still have to be secured, have to be won firmly. The success of UNPREDEP in the struggle for lasting peace and security is, to our knowledge, disputed by nobody. Therefore, in concluding Mr. President, let me again mention an old rule, which is valid not only in sports: "Never change a winning team."[25]

On 30 May, the Security Council adopted resolution 1058 extending UNPREDEP's mandate for six months, by a vote of 14 to 0, with Russia abstaining. The Council noted "that the security situation of the former Yugoslav Republic of Macedonia has improved," but recognized "that it is too early to be confident that stability has been established in the region." It welcomed the signing of the agreement between Macedonia and Yugoslavia of 8 April 1996 and urged "both parties to implement it in full, including the demarcation of their mutual border." Ambassador Sergey Lavrov, Russia's permanent representative, remarked, "It is strange that [the mission] is maintained in its present form," considering the "financial crisis of the United Nations and the need for operations in other areas, including real hot spots."[26]

THE BEGINNING OF THE END?

The need to justify the continuation of UNPREDEP was evident in the secretary-general's next report to the Security Council four months later. He underscored that peace and stability in Macedonia were still largely dependent on the regional situation: "The compelling arguments relating to the still uncertain situation in the wider region that led the Council to extend the mandate of the Force for a period terminating on 30 November 1996 are still valid."[27] The domestic scene had also not improved but had been "further aggravated" by the imprisonment of some of the leaders of the Albanian-language University of Tetovo. Boutros-Ghali concluded that "at the present time, only two months before the expiration of the current UNPREDEP mandate, it is neither appropriate nor necessary to recommend a change in the mandate."[28] With regard to a possible reconfiguration of UNPREDEP, he reported that the "least disruptive" option would be to revert to the original seven hundred–strong Force he had recommended in 1992, plus fifty engineers, since the operation could not call on engineering support from other parts in the theater. He noted, however, that

> the implementation of this option would result in insignificant savings and would seriously impair UNPREDEP's ability to carry out the monitoring of the Republic's western and northern borders, one of its core functions. Given the current fluid circumstances in the country and the region, I am not inclined at this stage to recommend such a change.[29]

The secretary-general indicated that before the end of November, he would submit to the Council, recommendations on UNPREDEP's future, including its mandate and the strength and composition of the force required to implement it. "My recommendation," he continued, "will be based on an evaluation of the general situation in the region and on an assessment of the specific threats, which continue to endanger the peace and stability of the former Yugoslav Republic of Macedonia."[30]

It seemed that UNPREDEP was approaching a turning point. In anticipation of the Security Council's forthcoming deliberations on the operation's future, Ambassador Sergey Lavrov visited Macedonia at the end of October, where he met President Gligorov and Foreign Minister Ljubomir Frckoski. During his stay, he visited UNPREDEP headquarters and toured two observation posts, one each in the areas of operation covered by the Nordic and U.S. battalions.[31] Ambassador Lavrov said that Russia was not seeking the termination of UNPREDEP but rather that it should be "adapted to changes in the region." In explaining the reasons for his country's position, the Russian envoy declared that the war in Bosnia-Herzegovina had ended, the relations between Macedonia and its neighbors had been normalized, and the negative effects of sanctions had ended. Therefore, UNPREDEP had to be reconfigured, performing the same mandate with fewer people. He maintained that this would be in line with the general trend of troop reduction in Bosnia and Croatia.[32] The President's Office released a statement saying that President Gligorov had explained the necessity of extending UNPREDEP's mandate to Ambassador Lavrov. It concluded diplomatically, "The Russian Federation is carefully following the situation and as a permanent member of the Security Council is interested in stability, security and peace in the region. This is the basis of Russia's position on the mandate of the peacekeeping force in Macedonia."[33]

Quite predictably, Ambassador Lavrov's visit was a major news story and the focus of the reports was on Russia's views on the future of UNPREDEP. *Nova Makedonija* carried the headline "Moscow still insists on UNPREDEP Reduction,"[34] *Vecher* declared, "Same Mandate, Fewer Peacekeepers,"[35] and *Dnevik* proclaimed "Russia is for a reconfigured and reduced UNPREDEP."[36] The press stressed two old themes. First, Russia's real objective in seeking the restructuring of UNPREDEP was to remove U.S. troops from Macedonia. Second, Russia was irked by Macedonia's determination to join NATO, whose expansion Russia opposed. In the words of *Nova Makedonija*, "Nobody in Macedonia or abroad is ready to accept the argument that the Russian commitment to a reconfiguration of the mission is motivated by the wish to save the UN budget some US$50 million per year for some other crisis zones."[37]

In his November 1996 report, Boutros-Ghali noted that although Macedonia's relations with its neighbors had improved considerably, progress had been slow in two areas. First, despite two meetings of the Joint Border Commission, little headway had been made in delineating the Serbian-Macedonian border; second, the dispute between Greece and Macedonia had not been fully resolved.[38] He acknowledged that improvements in the regional situation since the signing of the Dayton Agreement and "the enhanced international standing" of Macedonia had made the possibility of a spill-over of conflict "more remote." The secretary-general stressed that "the primary threat to the country's stability" was internal. Therefore, UNPREDEP had "accordingly devoted considerable attention to strengthening dialogue between the political forces and [had] assisted in monitoring human rights and interethnic relations."[39] Nevertheless, he stated that he was "conscious that, in this period of relative tranquillity, the Council might judge that economies are necessary."[40] Consequently, he recommended the extension of UNPREDEP's mandate for six months, but with a phased reduction of the military component by three hundred of all ranks by 1 April 1997. This timing would facilitate the reorganization after the winter and allow the Secretariat to consult with troop-contributing countries. However, although the reconfiguration would yield savings of $400,000 per month, it would have some operational costs. The Force would have to change from "an active and comprehensive patrolling capability to a more limited, and at times static, monitoring presence, particularly along the northern border, a number of observation posts being eliminated."[41] The secretary-general indicated that he would consult with UN agencies and other international organizations regarding continuing international support to Macedonia. "On this basis I will submit recommendations to the Council on the type of international presence that would be appropriate with effect from June 1997," he concluded.[42]

The Security Council's members were persuaded by the secretary-general's arguments, with the exception of Russia. Before the vote was taken on the draft resolution on UNPREDEP's mandate on 27 November, Russian Permanent Representative Sergey Lavrov addressed the Council. He observed that it was nearly four years since the Security Council had approved the deployment of UN peacekeepers in Macedonia. Other parts of the former Yugoslavia were then in the midst of war. UNPREDEP had played "an important role in preventing a widening of the Yugoslav crisis and in the stabilization of the internal situation of Macedonia." However, the original objective of the operation had been achieved and its mandate fulfilled. The regional situation had radically changed, the war was over, and the process of stabilization was under way. While recognizing that the secretary-general's recommendation to reduce the Force by one-third was "a definite step forward," Ambassador Lavrov said that it was "clearly insufficient." Russia saw no point in maintaining UNPREDEP after May 1997, which was why it had maintained that this should be its final extension. Given that its "principled position" had not been reflected in the draft resolution, Russia was unable to support it. However, taking into account the positions of the other members of the Council, the Macedonian leadership and the troop-contributing countries, Russia would not veto the resolution but would only abstain. Ambassador Lavrov emphasized that Russia firmly believed that this was the final extension of UNPREDEP but noted that this did not mean that it excluded the possibility of a further international presence in Macedonia. He concluded, "However, it is clear that the presence in that country of United Nations military contingents must cease after May 1997. We have no doubts whatsoever on that score and we do not want our partners to entertain any such doubts."[43]

Following the Russian ambassador's statement, the Security Council adopted Resolution 1082 (1996) by fourteen votes in favor and one abstention. It expressed, inter alia, the hope that developments in the region will contribute to increased confidence and stability in Macedonia, permitting the further drawing down of UNPREDEP toward its conclusion; reiterated its call on Macedonia and Yugoslavia to implement in full their Agreement of 8 April 1996, in particular regarding the demarcation of their mutual border; decided to extend UNPREDEP's mandate until 31 May 1997 with a reduction of its military component by three hundred of all ranks by 30 April 1997, with a view to concluding the mandate as and when circumstances permit; and requested the secretary-general to keep the Council regularly informed about any developments and to report to the Council by 15 April 1997 with its recommendations on a subsequent international presence in Macedonia.

The Security Council's decision to reduce the Force caused some degree of concern in Skopje. President Gligorov reiterated that the reasons for the mission's presence had not ceased to exist and warned, "a quick withdrawal of UNPREDEP can have very detrimental consequences." He urged members of the Security Council who supported the termination of UNPREDEP to take "a responsible view" of the situation.[44] Among the Macedonian press, *Nova Makedonija* asked, "Is this the beginning of the end for UNPREDEP in Macedonia, which has been carrying out its mission for the past four years under Security Council resolutions? Can Macedonia survive without UNPREDEP? Who will fill the security vacuum after the reduction (or withdrawal) of the mission?"[45] The onset of a winter of discontent in Serbia, Bulgaria, and Albania required that serious answers had to be given to these questions.

A TEMPORARY REPRIEVE

On 17 November, ten days before the adoption of Resolution 1082, the opposition Zajedno coalition had won the local elections in Serbia. The coalition was led by Vuk Draskovic of the Serb Renewal Movement (SPO), Zoran Djindjic of the Democratic Party (DS), and Vesna Pesic of the Serbian Civic Alliance (GSS). The results were as much of a shock to the opposition as to the government, for President Milosevic's ruling Socialist Party of Serbia (SPS) had a formidable political machine. The annulment of the results by the government-controlled courts and electoral commissions triggered a three-month political crisis. The Zajedno coalition and students organized daily mass demonstrations and protest rallies in Belgrade and most of the towns where opposition victories were overturned aimed at securing the reinstatement of the local election results.

In early December, the Belgrade authorities moved to muzzle the independent media. The broadcasts of the independent B-92 radio station were jammed and its operations subsequently declared illegal on the grounds that it lacked a broadcasting permit, and the student-run University Radio Indexs was taken off the air. Meanwhile, the SPS began employing a tactic, which it had used successfully in the 1991 disturbances, organizing counterdemonstrations in support of Milosevic. Workers and peasants in the countryside were bussed into towns to attend the rallies, sometimes with inducements such as a full day's pay.

The actions by Belgrade evoked widespread international condemnation. The U.S. State Department called on Belgrade to respect the results of the local elections which it had "flagrantly overturned" and warned that it would react "with outrage" against any use of force against the protesters. It called for a concerted international campaign against Belgrade's "antidemocratic actions." The United States reiterated that the outer wall of sanctions would be retained. The British, French, and German foreign ministries expressed concern over the annulment of elections and urged President Milosevic not to use force against the opposition. The EU and the OSCE also condemned Belgrade's actions, and on 6 December, EU foreign ministers decided not to extend to Yugoslavia the preferential trade terms already granted to other Balkan states.

NATO foreign ministers, meeting in Brussels on 10 December, deplored Belgrade's annulment of the elections and urged the authorities to reverse their decision. They also expressed dismay at the fact that Belgrade continued to ignore the appeals of the international community that it respect democratic principles. At the same time, the ministers commended the Zajedno coalition for its adherence to nonviolence and appealed to the Serbian government to refrain from using force against the demonstrators. In a separate statement, U.S. Secretary of State Warren Christopher said that if Milosevic were to honor his people's will, Serbia could expect recognition and the international support it needs, but if he chose to rule Serbia as an "unreformed dictatorship," he would only increase his own isolation and deepen the suffering of his people.

In a bid to deflect the vociferous condemnation from major world powers and international institutions, Milosevic decided to invite an OSCE delegation led by former Spanish Prime Minister Felipe Gonzalez to Belgrade. During its thirty-hour visit on 20–21 December, the delegation met with Milosevic, the Zajedno Coalition, the judiciary, and the media. The OSCE mission's report concluded that the local elections had reflected the will of the majority of Serbia's citizens and that the Zajedno coalition won the elections in nine municipalities in Belgrade as well as in thirteen others across the country. It recommended that the Serbian authorities accept and respect the election results.

Milosevic received an unwelcome New Year's present on 2 January 1997, when the Serbian Orthodox Church condemned his government for bringing the Serbian nation to its knees. It accused Milosevic of "falsifying votes," setting "Serb against Serb" and of "strangling political and religious freedoms."[46] The church's ruling council stated that only the recognition of the local election results could bring the Serbian nation hope for a better future and a peaceful life.

The sustained civic protests, the opposition's resolve, and international pressure prompted Milosevic on 5 February to request the government to draft a special law that would recognize the results of the November elections in line with the recommendations of the OSCE mission's report. One week later, on 12 February, the Serbian Parliament adopted the law. Following the election of DS leader Zoran Djindjic as mayor of Belgrade on 21 February, the red star was removed from the roof of Belgrade's town hall after more than half a century. It was really quite a small star and, despite the lights that illuminated it at night, not much noticed by the residents of Belgrade or the passing tourist. But its removal did have symbolic significance.

Although the local election crisis had passed, major problems remained in Serbia; the victory of the opposition was only the first step in the process of democratization. The media were still firmly under the control of Milosevic's government, there was no independent judiciary, and the creation of a market economy was yet to begin. The signs were not promising that concrete steps would be taken to ensure that parliamentary and presidential elections due in 1997 would be free and fair.

During the months of crisis in Serbia, Kosovo had experienced renewed unrest as well. The Kosovo Liberation Army (KLA) had increased its terrorist attacks against Serbs and "Serb-leaning" Kosovar Albanians. On 16 January, Pristina University Rector Papovic and his driver were seriously injured in a car bomb explosion. At the same time, KLA leaders were publicly advocating independence for the province.

January 1997 saw the collapse of the Bulgarian economy. As a result, the country faced a major crisis. The value of the national currency, the lev, fell from 495 to the U.S. dollar at the start of 1997 to between 1,730 and 1,900 to the dollar on 31 January.[47] Daily antigovernment demonstrations and strikes took place.

In Albania, the collapse of risky, high-yield pyramid investment schemes that same month provoked widespread popular protests that plunged the country into chaos and anarchy. The pyramid schemes, in which thousands of Albanians had invested an estimated $2 billion, were closely associated with President Sali Berisha's Democratic Party. It was widely believed that the party had used money from the schemes to fund its campaign during the fraudulent parliamentary elections held in May 1996. The Democratic Party was also blamed for failing to warn depositors of the perils of the schemes and to adopt legislation to control their activities.

The spontaneous protests began in the south of Albania, where people had suffered the greatest losses, but later spread to the north, including the capital Tirana. There was widespread violence, looting, and banditry as angry investors demanded compensation and the resignation of Berisha as preconditions for ending their protests. On 2 March, with the support of Parliament, Berisha declared a state of emergency. A nationwide dusk-to-dawn curfew was imposed, public meetings of more than four people were prohibited, and the police and army were authorized to use deadly force against demonstrators. The same day, in an ultimately unsuccessful attempt to mollify the protesters, Berisha sacked Prime Minister Aleksander Meksi and his cabinet and called for a new government. On 3 March, the DP dominated Parliament reelected Berisha to a second five-year term as president. Berisha subsequently fired the Army Chief of Staff General Sheme Kosova, blaming him for the army's failure to protect military bases from rebels, and replaced him with General Adem Copani, the president's military adviser.[48] Meanwhile, censorship of the media was imposed, the offices of the leading independent newspaper *Koha Jone* were destroyed by fire, and foreign journalists were attacked and ordered out of the country.

From the onset of the crisis in Albania, there had been growing anxiety and apprehension in Macedonia especially concerning a possible influx of refugees, which would upset the country's delicate interethnic balance and exacerbate the already tense relations between ethnic Macedonians and Albanians. Although most Albanian refugees were fleeing to Greece and Italy, as had been the case during the 1991 riots, the Macedonian authorities believed that it would be foolhardy to ignore the threat of a spillover of refugees. Following the Albanian government's imposition of a state of emergency Macedonia raised its army's level of combat readiness and put its troops on a state of alert.

While Macedonia's neighbors were being plagued by high, if varying, instability, UNPREDEP was preparing for the reduction of its military component to 750 personnel by 30 April as mandated by Security Council resolution 1082 (1996) of November 1996. According to the reduction plan, both the Nordic and U.S. battalions would be decreased to a strength of 350 each. Of the twenty-one observation posts, nine would be dismantled, three on the Albanian border and six on the border with the Federal Republic of Yugoslavia, leaving twelve in operation. Six of these would be manned by the Nordic battalion and the other six by the U.S. battalion. Macedonia's border with Serbia would be patrolled by formed infantry units, while its border with Albania would be monitored by military observers. In addition, the number of support personnel at UNPREDEP headquarters in Skopje and the headquarters of the Nordic and U.S. battalions in Petrovec, about twenty kilometers outside the capital, would be reduced.[49]

Coincidentally, UNPREDEP began implementing the reduction as the Albanian crisis intensified, dismantling the first observation post on the Albanian border, near Debar, on 3 March. Although UNPREDEP's patrolling of the border was not affected and the effectiveness of its monitoring and reporting activities was not diminished, the start of the closure of the observation posts attracted strong criticism in the Macedonian media.[50] In a front page article under the headline "Eruption in the Neighborhood-Reduction in UNPREDEP," *Nova Makedonija* stated that despite the chaos in Albania, UNPREDEP was reducing its observation posts on the border "as if nothing was happening."[51] It went on to say that recent developments in Serbia, Bulgaria, and Albania had confirmed that the Macedonian government had been correct in maintaining that UNPREDEP should not be reduced as threats to the country's stability had not disappeared. It asked, "Will the Security Council and all those who encouraged the withdrawal of UNPREDEP now admit that they have inaccurately assessed the situation around Macedonia?"[52] Similarly, *Vecher* contended that recent events had demonstrated that the Security Council's decision the previous November had been the result of a "blurred vision" of the regional situation.[53] The Albanian-language *Flaka e Vëllazërimit* carried the headline "Reduction Continues Despite Crisis in Albania."[54]

In light of the deterioration of the situation in Albania, the SRSG, Henryk Sokalski, and the force commander, Brig. Gen. Bo Wranker, conveyed their concern about the timing of the reduction to Secretary-General Kofi Annan and suggested that it should be temporarily suspended. The secretary-general readily approved their proposal.[55] On 7 March, Macedonian Foreign Minister Ljubomir Frckoski wrote to the secretary-general requesting that the Security Council be informed of the security risks to Macedonia of the Albanian crisis and of his country's request that the reduction of the UNPREDEP military component be urgently suspended.[56] Such a formal request to the Council was required if the reduction of troops was to be delayed beyond 30 April, the deadline mandated by Resolution 1082 (1996).

The situation on the Macedonian-Albanian border deteriorated sharply on 13 March when seven Albanian border police officers tried to cross the border at Kjafasan illegally after their watchtower was seized by rebels. They fired at the Macedonian border police, who returned fire. After an exchange of gunfire, the Albanian police officers fled, leaving their weapons and equipment behind. Immediately following the incident, Macedonia closed all its border crossings with Albania.[57] UNPREDEP observation posts along the border were put on an "Orange" state of alert for about forty-eight hours, the intermediate level between "Green" and "Red," and reinforcements were sent from the Nordic battalion to the observation posts. Five days later, on 18 March, UNPREDEP launched "Operation Black Lake" by which the military observers occupied three temporary observation posts close to three border crossings in the Lake Ohrid area, Kjafasan, Sveti Naum, and Stenje. The Nordic battalion also deployed Force Protection Teams backed by armored personnel vehicles to reinforce the military observers.

UNPREDEP's swift response to the tension on the Macedonian-Albanian border demonstrated the benefit of preventive deployment. The visible military observers and the troops at the three border crossings reduced confrontations between Macedonian and Albanian border guards. They also provided physical and psychological reassurance to ethnic Macedonians and Albanians living in the border towns. The twenty-four-hour UNPREDEP presence facilitated close observation, monitoring, and reporting of activities on the sensitive southwestern part of Macedonia's border with Albania.

On 3 April, Secretary-General Annan wrote to the president of the Security Council requesting a suspension of the reduction in UNPREDEP's military component until the end of its mandate on 31 May 1997. He recalled that "the relative tranquillity" in the region and the need for cuts in peacekeeping operations had prompted his predecessor, Boutros Boutros-Ghali, to recommend the reduction, which the Council had approved. The secretary-general observed that "recent developments in Albania and the resulting situation of lawlessness and banditry in certain parts of that country have demonstrated that stability in the Balkan region remains extremely fragile."[58] He noted that UNPREDEP had been "a most successful mission" but stressed that "proceeding with the planned reduction during a period when further regional instability continues to be a possibility could put at risk the credibility of the international community's first serious effort at preventive deployment."[59]

The members of the Security Council were united about the need to suspend the drawdown. The Council by Resolution 1105 (1997) of 9 April unanimously approved the secretary-general's recommendation. It welcomed the redeployment of UNPREDEP already achieved and encouraged the secretary-general to continue further redeployment, taking into consideration the situation in the region, consistent with UNPREDEP's mandate. The Council also decided to postpone the report on UNPREDEP due on 15 April by one month to take into account the latest developments in the region.

The strife faced by Macedonia's neighbors demonstrated the volatility of the countries in the southern Balkans. The Macedonian government viewed the upheavals as confirmation of the accuracy of its assessment of regional conditions and proof of the wisdom of continuing the UN preventive mission.

THE FORCE IS REDUCED

The concern with regional developments, especially the situation in Albania, was underlined in Kofi Annan's report in May, his first on UNPREDEP as secretary-general. He pointed out that few positive developments in the region had occurred: there had been public and social unrest, as well as tension in most of Macedonia's neighbors; there had been problems in implementing the civilian aspects of the Dayton peace agreement in Bosnia and Herzegovina; Macedonia and Yugoslavia had still not reached a final agreement on the demarcation of their mutual border; and the name-related dispute with Greece remained unresolved.[60] With regard to Albania, Annan said uncertainty still prevailed in the country, partly due to the absence of a constructive dialogue among the parties. Referring to doubts about the possibility of holding free and fair elections in June, he stated that the absence of a legitimate, elected, and representative government and of progress in rebuilding public institutions would undermine attempts to rebuild the economy. The secretary-general warned, "The lack of a perceptible and early change in the situation in Albania could lead to another explosion of internal violence, which may have a negative impact on neighboring countries."[61] He stressed that the large number of weapons circulating in the region, some of which had been interdicted in the border areas by the Macedonian authorities, posed a risk to stability, adding that "yet another potentially destabilizing factor in the coming months will be the outcome of the elections scheduled to be held in Bosnia and Herzegovina in September of this year."[62] The secretary-general's concluding observations were as follows:

> In the light of the strong views conveyed to me by the Government of the host country for a continued UNPREDEP presence, the continuation of the conditions that led to the suspension of the drawdown of the military component and the challenges to be faced in the region in the near future, I am of the view that it would be imprudent to recommend that the UNPREDEP mission be terminated. I believe it would be equally imprudent to recommend any immediate changes in the mandate or size of the Force at this time. I therefore recommend that the mandate of UNPREDEP be renewed for an additional six months until 30 November 1997. I further recommend that the present strength of the Force be maintained for a period of four months, up to 30 September 1997, with a view to starting as of 1 October

1997, taking into account the conditions prevailing at that time, a two-month phased reduction of the military component to the 750 troop level foreseen by the Council in resolution 1082 (1996).[63]

There was overwhelming support for the analysis and recommendations of the secretary-general in the Security Council. On 28 May, the Council unanimously adopted resolution 1110 (1997) renewing the mandate of the Force until 30 November and authorizing a two-month phased reduction of the military component by three hundred of all ranks, to start on 1 October. It was the first time the decision on the extension of the mandate of UNPREDEP had been unanimous since November 1995. Speaking in explanation of its vote, U.S. Permanent Representative Bill Richardson noted that the crisis in Albania had heightened the need for the continuation of UNPREDEP. However, other sources of instability and tension persisted in the region that also reinforced the importance of UNPREDEP. Accordingly, the United States supported a message of sustained, undiminished international commitment to UNPREDEP and the region. Russia expressed the view that the mandate originally given by the Security Council had been successfully implemented, and the main reason for the mandate's extension was the complicated situation in Albania, which had added a new element of risk. Japan indicated that it had supported the extension of the mandate, particularly in light of the situation in neighboring countries.[64]

The Security Council's extension of UNPREDEP's mandate was greeted with a palpable sense of relief by the Macedonian authorities. President Gligorov expressed his "pleasure" at the decision, stating that it was "yet another positive contribution of the international community for the preservation of peace and stability not only in the Republic of Macedonia, but also in the wider region."[65] In the same vein, Macedonian Permanent Representative Naste Calovski said that the extension "would make it clear that the Council and the international community continued to support preventive activities and peace efforts in the region. The activities of UNPREDEP and its clear message had greatly helped to prevent a spillover of the Balkan war toward the south and had also been an important factor in stabilizing the region."[66]

As a result of the reduction of the military component, which was completed by the end of November, the Nordic and U.S. battalions consisted of 350 personnel each, supported by a fifty-person Indonesian engineering platoon. However, the number of military observers and civilian police monitors remained unchanged at thirty-five and twenty-six, respectively. The number of observation posts manned by the two battalions was reduced from nineteen to eight, all of which were located at the most sensitive points on the border. Inevitably, the reduction affected the capacity of the Force to monitor the border areas despite increased patrols and greater use of temporary observation posts.[67]

Reporting on the reduction, the secretary-general stated that it "can be viewed as the commencement of a phased exit in response to the improved situation in the region."[68] Secretary-General Annan recommended two options to the Security Council to reduce the Force further: According to Option A, UNPREDEP would consist of two task forces of four hundred soldiers operating from three to four base camps and thirty-five military observers. The Force would also have a rapid, self-defense reaction capability. The military's "predominant task . . .would be to act, through their presence, as a psychological deterrent."[69] Under Option B, the Force would consist entirely of one hundred military observers operating from eight team offices located on Macedonia's northern and western borders, and it would have "a reasonably flexible patrolling and monitoring capability."[70] However, the secretary-general stressed that "the Council may wish to observe the effectiveness of this initial reduction before contemplating its next step. In this regard, Council members may wish to bear in mind that any decision to further downsize the military component could hardly be implemented before the spring of 1998 owing to the severe winter conditions in the region."[71]

On 4 December, acting on the secretary-general's recommendation, the Security Council by Resolution 1142 (1997) decided "to extend the mandate of UNPREDEP for the final period until 31 August 1998, with the withdrawal of the military component immediately thereafter."[72] The secretary-general was also requested to submit a report by 1 June 1998 "on the modalities of the termination of UNPREDEP. . .and to submit recommendations on the type of international presence that would be most appropriate for the former Yugoslav Republic of Macedonia after 31 August 1998."

A post-UNPREDEP presence in Macedonia was of particular interest to the United States. On 17 December 1997, U.S. Secretary of State Madeleine Albright suggested that the Euro-Atlantic Partnership Council (EAPC) should be involved in designing a security plan that would be implemented after the end of UNPREDEP's mandate:

> Another place where the EAPC can play an important role is the former Yugoslav Republic of Macedonia (FYROM). The UN mission in that country has served us well. But UNPREDEP's mandate will expire at the end of the next summer. So let us be imaginative in our thinking. Together, let us devise a new security arrangement that will contribute to stability in the FYROM and the surrounding region. Though we do not yet know how such an effort would be structured, we can say it would involve our Partners. And we believe that a link to NATO would not only deter conflict, but promote the integration of FYROM into Europe.[73]

As had happened before, events in the region, this time in Kosovo, would grant another lease on life to UNPREDEP.

THE MOST DANGEROUS PLACE IN EUROPE

In the summer of 1998, Richard Holbrooke described Kosovo as "the most dangerous place in Europe."[74] This was not an exaggeration. Kosovo is a province of Serbia, but Serbs were outnumbered nine to one by ethnic Albanians in a population of two million people. However, Serbs controlled the government and security services. Kosovo enjoyed considerable autonomy within former Yugoslavia, but in 1989 it was stripped of its political autonomy by President Milosevic. In that same year, which marked the six hundredth anniversary of the Serb defeat by the Ottomans at Kosovo, Milosevic delivered an inflammatory speech to one million Serbs at the Field of Blackbirds to fuel his nationalist rise to power. A nonviolent independence movement led by the moderate leader, Dr. Ibrahim Rugova, opposed Belgrade's repressive policies in Kosovo. However, in the face of Belgrade's uncompromising stance and perceived abandonment by the West, an armed resistance group, the Kosovo Liberation Army (KLA), had gained growing support among Kosovo Albanians.[75]

Conflict in Kosovo erupted in February 1998 when Milosevic ordered army and police units to begin a crackdown against the KLA. In March, a daylong battle between Serb forces and KLA rebels in the village of Prekaz in northern Kosovo marked the start of the undeclared war in the Serbian province. Adem Jashari, regarded by many Kosovars as the first martyr of the rebel cause, was killed together with several members of his clan.

On 31 March, the Security Council acting under Chapter VII of the UN Charter, adopted Resolution 1160 (1998) by which it banned the sale or supply of arms and related matériel to the Federal Republic of Yugoslavia, including Kosovo, and prohibited the arming and training for terrorist activities there. It condemned the use of excessive force by Serb police forces against civilians and peaceful demonstrators in Kosovo, as well as the terrorist acts by the KLA.

By early June, more than 250 people had been killed, tens of thousands left homeless, and 10,000 refugees had fled to Albania.[76] The crisis in Kosovo evoked fears that the violence would spread to Albania and Macedonia. NATO, the Contact Group, and the OSCE tried to defuse what was widely regarded as Europe's greatest security crisis since the Bosnian war. International diplomatic pressure and the threat of force were combined to pressure Milosevic to end his offensive and enter into negotiations with Kosovar Albanians.

In light of the crisis in Kosovo, UNPREDEP took measures to strengthen its monitoring and reporting of developments in the border region. It increased its ground and air patrols, established temporary observation posts for monitoring round the clock, and began patrols by boat at Ohrid and Prespa Lakes.[77] However, because of its reduced troop strength, UNPREDEP could not continue the same level of monitoring for a prolonged period of time, and the increased demands on the Force were putting at risk the implementation of its other tasks. As the secretary-general underlined in June 1998:

> within its current strength, any further escalation of the crisis in Kosovo could have negative operational consequences for the Force and undermine its impressive record of achievements to date. Consequently, it would be my intention to submit, by 15 July, should the Security Council so wish, specific proposals on a possible strengthening of the Force's overall capacity, taking into consideration the situation in the region and the relevant Security Council resolutions.[78]

In his July report, Secretary-General Annan recommended an increase in UNPREDEP's troop level by 350, 230 of whom would be deployed at nine new permanent observation posts along Macedonia's borders with Kosovo and Albania. In accordance with Resolution 795 (1992), the troops would monitor and report on developments in the border areas, including those developments relating to the implementation of Resolution 1160 (1998). The secretary-general also proposed the deployment of a reserve of two platoons composed of about sixty soldiers who would carry out limited ground and air patrolling duties. The reserve would be complemented by a thirty-five- person medical unit and three helicopters to enable UNPREDEP to respond promptly to emergencies involving its personnel. The military observers would be increased by twelve and the civilian police by twenty-four personnel in view of their "important confidence-building role."[79] The secretary-general recommended the extension of UNPREDEP's mandate for an additional six months, until 28 February 1999. One month earlier, on 11 June, NATO defense ministers meeting in the North Atlantic Council had expressed their support for the extension of the mandate of UNPREDEP.

Faced with the deterioration in the regional situation, the Security Council unanimously adopted Resolution 1186 (1998) on 21 July, extending UNPREDEP's mandate for a further six months and authorizing an increase in its troop strength up to 1,050. According to the Council, UNPREDEP would "continue by its presence to deter threats and prevent clashes, to monitor the border areas, and to report to the Secretary-General any developments which could pose a threat to the former Yugoslav Republic of Macedonia, including the tasks of monitoring and reporting on illicit arms flows and other activities that are prohibited under resolution 1160 (1998)."

The period between the extension of UNPREDEP's mandate and its expiration saw a dramatic escalation of the conflict in Kosovo. Violence and terror swept the Serbian province. In July and August 1998, KLA rebels seized control of 40 percent of Kosovo territory before being repelled by Serb security troops. Serb forces continued their offensive against Kosovar Albanians, destroying villages, killing civilians, and increasing the number of refugees.

Meanwhile, intense diplomatic efforts were under way to find a peaceful solution to the crisis. U.S. Ambassador to Macedonia Christopher Hill and EU Envoy Wolfgang Petrisch of Austria tried to negotiate a political settlement between the Serb authorities and Kosovar Albanian leaders.

In October, faced with the threat of NATO air strikes, President Milosevic agreed after talks with U.S. Envoy Richard Holbrooke to withdraw his troops and paramilitaries, allow thousands of refugees to return, and pursue a political settlement. He also agreed to the deployment of two thousand unarmed monitors to verify compliance with pledges. Milosevic, however, soon reneged on his commitments, and over the winter the cease-fire between the Serbs and the KLA broke down. On 15 January 1999, Serb police and paramilitary units summarily executed forty-five ethnic Albanians in the village of Racak. The Security Council issued a presidential statement condemning the massacre and calling for an end to acts of violence and the start of political talks.[80] A fortnight later, Serb police officers killed twenty-four Kosovar Albanians in a raid on a suspected KLA hideout. The deterioration in the situation and the massacres of Kosovar Albanians spurred international efforts for peace. Western governments issued an ultimatum to Milosevic and ethnic Albanian leaders to attend a peace conference or face NATO air strikes.

The threat worked. On 6 February, Serbs and ethnic Albanians met for talks in a fourteenth-century château in Rambouillet, thirty miles southwest of Paris. The main goal was to get the two sides to sign an autonomy agreement for Kosovo. Under the accord, Milosevic would withdraw all Serb special police forces from the province and permit the deployment of a NATO force for three years. However, after more than a week, there was no progress on the text of a possible agreement, and the talks collapsed.

A NEW MACEDONIAN ADMINISTRATION

As the conflict in Kosovo escalated, another key development was under way in Macedonia: a national election campaign began. It would lead to a change of government, and the changing of the guard would have far reaching repercussions on UNPREDEP. In the October and November 1998 general election, the opposition parties, VMRO-DPMNE and the Democratic Alternative, defeated the SDSM-led government. A new governing coalition was established including the Democratic Party of Albanians.

The electoral harvest having been safely gathered, the new center-right government of Prime Minister Ljubco Georgievski faced a difficult economic situation. For almost a decade, the Macedonian economy had stagnated, partly due to the Greek trade embargo and international sanctions against Serbia. An estimated one-third of the labor force was unemployed, the trade deficit was around $400 million, external debt was some $260 million (7 percent of gross domestic product), and central bank reserves totaled only $340 million.[81]

In February 1999, the Macedonian government decided to establish diplomatic relations with Taiwan. In return, it would secure an estimated $2 billion in Taiwanese aid and investment. China, which considers Taiwan a renegade province, lodged strong protests with the Macedonian government and decided to break diplomatic ties with Macedonia. It also halted implementation of all bilateral agreements. The die was cast, and the future of UNPREDEP now hung in the balance.

THE FINAL ACT

The new Macedonian government requested an extension of the mandate of UNPREDEP, despite its major diplomatic dispute with a permanent member of the Security Council. The government gave four justifications for its request: the danger of a spillover of the Kosovo conflict; increased tensions on the Albanian-Yugoslav border; the unstable situation in Albania, which had burdened its efforts to prevent arms trafficking to Kosovo; and the lack of progress in the demarcation of the country's border with Yugoslavia.[82] On 12 February 1999, Secretary-General Annan recommended that the Security Council renew the mandate of UNPREDEP for six months, the usual extension for peacekeeping operations. He stated:

It is a matter of satisfaction that, until now, the former Yugoslav Republic of Macedonia has not been adversely affected by the conflict in Kosovo. However, the potential serious repercussions that continued violence in Kosovo could have upon the external and internal security of the country cannot be ignored given the large proportion of ethnic Albanians in the population of the former Yugoslav Republic of Macedonia.[83]

The Security Council met to decide the fate of UNPREDEP at 3:51 p.m. (Eastern Standard Time) on 25 February. In a diplomatic coincidence, the Council was under the presidency of Canada, which had provided the first Blue Helmets, sent to Macedonia in 1992. Macedonian Permanent Representative Naste Calovski said that UNPREDEP was implementing its mandate success-fully in a region, which continued to be difficult, dangerous, and unpredictable. He urged the United Nations not to abandon the region and argued that ex-tending UNPREDEP's mandate would strengthen regional efforts toward peace.[84] Russian Ambassador Sergey Lavrov noted that UNPREDEP's role in monitoring compliance with the arms embargo against Yugoslavia should be-come its main function and be highlighted in its mandate. The draft resolution did not reflect this point, and therefore Russia would not support it. The vote on the eight-power draft resolution, authorizing a further six-month extension of UNPREDEP, was thirteen in favor, to one against (China), with one absten-tion (Russia).[85] China's veto blocked a renewal of the mandate of the UN mis-sion in Macedonia.

Speaking after the vote, Chinese Permanent Representative Qin Huasun said that the situation in Macedonia had stabilized, its relations with neighbor-ing countries had improved, and peace and stability in the country had not been adversely affected by regional developments. Reflecting a widely held view among UN member states, he said that Africa and other parts of the world were plagued by conflict and instability and needed greater attention from the United Nations. In view of the UN's financial crisis, it was unfair to continue to assess member states for UNPREDEP, and the organization's meager re-sources should be used where they were most needed. Notably, the speech made no reference to China's bilateral dispute with Macedonia.

The negative vote of China drew the criticism of other Council members. The United States, Germany (on behalf of the European Union), and Bulgaria said they deeply regretted the decision. Others, including Canada, considered it an in-appropriate use of the veto. Slovenia went further, saying that China's action had demonstrated the real need to reform the Council and the right of veto. The Se-curity Council's final deliberations on UNPREDEP were over at 5:10 p.m.

The Economist said that the mission had "worked surprisingly well."

> The timing of [UNPREDEP's termination] was unfortunate. More Serb troops have been taking up positions along Macedonia's border with Kosovo and, for the first time, have been shelling villages close to the frontier, driv-ing several thousand ethnic-Albanian refugees into the hills.[86]

Similarly, an editorial in the Ottawa Citizen called the ending of the mis-sion "premature."[87]

CONCLUSION

It was not easy for the Security Council to decide whether the threats to Macedonia's security and stability had ended, or at least sufficiently diminished, so that the presence of UNPREDEP was no longer necessary. The members of the Council were divided on their assessment of the internal and external dangers to Macedonia and therefore on the appropriate timing of the withdrawal of the UN mission. The Macedonian government put forward conditions, which had to be met before the termination of the operation would be warranted. Ultimately, the political decision to end UNPREDEP demonstrated that exit strategies for UN operations cannot be divorced from the foreign policies of key members of the Security Council.

NOTES

1. UN Security Council, 3716th Meeting, 27 November 1996.
2. "Report of the Secretary-General Pursuant to Resolution 908 (1994)," S/1994/1067, 17 September 1994, para. 50.
3. "Report of the Secretary-General Pursuant to Security Council Resolutions 981 (1995), 982 (1995) and 983 (1995)," S/1995/987, 23 November 1995, para. 22.
4. "Report of the Secretary-General Pursuant to Security Council Resolution 981 (1995), 982 (1995) and 983 (1995)," S/1995/987, 23 November 1995, para. 21.
5. "Report," S/1995/987, 23 November 1995, para.3 8
6. Tomislav Ivanovski, "Russian Winds," *Nova Makedonija,* 8 December 1995. For similar arguments see Mancho Mitevski, "Who Drinks, Who Pays in the Balkan Inn?" *Vecher,* 9–10 December 1995.
7. "Report of the Secretary-General Pursuant to Security Council Resolution 1027 (1995)," S/1996/65, 30 January 1996, para. 14.
8. "Report," S/1996/65, 30 January 1996, para.16.
9. "Report," S/1996/65, 30 January 1996, para.12.
10. "Report," S/1996/65, 30 January 1996, para.12.
11. "Report," S/1996/65, 30 January 1996, para. 25.
12. "Report," S/1996/65, 30 January 1996, para. 20.
13. For the text of the "Agreement on the Regulation of Relations and Promotion of Cooperation between the Republic of Macedonia and the Federal Republic of Yugoslavia," see S/1996/291, 17 April 1996.
14. "Report," S/1996/373, 23 May 1996, para. 41.
15. "Report of the Secretary-General Pursuant to Security Council Resolution 1046 (1996)," S/1996/373, 23 May 1996, para. 38.
16. "Report," S/1996/373, 23 May 1996, para. 26.
17. "Report," S/1996/373, 23 May 1996, paras. 27–28.

18. "Report," S/1996/373, 23 May 1996, para. 29.

19. "Report," S/1996/373, 23 May 1996, para. 31.

20. "Report," S/1996/373, 23 May 1996, para. 32.

21. "Report," S/1996/373, 23 May 1996, para. 36.

22. "Report," S/1996/373, 23 May 1996, para. 42.

23. "Report," S/1996/373, 23 May 1996, para. 42.

24. "Statement by Ambassador Madeleine K. Albright, U.S. Permanent Representative to the United Nations, on the Extension of the UNPREDEP Mandate, in the Security Council, in Explanation of Vote," USUN press release #79-(96), 30 May, 1996.

25. Permanent Mission of Germany to the United Nations, "Statement by Ambassador Dr. Gergard Henze, Deputy Permanent Representative of Germany to the United Nations," New York, 30 May 1996.

26. Quoted in Evelyn Leopold, "UN Mandate in Macedonia Extended; Russia Objects," Reuters report, 30 May 1996.

27. "Report of the Secretary-General Pursuant to Security Council Resolution 1058 (1996)," S/1996/819, 30 September 1996, para. 15.

28. "Report," S/1996/819, 30 September 1996, para. 11.

29. "Report," S/1996/819, 30 September 1995, para. 12.

30. "Report," S/1996/819, 30 September 1996, para. 16.

31. Ambassador Lavrov was the second permanent representative to visit UNPREDEP. The U.S. permanent representative, Ambassador Madeleine Albright, had visited the operation on 23 March 1996, on the same day that she officially opened the U.S. Embassy.

32. *MILS News,* 29 October 1996.

33. *Dnevnik,* 29 October 1996.

34. *Nova Makedonija,* 29 October 1996.

35. *Vecher,* 29 October 1996.

36. *Dnevnik,* 29 October 1996.

37. *Nova Makedonija,* 30 October 1996.

38. "Report of the Secretary-General on the United Nations Preventive Deployment Force Pursuant to Security Council Resolution 1058 (1996)," S/1996/961, 19 November 1996, para.18.

39. "Report," S/1996/961, 19 November 1996, para. 22.

40. "Report," S/1996/961, 19 November 1996, para. 24.

41. "Report," S/1996/961, 19 November 1996, para. 24.

42. "Report," S/1996/961, 19 November 1996, para. 25.

43. S/PV.3716, 3716th Meeting, 27 November 1996.

44. "Address of His Excellency Kiro Gligorov to the Parliament of the Republic of Macedonia," Skopje, 24 December 1996.

45. "Concession to Russian Pressure?" *Nova Makedonija,* 26 November 1996.

46. "Keesing's Record of World Events," *News Digest for January 1997,* 41454-55.

47. "Keesing's Record of World Events," 41453.

48. *Omri Daily Digest* 44, Part II, 4 March 1997.

49. United Nations Preventive Deployment Force, *The UNPREDEP Drawdown* (Skopje: n.d.).

50. "Letter of the Secretary-General to the President of the Security Council," S/1997/276, 3 April 1997.

51. *Nova Makedonija,* 5 March 1997.

52. *Nova Makedonija,* 5 March 1997.

53. *Vecher,* 5 March 1997.

54. *Flaka e Vëllazërimit,* 5 March 1997.

55. "Report of the Secretary-General on the United Nations Preventive Deployment Force," S/1997/365, 12 May 1997, para. 6.

56. "Report of the Secretary-General," S/1997/365, 12 May 1997, para. 6.

57. MIC, *Infomac-Daily News Service,* Skopje, 13 March 1997.

58. S/1997/276, 3 April 1997.

59. S/1997/276, 3 April 1997.

60. "Report of the Secretary-General on the United Nations Preventive Deployment Force," S/1997/365, 12 May 1997, paras. 19–21.

61. "Report," S/1997/365, 12 May 1997, para. 26.

62. "Report," S/1997/365, 12 May 1997, para. 26.

63. "Report," S/1997/365, 12 May 1997, para. 27.

64. UN Department of Public Information, press release SC/6376, 28 May 1997, 5-7.

65. "Address of His Excellency Kiro Gligorov at UNPREDEP's Changing of the Command Ceremony," Skopje, 3 June 1996.

66. Press release SC/6376, 28 May 1997, 5.

67. "Report of the Secretary-General on the United Nations Preventive Deployment Force Pursuant to Security Council Resolution 1110 (1997)," S/1997/911, 20 November 1997, paras. 3–4.

68. "Report," S/1997/911, 20 November 1997, para. 29.

69. "Report," S/1997/911, 20 November 1997, para. 29.

70. "Report," S/1997/911, 20 November 1997, para. 29.

71. "Report," S/1997/911, 20 November 1997, para. 29.

72. Secretary-General Annan had recommended that the mandate of UNPREDEP be extended for the customary further six months until 31 May 1998. See "Report," S/1997/911, 20 November 1997, para. 30.

73. U.S. Secretary of State Madeleine K. Albright, "Remarks to Euro-Atlantic Partnership Council Ministerial Meeting, NATO Headquarters, Brussels, 17 December 1997," as released by the Office of the Spokesman, U.S. Department of State, Washington, D.C.

74. Quoted in "Fighting Fire," *The (London) Times,* 7 July 1998.

75. For an excellent study on Kosovo, see Noel Malcolm, *Kosovo: A Short History* (New York: New York University Press, 1998).

76. William Drozdiak, "NATO Plans Exercises to Pressure Milosevic," *Washington Post,* 12 June 1998, A1.

77. "Report of the Secretary-General on the United Nations Preventive Deployment Force Pursuant to Security Council Resolution 1142 (1997)," S/1998/454, 1 June 1998, para. 5.

78. "Report," S/1998/454, 1 June 1998, para. 25.

79. "Report of the Secretary-General on the United Nations Preventive Deployment Force," S/1998/644, 14 July 1998, para. 9.

80. S/PRST/1999/2, 19 January 1999.

81. "Oxford Analytica East Europe Daily Brief," 26 January 1999.

82. "Report of the Secretary-General on the United Nations Preventive Deployment Force Pursuant to Security Council Resolution 1186 (1998)," S/1999/161, 12 February 1999, para. 32.

83. "Report," S/1999/161, 12 February 1999, para. 30.

84. Details of the Security Council's deliberations are from SC/6648, 3982d Meeting, 25 February 1999.

85. The resolution was sponsored by Canada, France, Germany, Italy, Netherlands, Slovenia, United Kingdom and the United States.

86. *The Economist*, 6 March 1999, 50.

87. *The Ottawa Citizen*, 8 March 1999.

EPILOGUE

UNPREDEP . . . has been a very successful operation, and we
hope this will serve as a model for many future activities of the
United Nations.[1]

Stevo Crvenkovski

I had two principal goals in writing this book. The first was to present a comprehensive study of UNPREDEP, the UN's first preventive peacekeeping operation. The prevention of conflict is at the core of the UN's mission. It is the
paramount responsibility of the Security Council and of the organization as a
whole. UNPREDEP's presence in Macedonia, the testing ground for preventive deployment, provided answers to many of the theoretical questions raised
about preventive diplomacy. Is it feasible? Is it effective? What factors determine
its effectiveness? What are its possibilities and limitations?

Preventive deployment only became a viable political and military instrument with the end of the Cold War. The end of the Cold War reinvigorated the
United Nations and ended the paralysis within the Security Council. The unprecedented unity of the Security Council, especially among the five permanent
members, enabled the United Nations to break new ground in international
peacekeeping. UNPREDEP demonstrated that preventive deployment can be
done, and that peacekeeping operations are an important tool to prevent crises.

In assessing the performance of UNPREDEP, it would be an error to give
it sole credit for maintaining Macedonia's security and stability, for other factors
have contributed to the country's stability. Most observers agree that an important role has been played by President Gligorov, whose political acumen has
helped to hold the country together. He has been a force for moderation in a
region racked by extremism. Moreover, governing Macedonia, which sits on a
key geopolitical and ethnic fault line, would challenge any leader. The country

is surrounded by neighbors who have historical claims on its territory, it is divided between an ethnic Macedonian majority and a restive Albanian minority, and in recent years its economy has suffered from international sanctions against Serbia, traditionally its largest trading partner, a trade embargo imposed by Greece, and the effects of the NATO bombing of Yugoslavia.

Macedonians of all ethnic groups deserve credit for the practical common sense they have demonstrated in confronting ethnic issues, which as ever are charged with emotion and prejudice. In addition, the horrors of war in Bosnia and Croatia have served as an object lesson for Macedonians of the consequences of interethnic conflict.

Other organizations, including the OSCE and the ICFY, have made valuable contributions to Macedonia's peace and stability. Local and international nongovernmental organizations are working to develop a civic culture of compromise, conciliation, and negotiation.

Nevertheless, UNPREDEP had a crucial impact on Macedonia. Judged against the stated terms of its mandate the operation achieved its goal. It deterred aggression against Macedonia, preserved the country's stability, and prevented conflict in other parts of the former Yugoslavia from spreading and igniting a wider Balkan war. Through its monitoring and reporting, the mission served as an early-warning mechanism to the UN. An unintended benefit of the presence of the Force was it reduced the pressure on the Macedonian government to divert scarce resources from social and economic development to military spending. Since the JNA took with it the bulk of its hardware when it withdrew from Macedonia, without UNPREDEP, the Macedonian government would have had to make heavy military spending at the same time that it was struggling to build a free market economy and raise living standards.

The good offices function of UNPREDEP helped to facilitate the resolution of underlying political, ethnic, and social problems. The mission took practical measures to foster dialogue among political parties and ethnic groups and monitor the observance of human rights. Its economic, social, and developmental programs served the overriding political objective of preventing conflict.

The presence of the UN mission was a force for social decency, interethnic tolerance, and democracy. In the words of Arben Xhaferi, a prominent ethnic Albanian politician, UNPREDEP exposed the country to positive political, moral and cultural values.

The second main goal in undertaking this study of UNPREDEP was to understand why the mission was successful and to see what lessons could be learned from the operation. Obviously, there is no ready-made or automatic formula for success in peacekeeping, especially as every peacekeeping mission operates in specific circumstances and conditions. Moreover, an axiom applica-

ble to peacekeeping is "The unexpected will happen." Nonetheless, the success
of UNPREDEP was not accidental but rather the result of certain key factors.

POLITICAL WILL

It is self-evident that preventing violent conflict is preferable than dealing with
it after it has erupted. The human and financial costs of a reactive approach to
armed conflict are much greater than those of a policy of conflict prevention.
However, the United Nations has missed many opportunities for conflict prevention because of the absence of political will by member states. The absence
of political will remains the main obstacle to mounting preventive operations.
The political will of member states is sine qua non for preventive action. In the
Macedonian case, a consensus prevailed in the Security Council on the need to
undertake preventive action and major governments believed it was in their national interest to do so. The Security Council seized the opportunity for preventive action in Macedonia because its members demonstrated the necessary
political resolve. The prompt and effective decision taken by the Council in December 1992 was instrumental in deterring aggression against Macedonia.

TIMING

As in politics and comedy, a fundamental requirement for successful preventive
diplomacy is timing. Too often, the United Nations has intervened after there
has been widespread destruction, gross and systematic violation of human
rights, and death. United Nations troops were on the ground in Macedonia before the outbreak of hostilities. The Force was also deployed swiftly. Speed is as
important as firepower and size in preventive deployment. Early preventive action by the Security Council helped to deter the spread of conflict.

CONSENT AND SUPPORT OF THE HOST COUNTRY

It is of fundamental importance that states must be willing to bring potential
conflicts to the attention of the Security Council. President Gligorov requested
a UN peacekeeping force when violence in the rest of the Balkans threatened
to engulf Macedonia. Thus, UNPREDEP, like traditional peacekeeping operations, was deployed after the request and with the consent of the Macedonian
government. In addition, the mission received the active support and coopera-

tion not only of the Macedonian authorities but also of all the political parties, the leaders of the various ethnic groups, and the Macedonian people.

THE MANDATE

UNPREDEP was a new form of peacekeeping that was also traditional in terms of its basic mandate. The mandate of UNPREDEP was relatively straightforward and clear, with realistic military and political objectives. Its mandate to monitor and report developments that might threaten Macedonia's peace and stability or increase tension provided the peacekeeping troops with a precise mission. The good offices mandate provided the flexibility required for political and other civilian initiatives.

RESOURCES

Evidently, the nature of a peacekeeping operation should be matched by appropriate resources. The principal resources provided to the Force, including personnel and equipment, were adequate to fulfill the mandate's military aspects. However, sufficient resources were not provided for the civilian functions of the mission, which restricted the implementation of good offices. If member states are not prepared to provide adequate human and financial resources to undertake effective conflict prevention, the UN will be unable to play a useful role in preventing the outbreak of violence around the globe.

COMPOSITION OF THE FORCE

The nationalities of the contingents were an ideal blend. Most of the Nordic troops had prior experience in UN peacekeeping operations, and the Nordic countries traditionally provide specialized training for their troops serving in peacekeeping missions. The U.S. battalion sent a strong message of the recognition by the United States of the importance of Macedonia to peace in the southern Balkans and U.S. commitment to helping to preserve stability in the region.

CIVILIAN AND MILITARY COORDINATION

The effectiveness of a peacekeeping operation is enhanced if coordination exists between the civilian and military components. In UNPREDEP, the civilian and military personnel collaborated closely on all matters of concern to the mission.

INTERORGANIZATIONAL COOPERATION AND COORDINATION

Effective preventive action requires joint action, cooperation, and coordination by various international actors. The efforts of different international organizations and agencies need to be complementary and to move forward in a coherent manner. The SRSG was responsible for the coordination of the activities of the UN system in Macedonia and to ensure that all agencies and programs contributed as effectively as possible to conflict prevention. UNPREDEP cooperated closely with the OSCE mission, the European Commission Monitoring Mission, and NATO on issues of mutual concern. The mission also cooperated with nongovernmental organizations to utilize comparative advantages and complement activities.

PUBLIC INFORMATION

An effective public information program is a key to success even when there is strong support from the government and citizens of the host country, as was the case in Macedonia. It is important for clearly explaining the mandate, conveying realistic expectations of the mission, and correcting misperceptions.

INTEGRATED PREVENTIVE STRATEGY

For a preventive operation to succeed, it must have an integrated preventive strategy comprising military, political, economic, humanitarian, and social action, as appropriate. A variety of tools and preventive techniques are required to deal with incipient crises, and preventive action can take many forms. In short, conflict prevention calls for a broad and comprehensive approach.

CONCLUSION

The preventive efforts of the United Nations contributed to Macedonia's survival and security. However, external and internal problems remain. The name dispute with Greece remains unresolved, although the two countries have been steadily increasing bilateral cooperation in the economic, defense, and cultural fields and in other areas. Macedonia's relations with Yugoslavia were strained during the NATO bombing, and there is still no agreement on the delineation of their mutual border. The greatest threat to Macedonia's stability, however, is internal, and the specter of ethnic conflict continues to haunt the country. Internal stability depends on the capacity of the Macedonian authorities to respond to the grievances of minority groups and their legitimate aspirations, as well as on the willingness of ethnic minorities to demonstrate a commitment to the Macedonian state in word and deed. Political leaders will have to affirm values, which will unite the state and transcend ethnic divisions that would split it asunder.

Despite these challenges, Macedonia has kept alive the hope that the future can be better than the past, even in the Balkans. That the country has survived despite difficult circumstances is an important achievement.

Since its foundation in 1945, the United Nations has usually intervened in conflicts after much damage had been done and finding a solution much more difficult. The great human and financial costs of conflicts in various parts of the world dramatize the continuing need for greater international attention to conflict prevention. The United Nations will continue to be faced with situations requiring preventive action, and the Security Council, as ever, will judge each case on its own merits. Conflict prevention must remain a priority of the United Nations, and the Charter is unequivocal about the organization's fundamental purpose: "to save succeeding generations from the scourge of war."

In establishing the mission in Macedonia, the United Nations took a major step toward translating the rhetoric of preventive action into reality. On the whole, UNPREDEP's role demonstrated the wisdom and efficacy of conflict prevention. It may be said that the record of UNPREDEP will help to ensure that the UN's first peacekeeping operation with a preventive mandate will not be the last.

NOTE

1. Speech at the Fortieth Session of the UN General Assembly, 4 October 1995.

SELECTED BIBLIOGRAPHY

BOOKS

Andreev, Velko, Aleksandr Candovski, Vasil Drvoëanov, Varica Hadûivasiléva-Markovska, Ljubomir Jakimovski, Dimitar Jurukovski, Melpomeni Korneti, Miki Kostovski, Spase Lazarevski, Kim Mehmeti, Pante Naumov, et al. *The Republic of Macedonia.* Skopje: GIT Goce Delcev, 1994.

Bennett, A, Leroy. *International Organizations: Principles and Issues.* 5th ed. Upper Saddle River, N.J.: Prentice Hall, 1991.

Blais, Giorgio. "Experiences with CSCE Monitoring in the Former Yugoslav Republic of Macedonia." In *Verification after the Cold War: Broadening the Process,* ed. Jurgen Altmann, Thomas Stock, and Jean-Pierre Stroot. Amsterdam: VU University Press, 1994.

Boutros-Ghali, Boutros. *Unvanquished: A U.S.–UN Saga.* New York: Random House, 1999.

Claude, Inis. *Swords into Plowshares: The Problems and Progress of International Organization.* 4th ed. New York: Random House, 1971.

Council on Foreign Relations Center for Preventive Action. *Toward Comprehensive Peace in Southeast Europe: Conflict Prevention in the South Balkans.* Report of the South Balkans Working Group. New York: Twentieth Century Fund Press, 1996.

Deacon, Bob. *Action for Social Change: A New Facet of Preventive Peacekeeping: The Case of UNPREDEP.* Report of the Intersectoral Mission on Developmental Social Issues, Helsinki: National Research and Development Center for Welfare and Health, 1996.

Diehl, Paul F. *International Peacekeeping.* Baltimore: Johns Hopkins University Press, 1994.

Durch, William J., ed. *The Evolution of UN Peacekeeping—Case Studies and Comparative Analysis.* New York: St. Martin's, 1993.

———, ed. *UN Peacekeeping, American Politics, and the Uncivil Wars of the 1990s.* New York: St. Martin's, 1996.

Fabian, Larry. *Soldiers without Enemies: Preparing the United Nations for Peacekeeping.* Washington, D.C.: Brookings Institution, 1971.

Fetherston, A. B. *Toward a Theory of United Nations Peacekeeping.* New York: St. Martin's, 1994.

Glenny, Misha. *The Fall of Yugoslavia: The Third Balkan War.* Rev. and updated ed. New York: Penguin, 1993.

Gutman, Roy. *A Witness to Genocide.* New York: Macmillan, 1993.

Holt, Victoria. *Briefing Book on Peacekeeping: The U.S. Role in United Nations Peace Operations.* Washington, D.C.: Council for a Livable World Education Fund, 1995.

Holbrooke, Richard. *To End a War.* New York: Random House, 1998.

Human Rights Watch/Helsinki. *A Threat to "Stability": Human Rights Violations in Macedonia.* New York: Human Rights Watch, 1996.

International Commission on the Balkans. *Unfinished Peace: A Report.* Foreword by Leo Tindemans. Washington, D.C.: Carnegie Endowment for International Peace, 1996.

James, Alan. *Peacekeeping in International Politics.* London: Macmillan, 1990.

Kaplan, Robert D. *Balkan Ghosts: A Journey through History.* New York: Vintage, 1993.

Krasno, Jean. *The Quiet Revolutionary: A Biographical Sketch of James S. Sutterlin.* New Haven, Conn.: Academic Council on the United Nations System, 1998.

Lehmann, Ingrid A. *Peacekeeping and Public Information: Caught in the Crossfire.* London: Cass, 1999.

Lund, Michael S. *Preventing Violent Conflicts: A Strategy for Preventive Diplomacy.* Washington, D.C.: U.S. Institute of Peace, 1996.

Malcolm, Noel. *Kosovo: A Short History.* New York: New York University Press, 1998.

Mickey, Robert W., and Adam Smith Albion. "Success in the Balkans? A Case Study of Ethnic Relations in the Republic of Macedonia." In *Minorities: The New Europe's Old Issue,* ed. Ian M. Cuthbertson and Jane Leibowitz. New York: Institute for East-West Studies, 1993.

Owen, David. *Balkan Odyssey.* New York: Harcourt Brace, 1995.

Perry, Duncan M. *The Politics of Terror: The Macedonian Liberation Movements 1893–1903.* Durham, N.C.: Duke University Press, 1988.

Poulton, Hugh. *Who Are the Macedonians?* Bloomington: Indiana University Press, 1995.

Renninger, John P. *The Future Role of the United Nations in an Interdependent World.* Dordrecht: Martinus Nijoff, 1989.

Roberts, Adam, and Benedict Kingsbury, eds. *United Nations, Divided World: The UN's Roles in International Relations.* Oxford: Clarendon, 1993.

Rohde, David. *Endgame: The Betrayal and Fall of Srebrenica, Europe's Worst Massacre since World War II.* New York: Farrar, Straus & Giroux, 1997.

Rosner, Gabriella. *The United Nations Emergency Force.* New York: Columbia University Press, 1963.

Silber, Laura, and Allan Little. *Yugoslavia: Death of a Nation.* Rev. and updated ed. New York: Penguin, 1997.

Stegenga, James. *The United Nations Force in Cyprus.* Columbus: Ohio State University Press, 1968.

Stremlau, John. *Sharpening International Sanctions: Toward a Stronger Role for the United Nations.* Report to the Carnegie Commission on Preventing Deadly Conflict. New York: Carnegie Corporation, 1996.

Urquhart, Brian. *Hammarskjöld.* New York: Knopf, 1972.

———. *Ralph Bunche: An American Life.* New York: Norton, 1993.

Weiss, Thomas, and Jarat Chopra. *United Nations Peacekeeping: An ACUNS Teaching Text.* Providence, R.I.: Academic Council on the United Nations System, 1992.

West, Rebecca. *Black Lamb and Grey Falcon.* New York: Penguin, 1982.

White, N. D. *Keeping the Peace: The United Nations and the Maintenance of International Peace and Security.* 2d ed. Manchester: Manchester University Press, 1997.

Woodward, Susan. *Balkan Tragedy: Chaos and Dissolution after the Cold War.* Washington, D.C.: Brookings Institution, 1995.

Zimmerman, Warren. *Origins of a Catastrophe: Yugoslavia and Its Destroyers.* New York: Times Books, 1996.

ARTICLES

Ackermann, Alice, and Antonio Pala. "From Peacekeeping to Preventive Deployment: A Study of the United Nations in the Former Yugoslav Republic of Macedonia." *European Security* 5, no.1 (Spring 1996).

Akashi, Yasushi. "The Dilemmas of Peacekeeping." *Brown Journal of World Affairs,* 3, no. 1 (Winter/Spring 1996).

Archer, Clive. "Conflict Prevention in Europe: The Case of the Nordic States and Macedonia." *Conflict and Cooperation* 29, no. 4 (1994).

Corry, John. "Why Are We in Macedonia?" *American Spectator* (November 1995).

Fromkin, David. "Dimitrios Returns: Macedonia and the Balkan Question in the Shadow of History." *World Policy Journal* 10 (1993).

Glenny, Misha. "Heading Off War in the Southern Balkans." *Foreign Affairs* 74, no. 3 (May/June 1995).

———. "The Birth of a Nation." *New York Review of Books* 16 (November 1995).

James, Alan. "Reluctant Heroes: Assembling the United Nations Cyprus Force, 1964." *International Journal* (Autumn 1998).

Lefebvre, Stephane. "The Former Yugoslav Republic of Macedonia (FYROM): Where to?" *European Security* 3, no. 4 (Winter 1994).

Lund, Michael S. "Response: Underrating Preventive Diplomacy." *Foreign Affairs* 74, no. 4 (July/August 1995).

Perry, Duncan M. "Crisis in the Making? Macedonia and Its Neighbors." *Südosteuropa* 43, nos.1–2 (1994).

Perry, Duncan M. "Macedonia: Balkan Miracle or Balkan Disaster?" *Current History* (March 1996).

Pettifer, James. "The New Macedonian Question." *International Affairs* 68, no. 3 (1992).

Russett, Bruce, and James Sutterlin. "The UN in a New World Order." *Foreign Affairs* 70 (1991).

Schmidt, Fabian. "From National Consensus to Pluralism." *Transition* 1, no.1 (1995).
Stedman, Stephen John. "Alchemy for a New World Order: Overselling 'Preventive Diplomacy.'" *Foreign Affairs* 74, no. 3, (May/June 1995).
Urquhart, Brian. "Beyond the Sheriff's Posse." *Survival* 32, no. 3 (1990).

UNITED NATIONS DOCUMENTS

Akashi, Yasushi. "Press Briefing." *Daily Public Information Summary*. Zagreb: Division of Public Information, United Nations Peace Forces Headquarters, 31 October 1995.
Annan, Kofi. "The Challenge of Conflict Prevention." Address to the James A. Baker III Institute for Public Policy at Rice University, Houston, Tex., SG/SM/6535, 23 April 1998.
Boutros-Ghali, Boutros. *An Agenda for Peace*. New York: United Nations, 1992.
———. "Supplement to *An Agenda for Peace*." A/50/60-S/1995/1, 3 January 1995.
———. *The 50th Anniversary Annual Report on the Work of the Organisation*. New York: United Nations, 1996.
United Nations. *Blue Helmets*. 2d ed. New York: Author, 1991.
———. *United Nations Peacekeeping: 50 Years 1948–1998*. New York: Department of Public Information, October 1998.
———. *The United Nations and the Situation in the Former Yugoslavia*. Reference Paper. New York: Department of Public Information, 15 March 1994.
———. *The United Nations and the Situation in the Former Yugoslavia*. DPI/1312/Rev. 4. New York: Department of Public Information, July 1995.
United Nations General Assembly. *Renewing the United Nations: A Program for Reform*. Report of the Secretary-General, A/51/950. New York: Department of Public Information, 14 July 1997.
———. *Report of the Secretary-General on the Situation in the Occupied Territories of Croatia*. A/50/648. New York: Department of Public Information, 18 October 1995.
United Nations Preventive Deployment Force. *Brief Summary*. Skopje: 30 May 1995.
———. *Youth as Bridge Builders in Multi-ethnic Communities: The Meaning of International Educational and Linguistic Standards*. Report of a Seminar Co-organized by the Macedonian youth structures and associations in cooperation with the United Nations Preventive Deployment Force. Skopje: 20 May 1997.
UNPROFOR FYROM Command. "Press Release." SP0055 Skopje: 21 November 1993.
———. Press release. SP0062. Skopje: 11 January 1994.
———. Press release. SP0072. Skopje: 6 April 1994.
———. Press release. SP0078. Skopje: 16 April 1994.
———. Press release. SP0080. Skopje: 27 April 1994.
———. Press release. Skopje: 28 September 1994.
———. Press release. Skopje: 20 October 1994.
———. Press release. Skopje: 18 February 1995.

———. Press release. Skopje: 22 February 1995.

———. Press release. Skopje: 16 March 1995.

———. "Statement by Mr. Kofi Annan, Under-Secretary-General and Special Representative of the Secretary-General." Skopje: 11 January 1996.

United Nations Protection Force—Macedonia. "Press Release." 00SP8. Skopje: 4 February 1993.

———. Press release. SP0017. Skopje: 5 March 1993.

———. Press release. SP0027. Skopje: 18 June 1993.

———. Press release. SP0028. Skopje: 25 June 1993.

———. Press release. SP0030. Skopje: 4 July 1993.

———. Press release. SP0033. Skopje: 10 July 1993.

———. Press release. SP0043. Skopje: 18 August 1993.

United Nations Security Council. Letter dated 23 November 1992 from the secretary-general addressed to the president of the Security Council, S/24851, 25 November 1992.

———. Letter dated 15 June 1993 from the secretary-general addressed to the president of the Security Council, S/25954, 15 June 1993.

———. Letter dated 6 February 1996 from the secretary-general addressed to the president of the Security Council, S/1996/94, 8 February 1996.

———. Letter dated 3 April 1997 from the secretary-general addressed to the president of the Security Council, S/1997/276, 3 April 1997.

———. "Report of the Secretary-General on the Former Yugoslav Republic of Macedonia." S/24923, 9 December 1992.

———. "Report of the Secretary-General Pursuant to Security Council Resolution 795(1992)." S/26099, 13 July 1993.

———. "Report of the Secretary-General Pursuant to Resolution 871 (1993)." S/1994/300, 16 March 1994.

———. "Report of the Secretary-General Pursuant to Resolution 908 (1994)." S/1994/1067, 17 September 1994.

———. "Report of the Secretary-General Pursuant to Resolution 947 (1994)." S/1995/222, 22 March 1995.

———. "Report of the Secretary-General Pursuant to Security Council Resolution 795 (1992)." S/26099, 13 July 1995.

———. "Report of the Secretary-General Pursuant to Security Council Resolutions 981 (1995), 982 (1995) and 983 (1995)." S/1995/987, 23 November 1995.

———. "Report of the Secretary-General Pursuant to Security Council Resolution 1026 (1995)." S/1995/1031, 13 December 1995.

———. "Report of the Secretary-General Pursuant to Security Council Resolution 1027 (1995)." S/1996/65, 30 January 1996.

———. "Report of the Secretary-General Pursuant to Security Council Resolution 1046 (1996)." S/1996/373, 23 May 1996.

———. "Report of the Secretary-General Pursuant to Security Council Resolution 1058 (1996)." S/1996/819, 30 September 1996.

————. "Report of the Secretary-General on the United Nations Preventive Deployment Force Pursuant to Security Council Resolution 1058 (1996)." S/1996/961, 19 November 1996.

————. "Report of the Secretary-General on the United Nations Preventive Deployment Force." S/1997/365, 12 May 1997.

————. "Report of the Secretary-General on the United Nations Preventive Deployment Force Pursuant to Security Council Resolution 1110 (1997)." S/1997/631, 11 August 1997.

————. "Report of the Secretary-General on the United Nations Preventive Deployment Force Pursuant to Security Council Resolution 1110 (1997)." S/1997/911, 20 November 1997.

————. "Report of the Secretary-General on the United Nations Preventive Deployment Force Pursuant to Security Council Resolution 1142(1997)." S/1998/454, 1 June 1998.

————. Resolution 724. 15 December 1991.

————. S/Res/817. 7 April 1993.

————. S/Res/842, 18 June 1993.

————. S/Res/908, 31 March 1994.

————. S/Res/983, 31 March 1995.

————. S/Res/1022, 22 November 1995.

————. S/Res/1027, 30 November 1995.

————. Statement by the president of the Security Council. S/PRST/1995/9, 22 February 1995.

————. Statement by the president of the Security Council. S/PRST/1995/26, 4 May 1995.————

MACEDONIAN DOCUMENTS

Assembly of the Municipality of Debar. Resolution, Sixteenth Session, 29 December 1992.

Cabinet of the President of the Republic of Macedonia. Press release, Skopje, 30 July 1996.

————. Press statement, Skopje, 20 September 1994.

————. Press statement, Skopje, 10 January 1996.

Gligorov, Kiro. Address to the Parliament of the Republic of Macedonia, Skopje, 24 December 1996.

————. Address at the UNPREDEP Change of Command Ceremony, Skopje, 29 February 1996.

————. Address at the UNPREDEP Change of Command Ceremony, Skopje, 3 June 1996.

Official Gazette of the Republic of Macedonia 25 (1994).

Official Gazette of the Socialist Republic of Macedonia 16 (1985).

Republic of Macedonia. *Constitution of the Republic of Macedonia*, Skopje, 1991.

———. *Facts about the Republic of Macedonia*. Skopje: Zumpres, 1996.

Republic of Macedonia: Independence through Peaceful Self-Determination. Skopje: Balkan Forum/Nova Makedonija, 1992.

Statistical Office of the Republic of Macedonia. *Census 94 Data for the Present and the Future: First Results*, Communication 1. Skopje: Author, 14 November 1994.

INDEX

Ackermann, Alice, 52
administrative support staff, 45
aggression, deterrence of. *See* deterrence
Ahrens, Geert, 114, 117
Aideed, Mohammed Farah, 11, 12, 13, 72
Akashi, Yasushi, 1–2, 60, 137; as SRSG, 68,
   111; during Tetovo University crisis, 124
Albania, 18; guerrilla support, 6; relations with
   Macedonia, 28, 29, 152; Tetovo University
   support, 122, 128; unrest in, 28, 164, 165,
   167, 173
Albanians, ethnic: Albanian support of, 128,
   148n84; attitude toward UN peacekeepers,
   90; discrimination against, 33, 91, 109, 113,
   119–20, 130; election boycotts, 23–24,
   114–15; in Kosovo, 44, 170, 172; in
   Macedonian population, 29, 39n29;
   number of, 32–33; opposition by, 57;
   relations with government, 124; residence,
   31–32; status and treatment of, 28, 32; view
   of UN good offices mandate, 110; view of
   UN preventive deployment, 48–49. *See also*
   interethnic relations; interethnic tensions
Albright, Madeleine, 54, 157; on post-
   UNPREDEP presence, 169; on
   UNPREDEP independence, 81
Alexander the Great, 18
Aliti, Abdurahman, 119, 129
Aliu, Eshtref, 126
Anderson, Norman, 114, 116
Andov, Stojan, 30, 80, 115; elections and, 112,
   116
Angola, 9
Annan, Kofi: on border delineation, 27–28; on
   human rights, 133; on interethnic relations,
   134; on preventive deployment, 1; on
   regional unrest, 167; on SOFAs, 58; in UN
   peacekeeping operations, 53, 84n30; on

UNPREDEP independence, 80; on
   UNPREDEP mandate renewal, 173; on
   UNPREDEP reduction, 166, 169
Anson, Hugo, 99; on Albanian population in
   Macedonia, 39n29; elections and, 113–14,
   116, 117; on need for economic assistance,
   99; on SOFA, 61; as SRSG-Macedonia,
   111, 112; in Tetovo University crisis, 124;
   on UN report misperceptions, 142–43
Archer, Clive, 47
armistice agreements, monitoring, 6
assassinations, 6, 31
authority, central, 13

Babic, Milan, 35
Balkan Wars (1912–1913), 19–20
Balkans, viii, 17
Banditer Commission, 24
Banks, Jimmy C., 55
Baril, Maurice, 46
Barre, Siad, 11
Belgium, 7
Berisha, Sali, 115, 164; on ethnic Albanian
   rights, 28
Berlin, Congress of, 19
Bernadotte, Folke, 6
Bismarck, Otto von, viii
Bocinov, Dragoljub, 93, 103
border crossings: Albanian–Macedonian, 165–66;
   illegal, 109; mistaken, 88–89, 93; monitoring,
   45, 49. *See also* Cupino Brdo border incident
border defense, 57
border delineation: with Albania, 28; with EU,
   27; with Greece, 18; Macedonia–Yugoslavia,
   88, 184; patrol line, 89, 93
border demarcation with Serbia, 27–28, 157,
   173; as continuing disagreement, 141, 143,
   159; lack of, 87, 89

border monitoring, 6, 88–91; ability for, 168; by military observers, 156, 165; patrol reduction, 160; patrols, 74, 87, 90–91, 155–56
Boris, King (of Bulgaria), 20
Bosnia, 1, 11; independence of, 23, 36; peacekeeping operations in, 68; UN troop reductions in, 159; UNPROFOR implementation in, 18, 57; US involvement in, 55; war in, 35–37, 78–79. *See also* Serbia; Yugoslavia, Federal Republic of
Bosnia-Herzegovina: conflict spread from, 26; elections in, 22; resolution of war, 155, 157; UNPROFOR in, 36–37; war in, 94; as Yugoslav republic, 20
Boutros-Ghali, Boutros: actions re Yugoslavia, 35; *An Agenda for Peace*, 2, 3–4, 11, 106n21; on Bosnian UNPROFOR, 57; on establishment of security, 157; on human rights, 133; on information programs, 138, 139; on need for economic assistance, 99; on need for UNPREDEP, 153, 154–55, 157, 158–59; on peace-building projects, 136; on peacekeeping operation separation, 77; on preventive diplomacy, 2, 3; on Somalia, 12; on standing of Macedonia, 152; on Tetovo University issue, 125, 133; on troop control, 83n9; UNPREDEP creation and, 43, 45–46; on UNPREDEP independence, 80–81; on UNPREDEP mandate, 110–11; on UNPREDEP reconfiguration, 156–57; on US troop involvement, 55; view of Macedonian stability, 135
Brioni Accords, 23
Britain, 6, 8
buffer zone, 93–94
buffers, 6
Bulgaria, 18, 19; guerrilla support, 6, 19; Macedonian occupation, 20; recognition of Macedonia, 28, 60, 152; relations with Macedonia, 28–29; in World War I, 20
Bunche, Ralph, 5, 6
Bush, George, 11, 12

Calovski, Naste, 168, 174
Canada, 174; troop/personnel contribution, 50–51
Carrington, Lord, 34
casualties: avoidance of, 74; peacekeepers, 7, 12
Catholic Relief Services (CRS), 103–4
cease-fires: in Cyprus, 8; monitoring, 6, 10; Sarajevo, 57; Serb-KLA, 172; Somalia, 11; Yugoslavia, 34, 35
census, 32, 141
Central America, 9
chief of mission, 77

chief of staff, 70
China, 152, 173, 174
Christopher, Warren, 54, 162
Churchill, Winston, 131
Civil Affairs component, 68–69, 82, 156; mandate, 110; during Tetovo University crisis, 124
civil affairs officers, 45, 68
civil wars, 9; El Salvador, 10; Somalia, 11
civilian chief of mission, 68
civilian police monitors (CIVPOL), 9, 69, 168; creation of force, 10; deployment, 46, 51–52; humanitarian needs reporting by, 91, 102; mandate, 45, 49; tasks, 90–91; training, 10; UN insistence on, 49, 109
Clinton, Bill, 13, 54, 55; on US troop control, 72
Cold War, 179; effect on United Nations, 5; peacekeeping during, 2
collaboration. *See* Catholic Relief Services; cooperation; coordination, military/civilian
collective security: and the United Nations, 4–5; and the Cold War, 5
command/control structure (UNPREDEP), 72–75, 82, 83n9
communications, 81, 138
Conference on Security and Cooperation in Europe (CSCE), 44, 46, 52; election monitoring by, 116–17
conflict, causes of, viii
conflict prevention, vii; cost of, 181; local capacity for, 137; methods of, 5; strategy integration for, 183; traditional peacekeeping and, 46; as UN core mission, 179, 184. *See also* preventive action
conflict spillover, viii, ix; from Albanian unrest, 164, 173; from Kosovo, 173; likelihood of, 160; Macedonian fears of, 41, 44, 109; preventing, 52, 155
conflicts, intrastate, 9. *See also* civil wars
Congo, 7
consent, xn2, 181–82; to humanitarian assistance, 3; lack of, 9; to mission, 7; to peacekeeping deployment, 42, 43; for troop deployment, 5
constitution, 23–24, 26; ethnic group recognition in, 32; protection of nonresident Macedonians, 29
cooperation: of host country, 111; international, 1; interorganizational, 104, 115, 183; Nordic countries, 47–48; regional, 29. *See also* coordination, military/civilian
coordination, interorganizational, 53, 183
coordination, military/civilian, 68, 182–83
Copani, Adem, 164

Cot, Jean, 103
Council of Europe, 153
Croatia, 1; agreement re regional reintegration, 79; consent re UNPROFOR, 75–76; elections in, 22; independence of, 23; peacekeeping operations in, 68; UN troop reductions in, 159; UNPROFOR deployment in, 35–36; UNPROFOR implementation in, 18; war in, 79; as Yugoslav republic, 20
CRS (Catholic Relief Services), 103–4
Crvenkovski, Branko, 22, 30, 44; on coalition government, 117, 145n24
Crvenkovski, Stevo, 30, 60, 77, 140
CSCE. *See* Conference on Security and Cooperation in Europe
Cupino Brdo border incident, 74, 87–88, 91–94
Cyprus, 7–8

Dayton Peace Agreements, 79, 101, 153, 157
de la Presle, Bertrand, 59
decolonization, 7
Demirel, Suleyman, 30
demobilization, 10
Democratic Alternative, 31, 173
Democratic Party, 113, 116, 131; election boycotts, 30; election code and, 114; on international institutions, 129; on national consensus, 132; re Tetovo University, 119, 126; UN report and, 142; view of UN good offices mandate, 110
Democratic Party of Albanians, 31
Denmark, 47, 137
deployment, preventive. *See* preventive deployment
deterrence: credibility for, 42; forces sufficient for, 56; internal stability and, 143; by patrolling, 91; success of, viii–ix; by UN, viii
development programs, 136, 151
Dika, Agni, 118, 122
Dioguardi, Joseph, 123
diplomacy, traditional, 4
disarmament, 12
discrimination against ethnic Albanians, 33, 91, 109, 113, 119–20, 130
dispute resolution means, 5
Djindjic, Zoran, 161, 163
Djindoruk, Husametin, 30
domestic problems, 31–33. *See also* interethnic tensions; internal stability
Draskovic, Vuk, 161
Durch, William J., 12

EAPC. *See* Euro-Atlantic Partnership Council

economy, viii, 33; free market, 30, 180; peacekeeping as boost to, 49, 76; reform attempts, 33–34; sanctions' effect on, 95, 97, 100; sustainable development of, 104; as threat to stability, 88; UNPREDEP development assistance, 136, 152; weakness of, 18, 173
education, 118. *See also* University of Tetovo
Egypt, 6–7
El Salvador, 10
election observation, viii, 10, 82; by CSCE, 116–17; invitation for, 116; Macedonia (1994), 30, 110, 112–18, 142–43
elections: Albania, 167; Bosnia-Herzegovina, 167; boycotts, 23–25, 114, 114–15, 116; challenges to, 153; code of conduct, 113–14; free and fair, 10, 113, 114, 115; Macedonia (1990), 22; Macedonia (1994), 30, 145nn22–24; Macedonia (1998), 31, 143, 172–73; presidential/parliamentary, 112–18, 140–41; problems in, 115–16; second round, 115–16; Serbia (1996), 161–62; Slovenia, 22
Emini, Abduseljan, 123
Engström, Juha, 89
escalation, 94
ethnic cleansing, 36
ethnic conflict, 180, 184; post-Cold War, 9. *See also* interethnic relations; interethnic tensions
ethnic groups, ix, 180; interethnic tensions; constitutional recognition of, 23–24; dialogue among, 124, 130–35; international standards of treatment, 109–10; in Macedonia, 20; multiethnic societies and, 33; tensions among, 18, 30, 31–33. *See also* interethnic relations
Euro-Atlantic Partnership Council (EAPC), 169
European Commission Monitoring Mission, 183

Faber-Rod, Christian, 128, 129
fact finding, 2
federalization, 121, 134
Fejziu, Miliam, 122, 123, 127
Finland, 47, 70
flags: Macedonian, 24, 26, 27, 39n23, 134; of national minorities, 134
force commander, 72, 81
force, use of, xn2, 5, 7, 42
France, 6
Franck, Thomas M., 111
Frckoski, Ljubomir, 122, 159, 165

Galbraith, Peter, 79
general officer commanding (GOC), 68

Georgievski, Ljubco, 29, 31; as Prime Minister, 173
Georgievski, Ljubisha: as candidate, 113, 115; on ethnic Albanians, 113
Germany, 20
Gingrich, Newt, 57
Glenny, Misha, 17
Gligorov, Kiro: assassination attempt, 31, 154; Bulgarian visit, 29; as candidate, 113; on CIVPOL monitors, 49; election of, 22, 115; on JNA withdrawal, 25; as leader, 31; meeting with Lavrov, 159; as moderating force, 179; on need for peacekeeping forces, 82; reelection of, 30; request for peacekeeping force, 41, 43–46, 181; on sanctions, 98; on Tetovo University, 126, 128–29; on UN border concerns, 141; on UNPREDEP extension, 168; on UNPREDEP independence, 80; on UNPREDEP withdrawal, 161; on US troop involvement, 54
GOC. *See* general officer commanding
Gonzalez, Felipe, 163
good offices functions, viii, 109–43, 180; authorization of, 110–12; during Cold War, 2; delegation of, 111; dialogue facilitation, 130–33; discretion re, 111; expectations of, 110, 134–35; Macedonian view of, 112, 135; mandate, 116, 182; SRSG mandate, 68; support for, 182; in Tetovo University crisis, 124–25, 128
good works projects, 103
Goshev, Petar, 142
government: coalition, 30–31, 113, 173; minority representation in, 117, 154
Greece: accords with Macedonia, 27, 153; border with Macedonia, 18; civil war in, 6; Cyprus and, 8; disputes with Macedonia, 159; guerrilla support, 19; involvement in Balkan wars, 44; recognition of Macedonia, 152; relations with Macedonia, 25–27, 29, 60; trade embargo by [*see* trade embargo (Greek)]; in World War I, 20

Halili, Nevzat, 123
Halimi, Musli, 123
Hammarskjöld, Dag, 2, 5, 7
Handziski, Blagoj, 78
headquarters, branches of, 70
Herzegovina, 57. *See also* Bosnia-Herzegovina
Hill, Christopher, 127, 172
history, 37
Hoglund, Kari, 51
Holbrooke, Richard, 79, 170, 172; Greek–Macedonian accords and, 27; on Serbian Yugoslavia, 23
human rights abuses, 133; monitoring, 10, 180; UNPREDEP action re, 134–35

human rights compliance, 10, 110
Human Rights Watch, 133
humanitarian assistance, viii, 3; hindrance of, 36; information gathering re needs, 91; social/economic development activities as, 137; by trip wire troops, 105; from Turkey, 30; UN role in, 8, 10; by UNPREDEP, 88, 102–4; in UNPREDEP mandate, 102
Humanitarian Committee, 102–3

ICFY. *See* International Conference on Former Yugoslavia
IFOR. *See* Implementation Force
IFRC. *See* International Federation of Red Cross and Red Crescent Societies
Ilinden Uprising, 19, 20, 97
impartiality, 7, 13, 93
Implementation Force (IFOR), 79
India, 6
Indonesia, 6
information programs. *See* public information programs
interethnic relations, 113; CIVPOL monitors and, 49; education and, 118; government portrayal of, 128–29; international organizations in, 129; Tetovo University crisis, 118–30; youth in, 132–33
interethnic tensions, 31–33, 130; CIVPOL monitors and, 109; as destabilizing force, 153, 157; factors exacerbating, 137; UN view of, 133–34, 141, 143. *See also* University of Tetovo
Internal Macedonian Revolutionary Organization (VMRO), 19
Internal Macedonian Revolutionary Organization-Democratic Party of Macedonian Unity (VMRO-DPMNE). *See* VMRO-DPMNE
internal stability: deterrence and, 143; economy and, 101; elections and, 116; external mediators and, 129; government/legislation for, 30–31; interethnic tensions and, 49, 114 (*see also* interethnic tensions); maintaining, ix; threats to, viii, 101, 137, 184 (*see also* stability, threats to)
International Conference on Former Yugoslavia (ICFY), ix
International Federation of Red Cross and Red Crescent Societies (IFRC), 44, 102–3
Isberg, Jan, 51
Ismail, Guner, 123
Ismaili, Murtezani, 118
Israel, 6, 7; Lebanese conflict, 8–9
Italy, 20
Izetbegovic, Alija, 22, 36

James, Alan, 2
Japan, 137, 168
Jashari, Adem, 170
JNA. *See* Yugoslav National Army
Jonah, James, 11

Kashmir, 6
Kosova, Sheme, 164
Kosovo, 118, 147–48n74, 155; 1997 unrest
  renewal, 163; 1998 crisis in, 170–72;
  conflict spillover from, 41, 44
Kosovo Liberation Army (KLA), 163, 170, 172
Kostov, Ivan, 29
Kovacevic, Blagoje, 92, 93
Kucan, Milan, 23

language: Albanian, 33, 110, 118 (*see also*
  University of Tetovo); for education, 119,
  121, 132; official, 21; recognition of, 28; of
  UN documents, 60
Lavrov, Sergey, 151, 158, 159; on UNPREDEP,
  160, 174
law and order, maintaining, 10
League of Nations, 4
Lebanon, 8–9
legal reform, 30, 31
Lehmann, Ingrid A., 138
Liberal Party, 30, 113, 132, 142
Lumumba, Patrice, 7
Lund, Michael, 1

Macedonia: anthem, 134; constitution (*see*
  constitution); defense capabilities, 44,
  155; disputes with China, 173, 174;
  disputes with Greece, 18, 24–25, 25–27,
  157, 159; economic assistance to, 98–99;
  education law, 120–21; elections (*see*
  elections); ethnic Albanians in (*see*
  Albanians, ethnic); ethnic groups in, 20
  (*see also* ethnic groups); flag, 24, 26, 27,
  39n23, 134; government change, 172–74;
  history of, 18–19; as independent
  country, 17–18, 23–25; legal system, 117;
  national consensus issues, 131,
  148–49n95; need for UNPREDEP, 152,
  154–55; partitioning of, 20; population
  composition, 19, 23, 32; relations with
  Bulgaria, 28–29; relations with Greece,
  27, 153, 183–84; relations with
  neighboring states, 29, 41; relations with
  Serbia, 126; relations with Turkey, 29–30;
  relations with United Nations, 77–78;
  relations with Yugoslavia, 184; sanctions
  enforcement by, 95 (*see also* sanctions);
  secession, 1; security plan for, 169–70;
  strategic importance of, viii, 17, 29; UN
  preventive deployment support, 48–50;

UNPREDEP independence and, 75–82;
  view of good offices mandate, 109–10;
  view of UN Yugoslavian intervention, 34;
  as Yugoslav republic, 17, 20–21. *See also*
  Gligorov, Kiro
Macedonia, international recognition of, 18,
  26, 152; by Greece, 24–25; increasing, 44;
  independent peacekeeping mission and, 75,
  76; name and, 24 (*see also* Macedonia,
  name of); UN presence and, 41, 44; by
  United States, 54
Macedonia, name of, vii, xn1, 18, 183–84;
  ethnic Albanians' use of, 128; Greek
  opposition to, 24–25, 27, 60, 152; for
  international recognition, 27; for
  peacekeeping operations use, 77; in SOFA,
  58–59; in United Nations, 18, 25–26,
  39n20
Macedonian Orthodox Church, 21, 26
Macedonian question, 19–21
Macedonians, ethnic, 128, 130; in Bulgaria, 29;
  symbols of, 134
Mahdi, Mohammed Ali, 11
Maleski, Denko, 80, 100, 142
mandates, xn2, 10, 182; clarity of, 11, 87;
  differences in, 76; expansion of, 12;
  explaining, 183; implementation of, 68, 87;
  implementation prevention, 42; nature of,
  87; nonmilitary aspects, 82; operations
  outside, 95, 96; success and, 87. *See also*
  UNPREDEP mandate
media: explanations to, 112; international, 140;
  local, 76, 139, 141–42; as UN information
  channel, 139. *See also* public information
  programs
mediation, 2; local capacity for, 137; in Tetovo
  University crisis, 128–29
medical emergencies, 103
Meidani, Rexhep, 28
Meksi, Aleksander, 164
Middle East, 6
military commanders, 77
military observers, 51, 71–72; number of, 168;
  reinforcement of, 166; tasks, 90–91; as
  UNPREDEP replacements, 151, 153,
  155–56, 169
Milosevic, Slobodan, 21; Dayton Agreements
  and, 79; Kosovo actions, 170, 172; response
  to election results, 162–63; on Slovenian
  independence, 23; on US troop
  involvement, 54; view of Macedonia, 25
mines, 10
minority groups. *See* ethnic groups
MINUSAL. *See* United Nations Mission in El
  Salvador
mission implementation, 68
Mitsotakis, Constantine, 26

monitoring functions, viii, 158, 180; armistice agreements, 6; borders (*see* border monitoring); cease-fires, 6, 10; civilian police, 45, 49, 51–52, 90–91; elections (*see* election observation); human rights abuses, 10, 180; human rights observance, 110; sanctions, 88, 94–102; UNPREDEP mandate, 87
Montenegro, 18, 20; sanctions against, 94–102
monuments. *See* Cupino Brdo border incident
Moussalli, Michel, 124
Muslims, 29

Nambiar, Satish, 45
Namibia, 9, 10
Nasser, Gamel, 7
National Democratic Party (NDP), 126; boycott of Parliament, 125; re ethnic Albanian rights, 153; on national consensus, 131
national identity, 17; as artificial, 28; creation of, 18, 19, 21; other nations' view of, 60
national institutions, 33
National Research Development Center for Welfare and Health, 137
nationalism: as election issue, 113; ethnic, 21
NATO. *See* North Atlantic Treaty Organization
NDP. *See* National Democratic Party
neutrality, 13, 93; re Tetovo University, 123–24
NGOs. *See* nongovernmental organizations
no-fly zones, 10, 37
Nolte, Georg, 111
nongovernmental organizations (NGOs), ix, 180; cooperation with UNPREDEP, 183
NORDBAT. *See* Nordic peacekeeping forces
Nordic Committee for Military UN Matters (NordSamFN), 47, 48
Nordic Economic Working Committee, 48
Nordic peacekeeping forces, 42, 46–48, 70, 168; composition of, 70–71; at Cupino Brdo, 93; initial deployment, 51; peacekeeping experience, 82; SCANDCOY, 67, 70
NordSamFN. *See* Nordic Committee for Military UN Matters
North Atlantic Treaty Organization (NATO), 183; air strikes by, 78; Macedonian membership in, 159; Partnership for Peace Program, 153
Norway, 47
Noyan, Süha, 29

observation posts, 51, 64n43, 87; at Cupino Brdo, 93; elimination of, 160, 164–65; infrastructure support for, 72, location of, 89–90, 168; military observers at, 156;

temporary, 166, 168; US troop deployment at, 74
observer missions, 6
ONUC. *See* Opération des Nations Unies au Congo
ONUSAL. *See* United Nations Observer Mission in El Salvador
Open Society Institute, 137
Opération des Nations Unies au Congo (ONUC), 7
Ordanoski, Sasho, 142
Organization for Security and Cooperation in Europe (OSCE), ix; cooperation with United Nations, 42–43; Macedonia as member, 153; Serbian election investigation, 162–63; in Tetovo University crisis, 127
OSCE. *See* Organization for Security and Cooperation in Europe
Osvald, Peter, 53
Ottoman Empire, 19. *See also* Turkey
Owen, David, 43, 99–100, 117

Pakistan, 6
Pala, Antonio, 52
Palestine, 6
Palestine Liberation Organization (PLO), 8
Papandreou, Andreas, 26
Party for Democratic Prosperity (PDP), 22, 114, 115; boycott of Parliament, 125; on national consensus, 131; re Tetovo University, 119, 129–30, 147n64; view of UN preventive deployment, 48
Party for Democratic Transformation, 22
PDP. *See* Party for Democratic Prosperity
peace-building activities, viii, 135–37, 152
peacekeepers: experience of, 70–71, 82; from neutral states, 42; training, 47, 56, 71
peacekeeping, vii; during Cold War, 5–9; cost of, 13; effectiveness of, 182–83; evolution of, 2, 5; financial aspects of, 48; improvisation in, 9; need for, 9; Nordic countries' involvement in, 47–48; personnel for, 9; post–Cold War, 2, 9–13; success in, 180–83; traditional (*see* peacekeeping, traditional)
peacekeeping operations: composition of, 5; conflict prevention methods, 5; control of, 7; coordination of, 77; multidimensional, 10; principles of, 7; Yugoslavia, 34–37
peacekeeping, traditional, viii; chain of command, 72; failure in prevention, 46; methods of, 87; principles of, xn2, 7, 13, 41–42
Pearson, Lester B., 5, 6
Pellnäs, Bo, 45
Perez de Cuellar, Javier, 34

Perry, Duncan, 19, 21
personnel, 9; contributors, 47, 50–51; service
   length, 70, 71; UNPREDEP, 136, 165
Pesic, Vesna, 161
Petkovski, Tito, 127
Petrisch, Wolfgang, 172
Philip of Macedon (Philip II), 18, 24
police, civilian. *See* civilian police monitors
political parties: opposition, 30–31, 110, 113,
   117; representation in Parliament, 131,
   147n63; in Tetovo University crisis,
   129–30, 147nn63–64
political prisoners, 10
political will, 61, 181
Popovski, Vlado, 49, 58
Press and Information office (UNPREDEP),
   139
preventive action, vii; effective, 143–44;
   social/economic development activities in,
   137. *See also* preventive deployment;
   preventive diplomacy
preventive deployment, vii; benefits of, 94, 166;
   cost of, 61–62, 151; effects of, 62;
   exploratory mission re, 43–44; Macedonia
   (December 1992), viii, 41 (*see also*
   UNPREDEP; UNPROFOR Macedonia
   Command); need for, 153; nonmilitary
   aspects, 118; reasons for, 44; requests for,
   43; speed of, 62, 181; theory of, 179;
   timing of, 181
preventive diplomacy, 2–4. *See also* preventive
   action; preventive deployment
privatization, 33–34
procurement, local, 69, 76
public information/affairs officers, 45, 139
public information programs, 45, 138–40, 183;
   re air traffic, 56; to correct misperceptions,
   138, 140–43; responsibility for, 68, 110; re
   UNPREDEP activities, 131

Qin Huasun, 174

Rambouillet talks, 172
Reform Forces of Macedonia-Liberal Party, 22
refugees, 10, 36; from Albania, 164; effects of,
   41, 44
regional cooperation, 29
religious groups, 20
reporting, viii, 180; re borders, 88–91; on
   humanitarian needs, 102; UNPREDEP
   mandate, 87
rescues, 103
resources: diversion to military uses, 180; lack
   of, 11, 144
Richardson, Bill, 168
road safety, 91
Rugova, Ibrahim, 170

Rusi, Arben, 123
Russia: objectives re UNPREDEP, 159; UN
   votes re UNPREDEP, 157–58, 160–61,
   168; on UNPREDEP reconfiguration,
   153, 154, 155–56, 159; on UNPREDEP
   replacement, 151, 161; war with Ottoman
   Empire, 19
Rwanda, 11

Saermark-Thomsen, Finn, 51, 58, 103; on
   peacekeeping mission, 56
safe areas, 10, 78
Sainovic, Nikola, 98
SAMs. *See* Sanctions Assistance Missions
sanctions: costs of, 106–7n21; economic, 36;
   effects of, 33, 95, 97–100, 180; enforcing,
   94–95; exceptions to, 95; maintenance of,
   162; monitoring, 88, 94–102; public
   reaction to, 95–96; suspension of, 101;
   weapons embargo, 34, 170, 173, 174
Sanctions Assistance Missions (SAMs), 94–95
sanctions violations, 96–98. *See also* smuggling
San Stefano, Treaty of, 19
Santayana, George, 37
SCANDCOY. *See* Scandinavian Company
Scandinavian Company (SCANDCOY), 67,
   70
SDSM. *See* Social Democratic Union of
   Macedonia
secretary-general, 72
Security Council, 174, 175; post–Cold War,
   179; powers, 5. *See also* United Nations
security, European, 47
self-defense, 5, 7, 42
Serbia, 18; aggression by, 21; claims to
   Macedonia, 21, 44, 49; domination of
   Yugoslavia, 23; elections (1996), 161–62;
   guerrilla support, 19; Macedonian
   occupation by, 20; problems in, 163;
   recognition of Macedonia, 27–28; relations
   with Macedonia, 25, 29, 126; sanctions
   against, 33, 94–102, 180; view of UN
   preventive deployment, 54; war with
   Bosnia, 36 (*see also* Bosnia); in World War
   I, 20; as Yugoslav republic, 20. *See also*
   Yugoslavia, Federal Republic of
Serbian Orthodox Church, 163
Serbians, ethnic, 24
Slovenia, 20, 22, 23
smuggling, 33, 96
Social Democratic Union of Macedonia
   (SDSM), 22, 30, 113, 114; on national
   consensus, 131; support for UN preventive
   deployment, 48
social development, 136–37, 151
Socialist Party, 30, 113
SOFA. *See* Status of Forces Agreement

Sokalski, Henryk J., 77, 128, 129; dialogue
meetings, 130–31; as Macedonian special
representative, 81; on peace building mission,
135; on UNPREDEP reduction, 165
Somalia, 11–13, 72–73
South Africa, 10
sovereignty, 42; legitimizing, 41, 44, 49;
respecting, 3, 111, 143
Special Representative of the Secretary-
General (SRSG), 183; command/control
by, 77; good offices functions, 111; Office
of, 69; Sokalski as, 82
stability: fragility of, 166, 167; human rights
abuses and, 133; internal (see internal
stability); promoting, 118; regional situation
and, 158; small-force effects on, 105; UN
view of, 175
stability, threats to, viii, 17–18, 151; economic,
97; external, 41, 109, 152–53, 164; internal,
41, 57, 109, 133–35, 144, 153, 160
standard of living, 180
statehood, concept of, 32
Status of Forces Agreement (SOFA), 58–61
Stoltenberg, Thorvald, 79, 99, 117
strategy, integrated, 183
Suez Canal, 6–7
Sulejmani, Fadil, 118, 119, 120; arrest, 122,
123; imprisonment, 126, 127, 128; on PDP,
130; trial, 125; as university rector, 122, 123
support for missions, xn2, 182
Sweden, 46, 47, 57
Switzerland, 137

Taiwan, 173
teachers, 118
Tellefsen, Tryggve, 71, 74; administrative
boundary negotiations, 89; in Cupino Brdo
incident, 92; as mediator, 87
territorial claims, viii, 25, 180; historical, 17
Tetovo, 118. See also University of Tetovo
timing, 181
Tito, Josip Broz, 17, 20–21
Todorova, Sofija, 132
trade embargo (Greek), 26–27, 33, 88, 180;
economic effects of, 99; end of, 153; UN
view of, 141. See also sanctions
Treaty of San Stefano, 19
trials, 125
trip wire function, 58, 105
troop contribution, 46; adequacy of, xn2;
voluntary, 7
troop contributors, 151; risk acceptance by,
xn2
truce supervision, 6
Tudjman, Franjo, 75, 76, 79
Tupan Hill border area, 74–75

Turkey, 19; Cyprus and, 8; involvement in
Balkan wars, 44; relations with Macedonia,
29–30
Turks, ethnic, 29

Ugglas, Margaretha af, 53
UNCRO. See United Nations Confidence
Restoration Operation
UNDP. See United Nations Development
Program
UNEF. See United Nations Emergency Force
unemployment, 33
UNFICYP. See United Nations Peacekeeping
Force in Cyprus
UNHCR. See United Nations High
Commissioner for Refugees
UNIFIL. See United Nations Interim Force in
Lebanon
UNITAF. See United Task Force
United Nations: actions in Yugoslavia, 34; areas
of concentration, 153–54, 174; armed
forces supplied to, 5; Charter, 2, 4–5;
command of UNPREDEP forces, 67; cost
savings for, 159; economic assistance
provisions, 98–101; financial problems, 153,
174; independence of, 9; Macedonia as
member, 25; mission, 4–5, 61, 179, 184;
preventive deployment by, 46, 61 (see also
preventive deployment); response
effectiveness, 10–11; role of, viii, 138;
secretary-general reports, 140–43; Security
Council (see Security Council); view of
Macedonian stability, 135, 140
United Nations Confidence Restoration
Operation (UNCRO), 79
United Nations Development Program
(UNDP), 136, 152
United Nations Emergency Force (UNEF), 6
United Nations High Commissioner for
Refugees (UNHCR), 36, 44
United Nations Interim Force in Lebanon
(UNIFIL), 8–9
United Nations Military Observer Group
(UNMOGIP), 6
United Nations Mission in El Salvador
(MINUSAL), 10
United Nations Observer Mission in El
Salvador (ONUSAL), 10
United Nations Operation in Somalia
(UNOSOM), 11
United Nations Peace Forces headquarters
(UNPF-HQ), 68, 77, 81; maintaining, 80
United Nations Peacekeeping Force in Cyprus
(UNFICYP), 8
United Nations Preventive Deployment Force.
See UNPREDEP

United Nations Protected Areas (UNPAs), 35, 84n25
United Nations Protection Force. *See* UNPROFOR
United Nations Transition Assistance Group (UNTAG), 10
United Nations Truce Supervision Organization (UNTSO), 6
United States: international responsibilities, 58; objectives in Macedonian involvement, 54; in Somalia, 11–13
United States forces, 71, 168; command restrictions, 67, 72–74; credibility of, 82; at Cupino Brdo, 93; ground troop deployment, 42; role of, 57; symbolic value of, 42, 55, 182; task restrictions, 73, 74; UN command of, 55, 70, 73–75; UNPROFOR Macedonia Command participation, 53–58; withdrawal of, 56
United Task Force (UNITAF), 11
universities, 118
University of Tetovo, 118–30; Albanian support of, 28; interethnic tensions re, 153; leaders' imprisonment, 125, 126, 127, 158; legality of, 120–21, 126; opposition to, 121, 126; as political venture, 141; recognition of, 33
UNMOGIP. *See* United Nations Military Observer Group
UNOSOM. *See* United Nations Operation in Somalia
UNPAs. *See* United Nations Protected Areas
UNPF-HQ. *See* United Nations Peace Forces headquarters
UNPREDEP, vii; administration, 69; civilian chief of mission, 68; command/control of, 72–75, 82, 83n9; composition of, 42, 182; cooperation with OSCE, 42–43; cost of, 153; creation of, 45–46; development programs, 136; duration of, 48, 152; explanation of, 138; exploratory mission preceding, 43–46; financial aspects of, 81, 136; as independent mission, 67, 68, 69, 75–82, 130; Indonesian engineers, 69, 72, 168; linkage to other operations, 75; in Macedonian internal affairs, 131, 151–52; Macedonians' objectives for, 44; military organization (*see* UNPREDEP military component); need for, 152–59 (*see also* UNPREDEP withdrawal/termination); Nordic troops in, 46–48; personnel, 136, 165; political direction of, 72; political interference by, 129; political objectives, 144; regional changes and, 79–80; reinforcement of, 171; relations with political parties, 131; request for, 43–46;

resources for, 144; response to Kosovo conflict, 171; review of mission, 154; sanctions monitoring by, 101; size of, 81; as stabilizing force, 133; success of, 2, 14n3, 174, 180, 184; tasks, 88 (*see also* UNPREDEP mandate); in Tetovo University crisis, 127; threat assessment by, 41; timing of deployment, 44; UN command of, 67; US role in, 42
UNPREDEP mandate, viii, 87–88, 102, 103, 134–35; conflict re, 151; core tasks, 103; extension of, 154, 157–58, 167–69, 171–72, 173; implementation of, 151; re internal situation, 110
UNPREDEP military component, 69–72, 88, 169; humanitarian assistance by, 103; size of, 69, 70; support for humanitarian aid, 103–4; withdrawal of, 169
UNPREDEP withdrawal/termination, 151–75; Chinese dispute and, 152; Macedonian opposition to, 165, 167, 173; military component, 169; phased reduction, 160, 164–65, 168; suspension of, 165–66, 171
UNPROFOR, 18; in Bosnia and Herzegovina, 36–37, 77; census assistance, 32; creation of, 35; liaison officers, 68; mandate, 35–37, 45, 140; relations with Macedonia, 142; restructuring, 68, 76, 77; sanctions monitoring by, 95; separation of missions from, 75–82; size of, 111; termination of, 79; in Tetovo University crisis, 123–25
UNPROFOR Macedonia Command, 50–52; composition of, 45; cooperation with OSCE, 52–53; size of, 56. *See also* UNPREDEP
UNTAG. *See* United Nations Transition Assistance Group
UNTSO. *See* United Nations Truce Supervision Organization
Urquhart, Brian, xn2

van den Broeck, Hans, 27
Vance, Cyrus, 26, 27, 43; Macedonian name mediation, 59; as UN representative, 34
Vance-Owen Peace Plan, 95
Velinovska, Mirka, 49
Vieira de Mello, Sergio, 59
VMRO (Internal Macedonian Revolutionary Organization), 19
VMRO-DPMNE, 22, 116, 131; in coalition government, 31, 113; re deployment request, 49, 64n40; election boycotts, 30; election code and, 114; election victory, 173; flag change opposition, 27; on

international institutions, 129; on national consensus, 131–32; no-confidence votes, 22, 26; re Tetovo University, 126; UN report and, 142; view of UN good offices mandate, 110

weapons availability, 167
weapons embargo, 34, 170, 173, 174
Wranker, Bo, 74, 165; on humanitarian assistance, 102; as UNPREDEP force commander, 81

Xhaferi, Arben, 28, 180

Yugoslav National Army (JNA), 23, 25
Yugoslavia, viii; disintegration of, 22–23; guerrilla support, 6; NATO bombing of, 180, 184; peacekeeping operations in, 68; UN action in, 34; war in, 1, 21–25
Yugoslavia, Federal Republic of, 18; recognition of Macedonia, 152; sanctions against (*see* sanctions); trade status, 162; weapons embargo, 34, 170, 173, 174

ABOUT THE AUTHOR

A biodun Williams is special assistant to the deputy special representative of the secretary-general, United Nations Mission in Bosnia and Herzegovina. He spent four years as the political and humanitarian affairs officer with UNPRE-DEP in Macedonia. Prior to that, he was assistant professor of international relations at the Edmund A. Walsh School of Foreign Service at Georgetown University. He is the editor of *Many Voices: Multilateral Negotiations in the World Arena*.

DATE DUE
